Social Learning Systems
and Communities of Practice

CW00918803

Chris Blackmore
Editor

Social Learning Systems and Communities of Practice

 Springer

Editor
Chris Blackmore
The Open University, Walton Hall
MK7 6AA Milton Keynes
United Kingdom

First published in 2010 by
Springer London

In association with
The Open University
Walton Hall, Milton Keynes
MK7 6AA
United Kingdom

Copyright © 2010 The Open University

All rights reserved. No part of this publication may be reproduced, stored in a retrieval system, transmitted or utilised in any form or by any means, electronic, mechanical, photocopying, recording or otherwise, without written permission from the publisher or a licence from the Copyright Licensing Agency Ltd. Details of such licences (for reprographic reproduction) may be obtained from the Copyright Licensing Agency Ltd, Saffron House, 6–10 Kirby Street, London EC1N 8TS (website www.cla.co.uk).

Open University course materials may also be made available in electronic formats for use by students of the University. All rights, including copyright and related rights and database rights, in electronic course materials and their contents are owned by or licensed to The Open University, or otherwise used by The Open University as permitted by applicable law.

In using electronic course materials and their contents you agree that your use will be solely for the purposes of following an Open University course of study or otherwise as licensed by The Open University or its assigns.

Except as permitted above you undertake not to copy, store in any medium (including electronic storage or use in a website), distribute, transmit or retransmit, broadcast, modify or show in public such electronic materials in whole or in part without the prior written consent of The Open University or in accordance with the Copyright, Designs and Patents Act 1988.

This book forms part of the Open University course TU812 *Managing systemic change: inquiry, action and interaction*. Details of this and other Open University courses can be obtained from the Student Registration and Enquiry Service, The Open University, PO Box 197, Milton Keynes MK7 6BJ, United Kingdom (tel. +44 (0)845 300 60 90, email general-enquiries@open.ac.uk).

www.open.ac.uk

Whilst we have made every effort to obtain permission from copyright holders to use the material contained in this book, there have been occasions were we have been unable to locate those concerned. Should copyright holders wish to contact the Publisher, we will be happy to come to an arrangement at the first opportunity.

ISBN 978-1-84996-132-5   e-ISBN 978-1-84996-133-2
DOI 10.1007/978-1-84996-133-2
Springer Dordrecht Heidelberg London New York

Library of Congress Control Number: 2010924628

Springer is part of Springer Science + Business Media (www.springer.com)

Acknowledgements

I am deeply grateful to all those who have contributed to this reader in their different ways. First and foremost I thank Richard Bawden and Etienne Wenger both for their insightful written contributions and for their encouragement, advice and support. This book would quite simply not have been possible without them. Many thanks also to all the other authors whose work appears in this book, both for their writing and their inspiraton. I am thankful also for the help of those who have acted on behalf of some authors in obtaining permission for the work to be reproduced.

My thanks go to Springer for the opportunity this publication has provided and to the Open University's copublishing department, particularly to David Vince who has been highly supportive.

I also greatly appreciate the comments and support I have received from other colleagues at the Open University. Kevin Collins, with whom I have developed some of my understandings of social learning systems over nearly a decade, was extremely helpful in his role as critical reader of the whole book and offering advice on its content. Pat Shah has skillfully styled the chapters, helped with drawings and generally been very supportive in getting the book finished. Thanks also to Karen Shipp for her critical reading of Part I.

The book contributes to an Open University course and a Masters Programme in 'Systems Thinking in Practice'. Associated with both the course and the programme are teams of people who have provided both the support and a conducive environment that have enabled me to complete this book. My thanks to all of them, particularly to Robin Asby, Gemma Souster, Penny Marrington, Magnus Ramage, Tony Nixon and Marilyn Ridsdale.

Last but by no means least, many thanks to Ray Ison and Janice Jiggins, with whom I have enjoyed a longstanding collaboration in my work concerning social learning systems and communities of practce. I value this collaboration a great deal and it has certainly influenced the content of this book.

Contents

List of Figures

Introduction to Social Learning Systems and Communities of Practice

Chris Blackmore

> ... how are we to regulate our responsiveness so as to preserve the stability of the manifold systems on which we depend, and how are we to make a collective world in which we individually can live?
>
> Sir Geoffrey Vickers (1980)

> ... we must invent and develop institutions which are 'learning systems', that is to say, systems capable of bringing about their own continuing transformation.
>
> Donald Schön (1973)

> The advantage of a systemic perspective [...] is the appreciation that actions are invariably also interactions. Thus what any one individual might actively do in the world, can, and frequently does have an influence on other humans as well as on the 'rest of nature', directly or indirectly. And this has ethical implications.
>
> Richard Bawden (2000)

> What if we assumed that learning is as much a part of our human nature as eating and sleeping, that it is both life-sustaining and inevitable? And what if, in addition, we assumed that learning is a fundamentally social phenomenon, reflecting our own deeply social nature as human beings capable of knowing?
>
> Etienne Wenger (1998)

The perspectives quoted above are just some of those considered in this book. Authors of the book's chapters explore actual and potential interconnections among people and their environments at different levels ranging from: individuals to groups, organisational to institutional and local to global. They also all consider the processes of learning as a system, and as a social phenomenon. This focus on *social learning* is concerned in different ways with managing or influencing systemic change. This book is therefore likely to be of interest to anyone trying to understand how to think systemically and to act and interact effectively in situations experienced as complex, messy and changing. It is mainly concerned with professional praxis, where theory and practice inform each other, but also includes aspects that apply at a personal level. The book is designed as a reader and as such is a

C. Blackmore (ed.), *Social Learning Systems and Communities of Practice*,
DOI 10.1007/978-1-84996-133-2_0, © The Open University 2010.
Published in Association with Springer-Verlag London Limited.

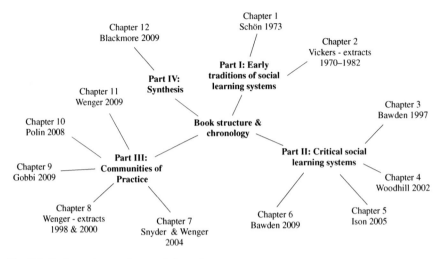

Fig. 0.1 Book structure, authors and chronology

collection of old and new writings. Some chapters have been written specifically, while others have been written earlier (see Fig. 1) and have previously appeared elsewhere. All of them have contemporary relevance.

Major changes have occurred over the past few decades in our environments, our institutions and the ways that many of us live our lives. These changes, for instance in our global economy, climate, communications, public health, technologies, governance and use of natural resources, are inevitably interconnected at different levels and scales. For example, countries such as Brazil, India and China have emerged as powerful in terms of the world's economy, while the roles of others have declined. In many parts of the world, crises have developed over the 2009 fall of the banking sector. Other examples of change are associated with: water, whether as a scarce resource linked with drought or its over-abundance at times of extreme weather events leading to flood damage and even loss of life; advances in information and communications technologies that have brought about changes in the role of experts and governments; and occurrence of pandemic diseases such as swine flu that have highlighted just how interconnected, complex and seemingly uncontrollable our ways of living and their effects have become. Some of the changes in these examples have occurred very suddenly and created or led to the emergence of problem situations. More gradual changes with systemic effects have occurred also, for example the build-up of levels of hormone-disrupting chemical pollutants that have led to feminisation of fish and mammals.

Such apparently unexpected occurrences and consequences are characterised at some levels by discontinuity and surprise. Yet with hindsight, analysis has often shown that preceding events, choices, capacities, responses and circumstances have led to these events. They are deeply embedded in particular historical and social contexts. How we view particular changes varies a great deal, depending on our points of view and what is at stake. As individuals and as groups, what we understand

and believe about the changes that have occurred, whether and how we are affected by them and affect them, both now and in future, are questions that evoke many different responses.

This book deals with one common response to such changes, which is to focus on learning. Being able to see what might have been done differently in such situations with the benefit of hindsight does not however mean that we can predict and control systemic effects and unintended consequences. But we can develop an understanding of how we might learn our way to make improvements in future and it is in this area that this book makes a contribution.

Gregory Bateson (1972, p. 283) said 'The word "learning" undoubtedly denotes change of some kind. To say what kind of change is a delicate matter.' This book aims to draw out various aspects of this delicate matter using a variety of theoretical and practice-based perspectives – on systems, learning and human activity in general. It uses the construct of a *learning system*, mainly in the sense of a 'system of interest' with the purpose of learning that can be identified by an observer and linked to a range of systemic theoretical and practice traditions. Systems thinking is at the core of this approach, acknowledging for instance: interconnections; systems, boundaries and environments; multiple causes and non-linear dynamics; multiple levels and emergent properties. Some authors in this book use systems theories and the language of systems explicitly. Others are more concerned with learning theories and systemic praxis, where theories and practice inform each other, but the language of 'systems' is less used.

All the chapter authors are concerned with social learning but what they mean by that varies. For some it is about societal learning generally, for others it is about multi-level and multi-stakeholder processes of interaction that lead to concerted action for change and improvement of situations. Others emphasise individual learning in their social contexts as well as group learning and are concerned with improving professional practice. De Laat and Simons (2002) explained some of these individual and collective distinctions by plotting learning processes against learning outcomes at both individual and collective levels. They distinguished four kinds of learning as a result: (i) individual learning; (ii) individual learning processes with collective outcomes; (iii) learning in social interaction and (iv) collective learning. In many situations different kinds of learning are likely to be ongoing at any time. The authors also use different theories of learning and identify different purposes. This diversity results in a variety of ways of distinguishing social learning systems. Some of the differences and commonalities of the approaches are discussed in the final chapter.

Part I of the book considers some of the early traditions of social learning systems. The description of 'early' is appropriate in that the contexts in which the ideas were formulated were of the mid-twentieth century, but these traditions continue to be widely influential today. Extracts of the work of two authors are included: Donald Schön's view of *learning systems* strongly influenced many of the early ideas of 'learning society' and 'learning organisations' and continues to be drawn on today, by a range of practitioners. Geoffrey Vickers' notion of *appreciative systems*, which captures many different facets of the dynamics of learning, is one of the influences of contemporary traditions of systemic and appreciative inquiry.

Part II explores a tradition that grew up in rural Australia – the Hawkesbury tradition of *critical social learning systems*. The work of Richard Bawden and his colleagues is central to this approach and they have synthesised many different theories in their work in systemic development which is distinguished by including ethical and epistemic dimensions. Taking ethics into account means that this approach addresses not just what *could* be done but what *should* be done. The epistemic dimension is manifest in the way different kinds of knowledge and ways of knowing are made explicit. Four chapters comprise this part, two from Richard Bawden (written at different times) and one each from Jim Woodhill and Ray Ison, both of whom worked as part of the Hawkesbury group before moving on to work in other locations and a range of domains of practice.

Part III concerns *communities of practice* which is a relatively recent coining of social learning systems but one that can be tracked back to the earliest times of humankind in the way that groups of people have collaborated and worked together. Communities of practice (CoPs) approaches have become very popular over the past decade though the CoPs idea is used in a range of different ways. The work of Etienne Wenger and his colleagues is central to this approach and is much cited in the CoPs literature. Five chapters are included in this part of the book offering varied perspectives on CoPs and social learning systems. Bill Snyder and Etienne Wenger consider our world as a learning system; some classical insights from Etienne Wenger's CoPs-based social theory of learning are included as extracts; and his new chapter gives an overview of the CoPs concept from the viewpoint of social learning systems. Mary Gobbi focuses on workplace learning and professional capital, from the perspective of professional communities which she also considers in relation to CoPs. Linda Polin is concerned with how the CoPs model and social computing applications support changing roles and activities.

Part IV comprises the concluding chapter which reflects on a context, for social learning systems and communities of practice, of *managing systemic change*, It draws together some of the main distinctions concerning social learning and social learning systems that are made in the book as a whole and discusses how they relate to each other. Fourteen common themes emerge from the book's chapters. Key points associated with each are summarised and synthesised. The chapter ends with a reflection on the potential roles for social learning systems and CoPs in addressing future challenges.

The book as a whole covers a wide range of domains of practice and some different parts of the world. Government and public policy are the main focuses for Schön and Vickers, in the USA and the UK. Sustainable development and natural resource management are the focus of the Hawkesbury group's tradition of critical learning systems, initially in Australia but also drawing on wider experiences including those in Europe, the USA and further afield. Over half the world's population now lives in cities, which are the focus of Snyder and Wenger's exposition of a communities of practice approach, drawing on examples from the USA and the Central American and Caribbean region. Practices of professional communities involved in nursing in the UK are explored by Gobbi and Polin focuses on graduate education and social and technical networking in the USA.

Each of the four parts of this book has its own introduction giving a brief overview and some chapters are introduced by a short description or editorial comment providing relevant contextual information. It is therefore possible to dip into parts and chapters at random or to engage with the book as a whole.

References

Bateson, G. (1972). *Steps to an Ecology of Mind.* New York, NY: Ballantine Books.

Bawden, R. (2000). Valuing the epistemic in the search for betterment: the nature and role of critical learning systems. *Cybernetics and Human Knowledge*, 7(4), 5–25.

de Laat, M.F. and Simons, P.R.J. (2002). Collective learning: theoretical perspectives and ways to support networked learning. *Vocational Training: European Journal*, 27, 13–24.

Schön, D.A. (1973). *Beyond the Stable State.* New York, NY: The Norton Library (first published in 1971).

Vickers, G. (1980). *Responsibility: Its Sources and Limits.* Seaside, CA: Intersystems Publications.

Wenger, E. (1998). *Communities of Practice: Learning, Meaning and Identity.* New York: Cambridge University Press, reproduced with permission.

Part I
Early Traditions of Social Learning Systems

Ideas about social learning, in the sense of individuals learning in a social context and the learning of groups, are part of a general discourse on learning that can be traced back to early philosophers, psychologists and biologists. However, the formal concept of a 'social learning system' with an explicit focus on both 'social learning' and 'system' emerged a lot more recently.

For much of the twentieth century ideas about social learning were heavily influenced by behaviourist approaches that focused on learning through imitation, observation and reinforcement through punishment or reward. Over time, recognition grew that most learning was not a linear process but relied on people's *interactions* with others. In analysing the interconnections associated with these interactions 'learning process' and 'systems' approaches were developed, mainly in the second half of the twentieth century. These approaches were heavily influenced by interdisciplinary study of *cybernetics* which focuses on systems, communication, control and regulatory feedback. Korten (1980) contrasted 'blueprint' and 'learning process' approaches in relation to community organisation and rural development, noting that the learning process approach, derived from a cybernetic paradigm, '. . . is appropriate for most areas of human activity. It assumes that neither the ends nor the means of social interventions can be fully known in advance, and that understanding and consensus on them must be built up through practical experience.'

Many practitioners and theorists have been involved in development of learning process and systems approaches that have contributed to ideas about social learning systems and just a few are mentioned here. From the 1950s onwards Bateson's work on learning theories using cybernetic principles influenced many other theorists. Learning and its context were seen by Bateson as inseparable and among his many contributions to learning theories were ideas about communication, logical types and learning levels (Bateson, 1972). Freire (1970) focused on learning through dialogue and informal interaction in his concern for oppressed people. Schön (1973), Hutchins (1970) and others were debating 'the learning society' and Vickers (1968) was writing about value systems, public policy making and social process.

Two of these twentieth century authors who focused quite specifically on social learning systems, in a variety of ways, were Donald Schön (1930–1997) and Geoffrey Vickers (1894–1982). Both were well known in different ways and their work and its derivatives still have many followers today. Although grounded in examples of the twentieth century some of their insights into social learning and systems apply just as much today as they did at that time. Hence it is some of their work that has been selected for the first two chapters of this book.

Donald Schön came from the USA. Initially he studied philosophy but became well known in a range of other disciplines. From the late 1960s he was associated with Massachusetts Institute of Technology (MIT) in a range of different roles connected with education and city planning though his writing extended to include technology and management. He was invited to give the 1970 Reith Lectures in London where he talked about 'Change and industrial society' and received much acclaim. His writing included, in Chapter 1, came from his book that succeeded these lectures. Schön's much cited later work included writing on reflective practice (Schön, 1983) and, with Chris Argyris, a focus on learning organisations (Argyris and Schön, 1978).

Geoffrey Vickers came from the UK. He worked as a lawyer, a wartime soldier and public administrator and held a range of roles on committees and Boards. His roles in public service were well recognised. He was awarded the Victoria Cross for action in 1915, the Croix de Guerre in 1918 and he was knighted in 1946. Later in his life he began writing to make sense of his many experiences and through his books and lectures, presented mostly in the UK and US, he made some major contributions to systems theories. One such contribution was his work in 'appreciative systems' which is one of the main focuses of Chapter 2. A book entitled 'Policymaking, Communication and Social Learning', published in 1987, after his death, is indicative of his legacy regarding social learning systems.

There are of course links that can be made between 'early' and 'later' traditions of social learning systems. The contexts of the authors of Chapters 1 and 2 were of earlier times than the contexts of the other authors in this book. But some of these earlier authors' observations and focuses on social learning and systems show similarities with later authors. In some cases this is because later work was influenced by the work of Vickers and Schön, among others, and in other cases some common roots to the work of several authors, whether past or present, can be distinguished. Links and contrasts between different authors' work are discussed further in the final chapter of this book.

References

Argyris, C. and Schon, D.A. (1978) *Organizational Learning: A Theory of Action Perspective.* Addison-Wesley, Reading, MA.

Bateson, G. (1972) *Steps to an Ecology of Mind.* Ballantine Books, New York, NY.

Freire, P. (1970) *Pedagogy of the Oppressed.* Seabury, New York, NY.

Hutchins, R.M. (1970) *The Learning Society.* Penguin, Harmondsworth.

Korten, D. (1980) 'Community organization and rural development: a learning process approach.' *Public Administration Review* 40(5), 480–511.

Schön, D.A. (1973) *Beyond the Stable State.* New York, NY: The Norton Library (first published in 1971).

Schön, D. (1983) *The Reflective Practitioner. How Professionals Think in Action.* Temple Smith, London.

Vickers, G. (1968) *Value Systems and Social Process.* Tavistock Publications, London; Basic Books, New York, NY.

Vickers, G. (1987) with Adams, G., Forester, J., Catron, B. (Eds.), *Policymaking, Communication and Social Learning: Essays of Sir Geoffrey Vickers.* Transaction Publishers, New Brunswick, NJ.

Chapter 1
Government as a Learning System

Donald Schön

Editor's Note: The following chapter is taken from Donald Schön's book 'Beyond the Stable State' which was first published in 1971. The first section comes from the start of the book and the rest is an edited version of his Chapter 5, leaving out some sections, his detailed notes and some of the specific examples of the times that would today be unfamiliar and require further description. Depending on the perspective taken, some processes and prevailing attitudes towards governments can be seen to have changed since this chapter was written, others remain unchanged. As the chapter concerns transformation and change, of various kinds, you might find it useful to read this chapter keeping the question in mind of what has changed since this was written. The concept of 'the stable state' is discussed further in the introduction to this part of the book. Schön's reference to the 'centre-periphery' refers back to an earlier chapter in his book in which he discussed how social systems resist change. He observed that changing elements near the periphery require least disruption whereas changing elements at the centre would mean re-structuring the whole system. In the chapter following this one in his book, he went on to discuss the decline of the centre-periphery model in our society in relation to growth and diffusion of organisations and the shift towards the concept of a network as pivotal to learning systems.

[Assumptions beyond the Stable State]

The present work [. . .] proceeds on the following assumptions:

- The loss of the stable state means that our society and all of its institutions are in *continuing* processes of transformation. We cannot expect new stable states that will endure even for our own lifetimes.

Source: Schön, D.A. (1973) *Beyond the stable state* pp. 30, 116–179. The Norton Library, W.W. Norton & Company INC, New York.

C. Blackmore (ed.), *Social Learning Systems and Communities of Practice*,
DOI 10.1007/978-1-84996-133-2_1, © The Open University 2010.
Published in Association with Springer-Verlag London Limited.

- We must learn to understand, guide, influence and manage these transformations. We must make the capacity for undertaking them integral to ourselves and to our institutions.
- We must, in other words, become adept at learning. We must become able not only to transform our institutions, in response to changing situations and requirements; we must invent and develop institutions which are 'learning systems', that is to say, systems capable of bringing about their own continuing transformation.
- The task which the loss of the stable state makes imperative, for the person, for our institutions, for our society as a whole, is to learn about learning.

> What is the nature of the process by which organisations, institutions and societies transform themselves?
>
> What are the characteristics of effective learning systems?
>
> What are the forms and limits of knowledge that can operate within processes of social learning?
>
> What demands are made on a person who engages in this kind of learning?

These are the questions we will be asking in the pages that follow
(Source: Schön, 1973, p. 30).

Public Learning

The problem of government as a learning system may be stated simply in these terms: how can we, as a society or nation, learn to identify, analyse and solve our problems?

There is more implied here than in the term social learning, as we have so far used it. A social system learns whenever it acquires new capacity for behaviour, and learning may take the form of undirected interaction between systems, as in the case of 'the system for keeping us in clean clothes'. But government as a learning system carries with it the idea of *public* learning, a special way of acquiring new capacity for behaviour in which government learns for the society as a whole. In public learning, government undertakes a continuing, directed inquiry into the nature, causes and resolutions of our problem.

The need for public learning carries with it the need for a second kind of learning. If government is to learn to solve new public problems, it must also learn to create the systems for doing so and to discard the structure and mechanisms grown up around old problems. The need is not merely to cope with a particular set of new problems, or to discard the organisational vestiges of a particular form of governmental activity which happen at present to be particularly cumbersome. It is to design and bring into being the institutional processes through which new problems can continually be confronted and old structures continually discarded.

Phrased in this way, the problem is government's version of the more general problem of response to the loss of the stable state.

Because many sorts of social system have governments, the requirements of public learning need not be limited to traditional political units. We have already examined what we could now call public learning in the context of the business firm. The concept of public learning applies as well to institutions such as the church, labour unions, schools, hospitals, and social welfare agencies. One way of increasing the capacity for social learning of such decentralised and disconnected social systems has been to equip them with governments – that is, with agencies capable of carrying out directed inquiry for the whole; this is, in fact, a way of describing the movement toward firms organised around business systems.

In our society, however, the most visible and apparently crucial form of public learning *is* carried out by traditional political units, and specifically by the governments of nations. The material of this chapter, whatever its broader implications for public learning, will apply directly to the Federal government of the United States.

Certainly the rhetoric of recent Federal administrations in the United States suggests or directly uses the language of public learning. New administrations enter on platforms made up of lists of public problems that demand solution and policies for solving them. We are forever being exhorted to face up to our problems, to learn from our past, to be wise and persevering in our inquiry, to try new solutions – or we are being reminded that our government is doing these things for us. And this is a use of language that cuts across political parties; it is part of the stock in trade of politics. We even speak of public learning from unexpected events, as in the statement that the United States learned some things from the Great Depression.

There have been over the last decade an increasing number of signs of concern with our capacity for public learning [. . .].

But it is also clear that as a nation we have been dreadfully inept at the process of public learning. This is not particularly attributable to a dearth of ideas for solving our problems. On the contrary, there is a plethora of suggested policies and programs for solving almost any social problem one might care to name. But we have proved ourselves – particularly in the last decade – to be singularly inept at bringing almost any new policy into effect. And we have proved to be equally inept at learning from the mistakes of the past.

The field of housing is a particularly rich mine of evidence for these assertions. Each of the last three presidential administrations has proclaimed its intent to solve the problem of housing supply, particularly for low-income citizens, and under each administration the housing situation has worsened. Moreover, there has been in the last 30 years a series of housing programs (public housing, urban renewal, large-scale rehabilitation) each of which turned away from the perceived failure of the old but was unable to learn from the old how to make its own operations successful.

One could as well have chosen the fields of health services, education, welfare reform, or programs aimed at the elimination of poverty. Each displays an analogous pattern. There is, to be sure, in every case an argument to be made that policies were never adequately tried because resources adequate to them were never made available. But there is also abundant evidence of lack of understanding of the means by which new policies might come into effect. And there is a prevailing attitude toward the recent past which seems to say that failures should be buried and forgotten, or that we should respond to them by a kind of over-learning which consists in veering away from the last in the series.

It is difficult to account for this systematic failure to learn, in view of the acknowledged astuteness of many of the people charged with implementing the new policies
land programs. Nor does the explanation lie simply in the familiar 'good people, bad
systems'. It seems, rather, to have at least one of its roots in prevailing theory about
the implementation of public policy.

If we now draw back to examine the structure of public learning on the part of
a specific government, we may regard it from several perspectives. It is at once an
informational process, an agent of the implementation and diffusion of policies and
programs, a manipulator of policies, and a complex of societies.

As an informational process, the federal government must somehow detect the
issues and problems around which it organises its efforts. It must sense the consequences of what it does. It must organise and transfer within its own system the data
and the directives on which policies and programs are based. It must undertake the
'book-keeping' tasks that go with taxation, regulation, and monitoring the state of
the systems that are seen to be the legitimate business of government. Moreover,
it must maintain this internal and external information system throughout shifts in
its environment and in its central problems. These functions fall under what Karl
Deutsch has described as the cybernetic model of government.

As an implementer and diffuser of policies, government must formulate and test
out policies answering to what it perceives to be the new situations in which it finds
itself, and cause these policies to be brought into effect and adapted to the range and
scale of situations to which they are relevant.

In manipulating policies, the Federal Government can be seen as an operator
of control systems. The 'levers' available to it are within the keyboard of policies
derived from acts of Congress and agency practices. These are constantly changing,
as Congress passes new laws, amends old, allocates funds, and as officials of the
executive branch construct, carry out and modify policies governing administrative
practice.

But the Federal Government is also a set of organisations – related to policies and
programs as instruments of action; related to one another as organisational neigh-
bours, competitors or collaborators; and related to the people in them as societies in
which their working (and much of their non-working) lives are lived.

Each of these ways of looking at the Federal Government reveals a different
aspect of the central problem of public learning:

- From the point of view of government as an informational system, how do new
  problems come to attention and ideas about them become ideas in good currency?
- From the point of view of government as an agent of implementation, how are
  new policies put into action? How are they extended, modified, scaled up? And
  how are the interconnections between policies understood and controlled as new
  problems and goals present themselves?
- From the point of view of government as a learning system, how are perceptions
  of the consequences of action fed back into the public learning process?

- From the point of view of government as a complex of societies, how are strategies designed and carried out by which resources can be organised to attack new problems, and old structures and mechanisms discarded as obsolete or inhibiting?

The prevailing theory of public learning answers these questions in the following way:

- The forming and implementing of public policy is a rational process which takes place in the centre-periphery mode.
- Issues, once mysteriously established, are taken as given. Inquiry addresses itself to the best policy for tackling an issue, but does not turn back on the relevance and apparent urgency of the issue nor on the processes by which that relevance and urgency came to be perceived.
- Similarly, government tends to act as though established policy were stable. Evaluation may address itself to the relative effectiveness or efficiency of the means by which a policy is to be accomplished but seldom (except perhaps on change of administration) to the appropriateness of the policy itself.
- The development of a new policy is sharply distinguished from its implementation. In spite of the language of experimentalism, government acts as though the process of invention and adaptation came to an end once a new policy had been legitimised.
- Inquiry into new policy, then, is conceived as the primary responsibility of the Federal centre. Implementation of policy consists in imposing established policy on a set of peripheral local agencies.
- Stable policy exists in compartmentalised units which have their parallels in compartmentalised government agencies. Once new policy has been established, public inquiry tends not to extend across agency boundaries.
- The inquiry involved in public leaning is conceived in terms of the methods of physical science. Hence, we have the widespread use of scientistic language in which 'problems are defined and quantified', 'hypotheses are developed', 'social experiments are undertaken', 'variables are identified', 'controls established' and 'quantitative measures of outcome formulated'. Finally, 'demonstrations are conducted' and the successful ones are 'replicated'. The answer to the question, 'How shall we undertake public leaning?' is increasingly, 'By applying what we take to be scientific method to the formation of public policy.'

Seldom is the prevailing theory made so explicit and seldom is it held in the pure form outlined above. Nevertheless, in one version or another the rational/experimental model of public learning underlies most current thought and practice in the field of public policy, and its inadequacies help to account for our failures in public learning.

It will be our business in this chapter to suggest alternatives to the rational/experimental model, taking as our starting points clues provided by fragments of actual behaviour.

The Emergence of Ideas in Good Currency

Underlying every public debate and every formal conflict over policy there is a barely visible process through which issues come to awareness and ideas about them become powerful. The hidden process by which ideas come into good currency gives us the illusory sense of knowing what we must worry about and do.

We pay attention to the visible conflicts over policy; but by the time such a conflict has crystallised, issues have long since been identified, ideas for solution have long since been available, sides have been defined and taken. These antecedent processes are as crucial to the formation of policy as the processes of discovery in science are crucial to the formation of plausible hypotheses. But our bias in favour of the rational, the 'scientific' the well-formed and the retrospective causes us to disregard the less visible process and to accept the ideas underlying public conflict over policy as mysteriously given.

The less visible processes, however, are essential to change in public policy and, in general, to public learning. A learning system must transform its ideas in good currency at a rate commensurate with its own changing situation. More broadly, the adequacy of a learning system is in part shown by how far its ideas in good currency are adequate to the situation actually confronting it.

It is surprising, in the light of these considerations, how little curiosity there has been about the emergence of ideas in good currency.

Some Preliminary Considerations

Ideas in good currency, as I use the term here, are ideas powerful for the formation of public policy. Among their most characteristic features are these: they change over time; they obey a law of limited numbers; and they lag behind changing events, sometimes in dramatic ways.

If we take an idea's effectiveness in getting money as a test of its good currency, ideas-in-good-currency in the mid-1950s included 'competition with the Russians', 'the space race', and 'basic research'. By the early 1960s these had given way to ideas about 'poverty', 'the disadvantaged', and 'unmet public needs'. By the early 1960s, the powerful ideas of the mid-fifties had lost their magic. In order to argue for new policies and to support requests for funds, public entrepreneurs required a new vocabulary and a new set of theories. There was a shift in the language by which people got their money. But there was also a process in which a new set of ideas began to exert its influence; in order to get or keep power, people had to serve these ideas.

The ideas of the early sixties did not simply take their places alongside the ideas of the mid-fifties. The later drove out the earlier, as though ideas in good currency in our society had a limited number of slots. But the process by which this happened was a tortuous one – so much so that at any point along the way we held ideas in good currency inappropriate to our times. City governments in the sixties, for example, failed to bring into good currency ideas adequate to the situation presented by the black centre-city. The universities lacked ideas in good currency adequate to the state of mind and behaviour of students. [...]

Ideas in good currency emerge *in time*, and the situations to which they refer change underneath the very process of deliberation. Not infrequently, the changes take place as a result of public debate and attention.

Ideas are often slow to come into good currency; and, once in good currency and institutionalised, they are slow to fade away. By the time ideas have come into good currency, they often no longer accurately reflect the state of affairs.

One of the principal criteria for effective learning systems is precisely the ability of a social system to reduce this lag so that ideas in good currency reflect present problems. It becomes all the more imperative, therefore, to gain an understanding of the ways in which this semi-visible process works.

Themes of the Process

I will not attempt here either a full-fledged theory or a complete case history. There are, however, some fairly general themes of the process which, taken together provide a projective model against which particular instances can be compared.

The essence of the model is this:

Taken at any given time, a social system is dynamically conservative in its structural, technological and conceptual dimensions. This last represents the 'system' of ideas in good currency. Characteristically, what precipitates a change in that system of powerful ideas is a disruptive event or sequence of events, which sets up a demand for new ideas in good currency. At that point ideas already present in free or marginal areas of the society begin to surface in the mainstream, mediated by certain crucial roles. The broad diffusion of these new ideas depends upon interpersonal networks and upon media of communication, all of which exert their influence on the ideas themselves. The ideas become powerful as centres of policy debate and political conflict. They gain widespread acceptance through the efforts of those who push or ride them through the fields of force created by the interplay of interests and commitments. Inquiry now becomes a political process in which the movement of ideas to power goes hand in hand with bids for dominance. When the ideas are taken up by people already powerful in society this gives them a kind of legitimacy and completes their power to change public policy. After this, the ideas become an integral part of the conceptual dimension of the social system and appear, in retrospect, obvious.

Crisis There is, to begin with, some critical shift situation which threatens the social system and sets up a demand for new ideas which will explain, diagnose or remedy the crisis. The analogy with scientific inquiry is helpful. The 'crisis' here is a piece of disruptive evidence incompatible with accepted theory which for some reason cannot be ignored. The Michelson-Morley experiment concerning the speed of light was a famous case in point, as was Galileo's observation of the mountains of the moon, Ticho Brahe's observations of the orbits of the planets, the recent discoveries of multiple subatomic particles, in Darwin's time the geological data concerning the age of the earth. Each of these confronted the scientific community with the failure of accepted theory and raised the potential for new ideas in good currency.

There is a social system of science, underlying its visible theoretical dimension, and there is conversely a theoretical dimension to every social system which contains the social system's view of itself, its role and function within some larger system, the nature of its environment, its own operation, and the norms which govern its behaviour. As in the case of scientific theory, then, a 'crisis' for the social system is any happening perceived to be incompatible with this prevailing theory.

But, as we have seen, dynamically conservative systems normally protect themselves against ideas which cannot be brought to public attention without disruptive consequences. Think, for example, of the history of the concepts of psychoanalysis or of the welfare state, or indeed of any set of ideas perceived as threatening prevailing institutions. The means of protection vary. Ideas may be relegated to private spheres or to the margins of society. Where ideas have not yet penetrated the general consciousness but suggest themselves on all sides, they may be repressed – that is, held back from conscious attention – or, like ideas discussed under headings such as philosophy or change, they may be relegated to a kind of intellectual never-never land, disconnected from action. Where ideas have become subjects of explicit attention, at least on the part of a few, those people may be suppressed, forcibly prevented from entering the arenas of public inquiry and debate. The movement from repression to suppression is a characteristic pattern in the emergence of ideas in good currency; as the ideas become more powerful, the defence against them shifts.

Events come to function as crises in the sense used here only when forces working towards the perception of them somehow overcome these protective mechanisms. For American society at large, the war in Vietnam is such an event, as is the revolutionary behaviour of a large part of American youth. These events disrupt not only by rocking the boat of civil order but by jarring settled ways of looking at society.

Such a disruption does not immediately overturn established theory. There is usually a substantial lag between perception of the disruptive phenomena and reorganisation of prevailing theory. The lag may be counted in months, years (as in the case of the ideas relating to policy for science and technology) or decades. Gradually, efforts to ignore or repress the crisis give way to a realisation of its existence, its incompatibility with settled ways of looking at things, and its danger to the social system. At this stage, there is widespread readiness for new ideas.

Attention turns then to certain free areas within the social system. These are backwaters in which ideas have been able to germinate without encountering massive defences. They are the margins of society. Freud, for example, during the time he was working on *The Interpretation of Dreams* existed, in the medical and the larger social worlds of Vienna, as a marginal man. Norman Thomas occupied a marginal position in American life for decades until his ideas (not his person) found their way into the mainstreams of public policy.

The social system tolerates, to a greater or lesser extent, in marginal areas or in playful or innocuous form, or in relatively insulated groups, ideas which would be virulent and disruptive if released into the main arteries of the culture. Then, crises in the system permit or compel these ideas to come to public notice and to begin their progress towards public awareness, currency, and acceptance. Ideas about mystical experience, communes and enhancement of experience through drugs survived in the United States for generations in small sects only to be taken up in a massive and public way in the sixties. In the forties and fifties, radical critiques of America's poverty, decaying cities, and neglected needs in the public sector, survived in a submerged and compartmentalised way to emerge in the sixties as broad-based critique and (in the Kerner Commission Report) as public gospel. Throughout America's sexually conservative years, liberal attitudes towards the human body survived in relatively invisible enclaves because most people were able to regard their adherents as cranks. In the sixties these attitudes emerged as a powerful threat to established morality.

Vanguard roles The movement of ideas from free areas to the mainstream has nothing automatic about it. Ideas do behave as if they had a life of their own, but only through the efforts of those who use and are used by ideas. Vanguards move ideas to public awareness, supplying the energy necessary to raise them over the threshold of public consciousness. But within and among these vanguards, there is a multiplicity of roles.

The muckraker forces us to look at the disruptive instance, takes it out of the domain of private experience and thrusts it into broad public view [...]. The muckraker is like the scientist who forces the scientific community to pay attention to a piece of evidence incompatible with prevailing theory.

The artist gives us new ways of looking at our experience, new ways of defining ourselves in relation to reality, and in the process frees our awareness of phenomena incompatible with settled theory. In Marshall McLuhan's language, he shifts our gaze from the 'rear view mirror' to experience of the here-and-now, as Cubism gave us a vision of things in the image of the new industrial forms, or as James Joyce helped us to become attentive to things in our own experience that depth psychologists were at roughly the same time beginning to explain.

The utopian presents us with a vision of what might be, in such a way as to focus attention on the inadequacy of what is – either directly, by contrasting a better future with an inadequate present, or ironically, by presenting as future a concentrated picture of present evils. [...].

The prophet – whether in his Old Testament form or in the current ecological style – tells us where we are going, makes us treat as real and present the distant consequences of our current behaviour, and through appeal to morality confronts us with sins we would otherwise have ignored or repressed.

The vanguard roles need not be mutually exclusive, of course. Samuel Butler was both prophet and utopian. But the nature of the vanguard roles and the crises to which they call attention vary with the type of idea in good currency.

The idea may be a way of looking at a particular situation, one that has implications for public action: for example, the pricing policies of the drug industry, the condition of mental hospitals, hunger and malnutrition in rural America. Then the crisis is a particular event, practice or institution incompatible with prevailing theory, and the muckraker's role is primary.

Or the idea may be in the nature of an invention. In this case, the *idea* of the invention undergoes a process of coming to awareness, diffusion, debate and acceptance which is at once distinct from and interdependent with the innovation and diffusion of the invention itself. The crisis may be a particular inequity to which the invention is a response; the scandalous condition of mental hospitals, for example, led to the invention of community mental health centres. Or it may be a disruption of some functional system; automobiles changed patterns of settlement and access to the centre city, and the suburban shopping centre has been a responsive invention. The important vanguard role here is a kind of prophet; Buckminster Fuller, with his 'Dymaxicon' car and house, has been a prophet of technological change.

The idea may be in the nature of intermediate theory, theory that serves as a bridge connecting views of particular situations to what we will later call paradigms of change. The bridging function of intermediate theory is essential to public learning. For those who operate under a revolutionary paradigm in a particular community, 'there must be a theory of the community that connects it to the paradigm'. If the paradigm requires 'establishment', 'disadvantaged', and 'community leadership', then an interpretive process must identify these elements within the community. Otherwise the paradigm cannot engage the community situation. [. . .]

Within the theoretical dimension of a social system, ideas operate at different levels. At the most fundamental level, every social system has root concepts which underlie all theory-making. These are in the nature of metaphors like mechanism, technique and progress which in the last several hundred years have cut across most sectors and subcultures of society. As new root concepts move into good currency their influence on the larger social system is enormous, since they influence not only a particular public policy, practice or situation, but the entire range of activities and practices of the system as a whole. These root concepts are like the largest overriding waves of change. They overshadow the smaller perturbations due to innovations related to particular institutions, inventions, or pieces of intermediate theory. The vanguard roles associated with root concepts are those of artist, scientist, philosopher, whose contribution is to make us alter our most fundamental views of things; and the crises to which they respond are the disequilibria associated with the deepest patterns of structural, theoretical and technological change.

Where 'idea' may have four such disparate meanings, not only the nature of the vanguard roles and related crises but the time-scales for emergence in good currency must vary enormously [. . .].

Implementation of Policy [. . .]

Implementation of Policy in a Learning System

The problem of implementing policy in a learning context is the problem of setting in motion and guiding, around central policy themes, a network of related processes of local public learning.

Within this process, the formation of policy cannot be neatly separated from its implementation. Every alleged example of local implementation of central policy, if it results in significant social transformation, is in fact a process of local social discovery. After-the-fact, there may be a way to state the new social policy to which all the local discoveries conform. But before the fact, there is no single policy statement which can be used to induce them.

Hence, the fostering of these processes cannot take the form of pre-defining policy and causing it to fan out from a centre. Central may provide first instances or policy themes which are take-off points for chains of transformation in localities. It may help local agencies to learn from one another's experience. It may even lend its weight to shifts in power structure which seem likely to lead to social discovery at the local level.

Also, the transformations of local systems influence one another, and may be supported in doing so. Moreover, the gradual transformation of the system as a whole influences the context in which each local system experiences its own transformation. The broad process can 'go critical' as ideas underlying the family of transformations come into good currency and as the numbers of learners and extenders multiply.

A system capable of behaving in this manner is a learning system. Within it, central's role is that of initiator, facilitator and goad to local learning. Such a process comes inevitably into conflict with demands for stable adherence to specific policies, and with demands for uniformity in the application of policies. It comes inevitably into conflict with many traditional procedures of the legislative and administrative process. It places special demands on the social systems of the agencies and on the networks through which information, people and money flow from central to local agencies and from all of these to one another. [...]

Conclusion

Government is an institution for performing public functions and an agent for inquiring into public problems affecting society as a whole.

As an instrument of public learning, the federal government of the United States rests largely on a theory of the stable state. It accepts as mysteriously given the issues around which policy and program must be shaped. It treats government as centre, the rest of society as periphery. Central has responsibility for the formation of new policy and for its imposition on localities at the periphery. Central attempts to 'train' agencies at the periphery. In spite of the language of experimentation, government-initiated learning tends to be confined to efforts to induce localities to behave in conformity with central policy. Localities learn to beat the system. Government tends to bury failure or to learn from it only in the sense of veering away from it. Evaluation, then, tends to be limited to the role of establishing and monitoring the extent of peripheral conformity with central policy.

The social systems of the agencies mirror the theory underlying the implementation of policies. Agencies are the social embodiment of policies, and in their efforts to sustain and protect themselves they also sustain and protect established policy. New problems fragment established agencies just as they fragment established policies. With the loss of the stable state, policies must be viewed as transient, their change being the foreground condition, and continuing fragmentation of agencies and policies becoming the rule.

For government to become a learning system, both the social system of agencies and the theory of policy implementation must change. Government cannot play the role of 'experimenter for the nation', seeking first to identify the correct solution, then to train society at large in its adaptation. The opportunity for learning is primarily in discovered systems at the periphery, not in the nexus of official policies at the centre. Central's role is to detect significant shifts at the periphery, to pay explicit attention to the emergence of ideas in good currency, and to derive themes of policy by induction. The movement of learning is as much from periphery to periphery, or from periphery to centre, as from centre to periphery.

Central comes to function as facilitator of society's learning, rather than as society's trainer.

Such a role is not appropriate to the stable areas of society in which steady, routine functions of government continue to be carried out; but it is appropriate to the areas in which public learning is required. Such a role deprives central of its monopoly on the formation of new policy. It demands a shift in the social system of government, which now serves and reinforces stable, compartmentalised policy. The concept of a government 'project system', made up of task forces and competence pools, serves only to illustrate what government as a self-transforming system might become.

When applied to government, this view of learning raises serious problems:

- The concept of legislation as a basis for policy tends to be accompanied by commitment to policy which remains stable over long periods of time. This view of public learning threatens established patterns of legislation, as well as processes for generating legislation and for relationships between administrative and legislative agencies.
- Arguments for the uniform application of policy (a phrase easier to state than to define) often rest on concepts of equity. What is the likelihood that the network of systems transformations at the periphery will result in policies which are equitable from region to region?
- Central government has as one of its functions the correction of inequities practiced in the regions – a function dependent, ostensibly, on its greater leverage and on its distance from the interests of established power in the regions. How is this function compatible with central's facilitative role?

These issues are real and they go to the roots of our governmental system. There may, indeed, be a conflict between the demands of public learning and the demands of legislative stability and governmental equity. If so, it conflict we must meet head on.

Chapter 2
Insights into Appreciation and Learning Systems

Geoffrey Vickers

Editor's Note: Geoffrey Vickers developed a set of concepts around the process of 'appreciation' in the sense of 'appreciating a situation'. Vickers wrote about appreciation over many years, with the purpose of making sense of his many public and private sector experiences of appreciating situations both alone, and with others, for instance in board room and committee meetings. In so doing he revealed much about what occurs in group processes of interaction. Vickers also wrote about other topics of relevance to social learning systems, including how humans affect and are affected by our contexts; institutional and personal roles in relation to our expectations and bringing about change; communication, and the principles of regulation of systems. His insights into appreciation and social learning systems are distributed across his writing. This chapter therefore comprises six edited extracts, five are from Vickers' work, from a range of different sources. The original footnotes have not been included. One extract is a diagram from Peter Checkland and Alejandro Casar that is an interpretation of Vickers' appreciative systems model. The chapter starts on a personal note that explains some of the author's context.

Extract 1 Foreword

[. . .] I grew to manhood before the First World War in an England that took stability for granted and regarded order – national and international – both as a self-regulating process of betterment called *progress* and also as a field for human design directed to the same end. These two not wholly consistent ideas applied in the political-social, the financial-economic, and the scientific-technological fields; all these fields are regarded as benign partners, the first still the most prized.

Of the 30 years following 1914 ten were spent in intensive warfare and twenty in the vain search for both national and international stability. By 1944 all my early assumptions were shaken, if not destroyed. Stability could not be taken for granted, could not even necessarily be assured by even the greatest conscious effort. Still,

Source: The sources of the extracts in this chapter are indicated at the end of each extract and in the references.

C. Blackmore (ed.), *Social Learning Systems and Communities of Practice*,
DOI 10.1007/978-1-84996-133-2_2, © The Open University 2010.
Published in Association with Springer-Verlag London Limited.

neither automatic regulation nor human design could be trusted to achieve 'betterment' by any of the diverse criteria that had emerged.

Worse was to come, but before it came an event occurred in the intellectual world that had a profound effect on me. In the decade following the war, a set of concepts about systems and their control that had been maturing in technological contexts during the previous decade was set loose in the general intellectual community by such writers as Norbert Wiener, Ludwig von Bertalannfy, and Ross Ashby. The effect on me was not so much revelation as liberation. The ideas did not seem surprising or even new, but they provided a new language in which to talk about the perplexing experience of my lifetime and a new point of view from which to regard it. The result was immensely illuminating. The relation between stability and *betterment*, the nature of the dialectic process of history, the extent of human initiative in influencing the course of a process of which it was itself part, the inescapable increase in constraint as well as enablement in every increase in organization, all this and much more, previously sensed chiefly as paradox, became understandable and discussable. I did not assume that this would make human affairs more controllable; but even if it did not, we should, I thought, be much the better for understanding the limits and conditions of human control. [. . .]

(Source: Vickers, 1987, pp. vii–viii)

Extracts 2 Appreciation, Appreciative Systems and Social Learning

Editor's Note: The following is a series of six short extracts taken from a range of Vickers' writing. My purpose here is to try and indicate as succinctly as possible what Vickers meant by appreciation and appreciative systems and how this relates to social learning.

Extracts begin here:

[. . .] It has been my experience that the debate which occupies hours, days, even months between the posing of some problem and its disposal serves not so much to produce a series of possible new solutions as to alter what those concerned regard as the relevant facts and the way in which these are classified and valued.

I recall an occasion when an important governing body debated for a year what should be done in a situation which seemed to require some radical solution. They finally decided that there was nothing to be done. No action followed – yet nothing was ever the same again. The mental activity which reached this negative conclusion radically changed their view and valuation of their situation. In particular, it changed their idea of what can be tolerated; a most important threshold in the regulative cycle.

Men, institutions and societies learn what to want as well as how to get, what to be as well as what to do; and the two forms of adaptation are closely connected. [. . .]

(Source: Vickers, 1987, p. 16)

We are changed not only by being talked to but also by hearing ourselves talk to others, which is one way of talking to ourselves. More exactly, we are changed by making explicit what we suppose to have been awaiting expression a moment before [. . .]. we know very little about how we carry on this extraordinary activity. We have not even a name for this state of affairs in our heads which is the fruit of past communication and which is both the target and the interpreter of present communication [. . .]. Nearly all our communication is directed to changing its state in others or in ourselves. It is strange that neither scientific nor common speech should have a word for it. I have taken to calling it an appreciative system, because the word *appreciation*, as we use it when we speak of appreciating a situation, seems to me to carry with it those linked connotations of interest, discrimination and valuation which we bring to the exercise of judgment and which tacitly determine what we shall notice, how we shall discriminate *situations* from the general confusion of ongoing events and how we shall regard them. I conceive it as consisting largely of categories for classifying and criteria for valuing experience [. . .] I call it a system because these categories and criteria are mutually related; a change in one is likely to affect others. The actual state of this system at any one time I will call its current setting. And I shall use these terms both for individuals and for those common settings which distinguish and give coherence to groups, societies and cultures.

(Source: Vickers, 1987, pp. 98–99)

This [appreciative] setting cannot be observed; it can only be inferred after the event and it changes with the events which reveal it. To take a very simple example – the meaning for me of a communication which I am about to receive will depend in part on whether I believe it; but my belief in it will depend in part on the impact which it makes on me when I hear it. So the appreciative system with which I await it may be radically reset by the activity of responding to it. Thus the setting of the appreciative system, personal and collective, is more uniquely self-determined by the cyclical process already noticed and thus more 'historical' than any other phenomenon which we need to understand.

(Source: Vickers, 1970, p. 207. © Sir Geoffrey Vickers Archives)

In the field of learning, I find it useful to draw two distinctions. The first is between learning to *appreciate* and learning how to act. Learning how to act has been intensively studied by psychologists and by students of artificial intelligence [. . .]. We have a fairly explicit model of the way in which both nervous systems and electronic systems develop *readiness-to-do*, awaiting appropriate signals. Within the field of appreciation I draw another much more difficult distinction between seeing and valuing. Ethologists recognize that even creatures much simpler than man [. . .] set up in their nervous systems some kind of map of their home ground, sufficient to guide them, wherever they may be within it. [. . .] In man, this capacity for representing to himself his manifold contexts and using these representations as a basis for communication and for forethought is his most striking characteristic, distinguishing him from other creatures far more sharply than his ingenuity as a doer. This kind of learning has received curiously little attention from psychologists, compared with the obsessive attention given to readinesses-to-do. [...] Readinesses-to-value are still further from the drawing boards of both psychologists and intelligence simulators [...]

(Source: Vickers, 1987, p. 94)

Most psychological research has concentrated on problems concerned with the selection of action, and for this purpose has held constant and made certain the relevant reality and value judgements. If we want to know how a rat solves a problem, we must know for certain what problem it is trying to solve; so we make it hungry enough to ensure that finding its food is its dominant problem. But most of the problems which humans try to solve are set by their own appreciative judgments and cannot be guessed without making assumptions about how reality and value judgments are formed.

(Source: Vickers, 1970, pp. 150–151. © Sir Geoffrey Vickers Archives)

The norms which regulate biological growth change only on an evolutionary time scale and are data for the individual [...] The learned responses of even the simplest organism are an individual achievement; but the criteria of success and failure which endorse them are largely given. Creatures capable of social learning, on the other hand, are exposed to two streams of education, one stemming from social experience and transmitted usually by the parents; the other stemming from individual experience (and lack of experience); and the two can often be seen in open conflict at levels far below the human. In human beings, both social and individual experience have been vastly amplified through the development of symbolic communication; and (probably from the same cause) the individual has developed means and needs to organise his own experience in the interests of inner consistency and acceptability, as well as external efficiency. Thus in each of us the appreciative system is in endless development, under the far from consistent demands of three hard masters. [...] the physical world of biological survival; the social world of communicating persons; and the personal world of conscious experience. We have to live with the realities of all three worlds, all equally real. And in all three dimensions, experience is constantly at work to develop that appreciative system which is the supreme artifact of individuals and societies.

(Source: Vickers, 1987, pp. 92–93)

Extract 3 Checkland and Casar's Interpretation of Vickers' Appreciative Systems Model

Editor's Note: Vickers never represented his idea of an appreciative system pictorially but the main idea might be followed more easily with the help of a diagram (see Fig. 2.1). Checkland and Casar (1986) devised a model of an appreciative system compatible with Vickers writings, reproduced here. They note (ibid, p. 3) that 'the appreciative system concerned may be that of an individual, an institution or a less formal human group'. Further details of what is included in each part of the process

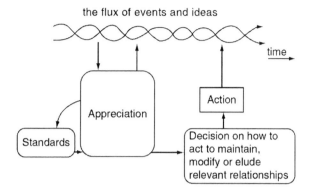

Fig. 2.1 Diagram of Vickers' appreciative systems model.
Checkland and Casar. (1986). *JASA*. 13(3–17), P. 6. Reproduced with permission from Peter Checkland

can be found in Checkland and Casar's paper. Some later versions of this model (e.g. Checkland, 1994) did not separate out the 'decision' part of the process.

Extract 4 Our Appreciated World and Our Appreciative System

Editor's Note: The following extract is almost all of a chapter called 'The Human Context' that appeared in Vickers book 'Freedom in a Rocking Boat', first published in 1970. It is one of several more detailed explorations that were part of his development of the concept of appreciation. Here the main emphasis is on 'the appreciative world' with some discussion of appreciative systems, settings and judgement. In this and following extracts I have sometimes changed Vickers use of 'men' which reflects his times. I have done this where I think that read today, it distracts from the point he is making.

Extract begins here:

[...] The most striking feature of [people], when compared with other animals, is not their ingenuity in doing – that 'goal-seeking' of which we have heard too much – but their capacity for knowing where they are. They can represent to themselves what I will call their contexts – all those manifold relations with the world around them which they pursue and on which they rely and which help to define their meaning to themselves and others. These include not only the private contexts of individuals at home, at work and at play but also the public contexts which concern both statesmen whose roles engage them personally and every citizen who feels him [or her] self personally concerned.

I have in mind the power of conscious reflection which enables us to represent to ourselves our relations with people and events and the relations of others which involve us. This enables us both to 'understand' – or perhaps misunderstand – them and to exercise judgement about them by comparing them with standards at which we have somehow arrived, of what we expect or desire or think right or acceptable. It thus affects our attitudes towards these relations and helps to determine what they actually are.

These representations – and this is a strange and most important point – include the dimension of *time*. We can represent to ourselves the real or hypothetical course of events, past, present and future, and the engagement of our hypothetical selves. It is a limited and fallible instrument, supported by subconscious processes which we may never be able to identify, and is far too weak for our present needs; but it is none the less potent and astonishing.

This faculty is, of course, very useful in deciding what to do, though this is not, I think, its most important function. Rehearsing possible futures on the stage of the mind, we can play out a dozen alternatives, based on different assumptions, including the assumption of different interventions by ourselves; and we can defer decision until their probable outcomes have been anticipated and compared. This procedure relieves trial and error of its usual costs and extends its use far beyond its normally narrow range. Having rehearsed some possible future where the curtain falls on disaster, we have only to dismiss the phantom actors and rewrite the script.

Knowledge gained from such an exercise is sometimes called 'feed-forward', to distinguish it from the feedback of actual experience. In all deliberate human action, feed-forward plays a far larger *direct* part than feedback. The signals of match and mis-match which alert our regulators are generated on the stage of the mind, usually by representations of the future.

Feedback is none the less incessant and indispensable; but it serves a different purpose. It monitors our representation of our context, confronting every expectation, as it matures, with the actuality to which it may or may not correspond. It corrects or at least criticizes – not only unsuccessful actions but, much more often, inept appreciation.

This control may operate at subtle and sophisticated levels. Suppose that in conversation the other party answers me 'angrily'. If this corresponds with one of the possible responses which my representation of his state of mind would lead me to expect, I am not surprised – but I am informed, for I am confirmed (perhaps wrongly) in that view of his state which makes sense of his response. If, on the other hand, I am surprised, I am still informed, though much less positively. I am told only that something is wrong with my appreciation of my context. I shall be led to wonder why my communication meant something to him which it did not mean to me.

More commonly, communication is expressly directed by the parties to it to comparing and bringing into conformity their appreciation of some context common to them all. This is the object of almost every rational argument in politics, business or private life. This again immensely extends the capacity for common action, which would otherwise be limited to [particular] situations [. . .] where the whole complex of 'contexts' is visible to all. It also extends, reciprocally, the power to communicate, since the understanding of communication depends on the possession of a shared viewpoint – as distinct from a shared view – of the matter under discussion.

This world of represented contexts is, I suggest, the world in which we effectively live. It is our supreme mental achievement. Most of our communication is directed to developing it, revising it, trying to reduce its inconsistencies, to test its accuracy and to extend its scope. I will call it our appreciated world.

The appreciated world is selected by our interests; for only some interest would lead us to notice any of its constituents. Of course, we have many contexts which we fail to notice. We of the West, for instance, had been polluting our air and water for several decades before this aspect of our relations claimed our attention. These neglected relations force themselves on our attention in time and thus become part of our appreciated world; but we may be sure that at any time important aspects of our relations are hidden from us, because we have not noticed them. At the personal level, we often notice in our friends and especially in our children these distressing discrepancies between their 'appreciated worlds' and aspects of the real world which they are unaccountably ignoring. They often notice the same in us.

This appreciated world, thus limited, is given form by our expectations. For it is these which, matching or mis-matching the unrolling stream of events, confirm it or call it into question. Matching, no less than mis-matching signals convey important information. They reassure us that our appreciated world is sufficiently in accord with the real world to be serviceable. They thus minister not only to the assurance of our actions but to the assurance of our lives. They make us feel at home in our appreciated world. (This is a major function of ritual and ritualized response, such as formalized greetings and conventional social behaviour.) The mass media of communication, in addition to more familiar disservices, render one which has not yet been charted and which in any case they could hardly avoid. By recording only the newsworthy, that is, the unusual, they radically alter the proportion between match and mismatch in the stream of our input and make the world seem even more unexpected than it actually is. How much this contributes to our anxiety and confusion we have no means of knowing.

Our appreciated world is given meaning by our standards of judgement, ethical, aesthetic, political and other. However these standards are generated and changed, there is no doubt that they give meaning to our experience. What happens – or might happen – is compared not only with our expectations but with this battery of standards by which we judge it to be welcome, important, acceptable, good, right or the reverse.

I thus conceive our appreciated world as carved out by our interests, structured by our expectations and evaluated by our standards of judgement. I find it confusing to give the word 'values' any narrower meaning than will comprehend interests and expectations, as well as standards of judgement. Without some 'standards' we could not notice anything at all – nor did we, when we lay in our cradles, before the whole build-up began. I have already stressed that 'standards', 'norms', by whatever name called, are fundamental to any kind of control, biological, psychological or sociological. The generation of multiple and partly conflicting standards is the distinguishing mark of [people] and their management is [their] human business.

'Values' in this sense discriminate and select facts, as well as give meaning to them. The antithesis between facts and values which has haunted Western science and philosophy for so long is due, I believe, to a radical misunderstanding of the meaning of both, to which I will return.

The appreciated world, as it grows, organizes our further experience and mediates our communication, as well as guides our actions. It is an hypothetical world, in the sense that it is largely built up on hypotheses, more or less developed, about how and why things happen as they do. It is also hypothetical in the sense that it is never completely validated, much of it is highly uncertain and some of it may be and may remain radically, undiscoverably and irremediably wrong – if only because it is sometimes ahead of and sometimes behind the constantly changing 'realities' that it selects and interprets. When events are inconsistent with it, they seldom throw light on what is wrong with it; feedback is often no more informative than the return of an undelivered letter. Though personal, it is a social construct; it would barely exist but for human communication. It is the major social, no less than the major personal, creation.

Above all, the appreciated world is both a *composite* and an *inexhaustible* world. It is composite because it is composed of views seen from different viewpoints, which cannot be simply added together. It is inexhaustible because these viewpoints may change and multiply without any obvious limit. We can see our surround as a source of support, a field of opportunity, a multiple threat, an intellectual puzzle. We can see ourselves acting and suffering simultaneously in a score of different roles. Each view selects its own relevant facts, in relation to its own relevant 'values'. Each view needs to be described from its own viewpoint, sometimes in its own language – as a sociologist, a rioter, a bystander and a policeman *need* to give different accounts of the 'same' riot. Accounts given from the same viewpoint may be more or less subject to ignorance and error and every effort is needed to make each conform to 'the facts'. But the differences between them are due not only to ignorance and error but to a difference in viewpoint which, by making different facts and values relevant, ensures that the resulting accounts will at best be neither conflicting nor cumulative but complementary.

The expectations which order our appreciated world are rules derived from regularities which we abstract from experience. As a simple example, to sighted creatures whose lifespan is measured in years, one of the most conspicuous regularities of nature is the alternation of day and night. This dramatic but regular change soon becomes recognized as a pattern, so that departure from it, as in an eclipse, becomes an alarming deviation. Except in low latitudes, another change is conspicuous, comprehending the first in an ampler pattern – the cyclical change in the proportions of light and darkness; and from this in time is abstracted the pattern of the seasons. To measure this alternation with sufficient precision is an early scientific achievement of the agricultural epoch, making possible the predictions involved in the sowing and storage of grain; but the pattern is sufficiently gross to be derivable from ordinary experience, given sufficient exposure to it.

The abstraction of rules from regularities like these is an example of that capacity for *pattern recognition* on which we rely not only in everything we do but in building the representation of our manifold contexts within which we live. This is the process of discovering order in – or imposing order on – the environment, which science has carried so far.

Not all the aspects of our environment are equally predictable. Rain and wind over the British Isles can be forecast, even by modern meteorology, only roughly a few days in advance. None the less, human experience, without benefit of any science, abstracts some useful generalizations – for example, that winds are not likely to exceed a given force or rain a given intensity and duration or floods a given height or annual rainfall to stray outside given limits – rules of which, in an old legal phrase, 'the memory of man runneth not to the contrary'.

These two kinds of regularity have been developed by Western science into its imposing structure of general and statistical laws.

Both science and common sense can contribute more than general and statistical laws to our understanding of where we are. A meteorological map, for example, shows variations in barometric pressure as a *system* of depressions, ridges and so on, moving and generating movements which will reverse them. The direction and force of the wind in an area over a period is represented as largely a function of these pressure gradients, of their movements and the speed of their change. The actual state of the field, still more its future changes, are not accurately known and perhaps may never be, but the concept serves to model the process and thus to give both a better understanding of what is and a better forecast of what will be.

[People] without benefit of science were familiar with such systematic relations – often more familiar than Western [people] are now. The relations between the size of the pastoral tribe, the number of its animals, its maximum rate of movement and the pasture available are systematic relations. Pastoral tribes must have been well aware of them and of the relative costs of the different ways, of keeping them in balance.

[Individuals] in their dealings with [others] create and recognize another kind of regularity – rules of their own devising, imposed and accepted consciously and unconsciously. The only reason why [people] are by and large more predictable than the weather is that they are *concerned to be predictable*; concerned to meet each other's expectations by accepting common self-expectations. This web of mutual expectations, [. . .] creates an order of which the regularities obey neither general nor statistical laws. They do not even show the regularities to be observed in simpler systems such as the weather. They evolve by an historical process which is neither reversible nor repeatable, because it generates those constantly changing standards to which I have referred and in consequence is constantly resetting its own regulators.

The description which I have given of the way in which we learn to appreciate our contexts is not, I believe, inconsistent either with common experience or with accepted views about knowing and learning, so far as they go. Yet it may seem to run counter to the deeply ingrained assumption that knowing is or ought to be an activity independent of any kind of human views or values; that these intervene only to distort or obscure our knowledge of 'reality as it really is'. To cast doubt on this may seem to question the 'objectivity' of science and the whole heritage of assurance which has been built on it.

I think this is mistaken [and discuss that elsewhere]. [. . .] I will [here] define a little more clearly the terms which I am using to describe both the process and the result of the process which I call 'appreciating', a word which I use because I want to escape from what seem to me the unduly narrow connotations of our ideas of knowing and of learning and from the distinction between them.

To account for the appreciated world – which is, after all, one of the most assured facts of our experience – I postulate that experience, especially the experience of human communication, develops in each of us readinesses to notice particular aspects of our situation, to discriminate them in particular ways and to measure them against particular standards of comparison, which have been built up in similar ways. These readinesses in turn help to organize our further experience, which, as it develops, becomes less susceptible to radical change. Circular relations of this kind are the commonest facts of life, though we are handicapped in accepting them by our long conditioning to the idea of causal *chains*, linearly linked in time. Since there are no facts, apart from some screen of 'values' which discriminates, selects and relates them, just as there are no values except in relation to some configuration of fact, I use the word appreciation to describe the joint activity which we call knowing and which we sometimes suppose, I think mistakenly, to be a separable, cognitive activity which is 'value-free'. Since these readinesses are organized into a more or less coherent system, I speak of them as an appreciative system. I sometimes refer to their state at any point of time as their appreciative setting and to any act which expresses them as an appreciative judgement. The appreciative world is what our appreciative system enables us to know.

(Source: Vickers, 1972, pp. 95–102. © Sir Geoffrey Vickers Archives)

Extract 5 Institutional and Personal Roles

Editor's Note: This extract is part of a chapter by the same name that appeared in Vickers' book 'Making Institutions Work' first published in 1973. That book consisted of three parts: part one was about 'The Institutional Explosion', part two, where this chapter appeared, was called 'Institutions and Persons' and part three was entitled 'Education for Multiple Membership'. The full version of this chapter included further examples from the times of writing and further sections on conceptual innovations, self and mutual expectations, changing the institutional system, bearing the institutional system and the personal role.

The Institutional and the Personal

We recognise that the institutions of government and business in America and other Western countries have become so closely interwoven that we may regard them as a system. This system is run by [individuals], but by [individuals] playing institutional roles. Their criteria of judgment and their standards of success seem to us to be those of the institutions which they serve. So when the system produces threats which alarm us or wrongs which outrage us, we may conclude that the system's ideas of success are quite different from our own. Some people feel so about the Vietnam war. Many people are equally offended at the way the system distributes incomes, wealth and power.

Apart from criticisms of what it is trying to achieve, we may also become anxious at the system's failure to do even what it is trying to do. We can see that the greatest cities are becoming ungovernable. And when we hear of great enterprises threatened with bankruptcy, we may question whether they have become unmanageable. Like men at sea, we may become anxious either about the course the ship is taking or about its ability to keep afloat, or both. Either is sufficiently alarming.

The managers of every kind of institution are equally familiar with both anxieties. They are expected to keep the institution in being and at the same time to realise the most acceptable mix of all the various things they are trying to do. The goals of balancing and optimising (or even 'satisfying') always conflict; yet the same set of decisions must serve both.

Our present institutions can be criticised both on grounds of responsiveness and on grounds of efficiency. They may need radical change. But unhappily we cannot assume that all our troubles are due to these defects. There are problems which attach to human governance as such and they are mounting. They would be making greater demands on our institutions and on us, whatever our institutions. We have no reason to be surprised at the mounting instability of the system.

The first of these general factors is the enormous expansion of the ethical dimension. The question of who gets what becomes an ethical question whenever the answer depends, or is thought to depend, even in part on human decisions. As our environment becomes increasingly human, so an increasing proportion of our threats and blessings seem to stem from the decisions of other [people] and so fall into the class about which we can argue that they ought to be different and which we can change, if at all, by the techniques which influence [people], rather than by those which manipulate the physical world.

The present storm of ethical protests is largely due, I believe, to the huge expansion of issues which are rightly deemed to be ethical. The wilderness does not owe us a living. Even the market does not owe us a living. But between us and those impersonal worlds is spread an institutional world on which we subsist, all of us as members, most of us also as employees. And all our individual rights as members, even as employees, have an ethical dimension. We can meaningfully argue about what they ought to be.

A second factor is the ambiguity which surrounds the concepts of forecasting and planning when we apply them to human affairs. Nothing human is predictable in the sense in which the movements of the moon are predictable; and no operations on them are plannable in the sense in which moon landings are plannable. Some years back an English study showed that the population of southeast England would increase by 5 million in the next 20–30 years. Plans were proposed for new towns, new highways and so on. But the already overcrowded people in southeast England refused to accept this figure as a prediction. If the towns were not built, the population would not expand. Of course this view, like the other, was only partly true; demographic changes are not wholly obedient to a planner's will.

But equally they are not unaffected by a planner's plans or even by a forecaster's forecasts.

A third factor is the growing disparity in scale between problems, agencies and beneficiaries. In 1961 a British minister of transport commissioned a report on urban traffic congestion. The report pointed out that this congestion was not a problem but a symptom of the problem that modern cities generate more activity than they can contain. The smallest system worth studying was the city, not just its roads. Cities could indeed be redesigned to contain more activity than they do now. But any such redesigning would have to take account not just of accessibility by vehicle but of access on foot, safety, parking, amenity and so on; of which disparate and conflicting goods different partial satisfactions were to be had at varying prices.

The problem involves a whole physico-social system. But the agency which commissioned the study was a functional department responsible only for transport. And the people for whose benefit the exercise was being done were concerned with even smaller fragments, differing radically with their position. Those who lived in the restricting houses were frustrated by the encroaching cars. Those who used the encroaching cars were frustrated by the restricting houses.

The example brings out a fourth factor – conflict between the divergent interests of the beneficiaries, bred by this disparity of scale. These conflicts must grow greater as larger scale problems impose larger scale solutions.

So apart from any defects of our present institutions, any future institutions are going to make greater demands on their beneficiaries, who in some capacities must also be their victims – greater demands on their intelligence; greater demands on their breadth of interest; greater demands on their confidence; and greater demands on their ability to reconcile conflicts, including conflicts of role; greater demands in fact on their humanity. As human beings we should not object to that.

But it sets us thinking about the nature and the limitations of these nets of mutual dependence in which we are enmeshed and so about the expectations on which they depend. And this brings us to the ubiquitous concepts of role; because role systems are precisely nets of self- and mutual expectation.

From varied experience of playing institutional, professional and personal roles and reconciling their conflicting demands, I have reached some conclusions which are currently unfashionable.

First, I attach a wider meaning to the concept of role playing than some may find familiar. What I have come to expect of myself and of others and to regard as legitimate expectations by them from me seems to describe a good deal of what I am and what others trust me to be. So I do not hesitate to talk of personal roles, which some people today may regard as a contradiction in terms.

Next, I think of role playing as a creative activity and of role players as agents of change. This is partly but by no means wholly because I have been lucky in playing roles in new and fluid organisations, apart from the role of being myself, which was once more new and fluid than any.

Third, I attach great importance to the element of conflict which is present in all role playing. There is conflict between institutional and personal roles. There is conflict between institutional roles and within each individual role, whether institutional or personal. But this does not frustrate them or make them unplayable. The resolution and containment of conflict is what role playing is all about.

Finally, I have learned from personal experience, as well as from observation, that the capacity for resolving and containing the conflicts inherent in roles varies with the role player, no less than with the role. I am thankful that there should be men and women willing and able to play, even badly, all the roles I cannot play at all. [...]

[...] any world which generations younger than mine may create or preserve on the other side of the dark decades ahead will include an institutional dimension and will make the same demands on us as players both of institutional and of personal roles. It will generate the same tensions and will require at least as much mutual trust as ours today. No organisational panacea will relieve any of us of the duty to sustain these tensions or to generate that trust. Institutional roles may impoverish or enrich us; and so, as they develop, may the personal roles which are so much a part of our personalities. But equally, both are our opportunities for making ourselves and our societies. [People] without role conflicts would be [people] without roles and [people] without roles would not be [people].

(Source: Vickers, 1973, pp. 105–108, 121. © Sir Geoffrey Vickers Archives)

Extract 6 The Limits of Government

Editor's Note: This extract comes from a long and detailed chapter in Vickers' book 'Value Systems and Social Process' that was first published in 1968. I was unable to include the chapter in its entirety within my word limits here so have edited it, picking up on the main points but not including the detailed examples. This might make it somewhat hard to follow in places – this is my doing not Vickers'! When reading, it is worth remembering (i) that Vickers' time of writing preceded digital communications technologies and (ii) that his deliberations are offered in the spirit of exploring human limitations and what we can and cannot control, which he has extended here to our political and social systems. In the latter part of the extract he refers a lot to 'regulation' which he discussed earlier in his book from ecologists' and engineers' viewpoints of reaching 'steady state' in terms of population dynamics and developing feedback devices through modelling patterns observed in nature.

Extract begins here:

I am not a political scientist; only a student of communication, and, in particular, of the part which human communication plays in the regulation of human societies. This study leads back – or on – along two closely related paths. One is the study of systems generally, in the search for principles of regulation common to them all. The other is the study of communication generally, in the search for better ways of understanding those levels of communication which distinguish human societies from other types of system. These studies are new, many-sided, and rapidly growing;

I claim no expertise in either. But they seem to be the fields in which I can most usefully think aloud in the presence of political scientists.

They have also a topical relevance, for they seem to me to provide apt language for describing simply and sharply the principal threat which shadows the world's political perspectives and the principal dimensions along which escape will have to be sought. I will first describe this threat as a breakdown in the conditions which make possible the regulation of political systems such as support us now. Then I will analyse this breakdown a little further, first as an ecological trap and then as a failure of communication.

Let me begin with a rather arid summary of what I understand by the regulation of a political system.

By a social system I understand a set of ongoing relations between persons and organizations, governed by mutual expectations which are usually embodied in roles. It is, of course, a very complex pattern. Each of us forms part of several subsystems and each of these is incorporated in varying degrees in others. Whether we focus our attention on the family, the neighbourhood, the city, or on the factory, the university, the trade union, we distinguish something which we regard as a continuing entity but only to the extent and in the field in which it maintains through time two sets of relationships which are themselves intimately linked – the internal ones which relate its members to each other and the external ones which link it, as a whole, to its surround. The entity is in fact a pattern of relationships, subject to change but recognizably extended in time. This way of regarding the objects of our attention helps to resolve the ancient dichotomy between the individual and society and many other pseudo-problems resulting from the tendency, built into our language, to regard the objects of our attention as 'things', rather than systematically related sequences of events.

Within this comprehensive picture I will distinguish a political system as constituted by those relations which a society seeks to regulate by the exercise of public power. This definition would be too narrow for some purposes but it distinguishes one group of relations which deserves a name. The departmental organization of central and local government distinguishes a host of relations which it is the function of these departments to regulate – the relation of roads and road-users, houses and home-seekers, schools and school-children, sickness and hospitals; the level of employment, the balance of trade, the balance of payments, the balance of international power, and so on. Every political activity is directed to the regulation of some set of ongoing relations, whether internal to the system controlled by the regulator or external, between that system and other systems.

Regulation operates by manipulating one or other term of the relationship or both. We may build roads or restrict traffic, build schools or abstain from raising the school-leaving age, increase the armed forces or cut our international commitments. Equally, of course, we may fail, partly or even wholly, in our regulative efforts. But even where we fail, I regard the relations in question as having been brought within the political system by the decision to treat them as regulable by acts of public power and thus to separate them from the host of other relations which are left to the regulation of the market or the family or of other determinants.

Even my casual list of examples shows how changeable is the content of a political system thus defined; for most of the relations it mentions were not regarded as necessary or even proper subjects of regulation a few decades ago. If we tried to distinguish the changes which forced these new regulative tasks on to the public power, we should have, I think, to distinguish at least three kinds, the physical, the institutional, and what I will call the appreciative. In the first I include all the changes of an island increasingly urbanized, mechanized, and populated; in the second, all the changes in the institutions by which we carry on our collective living. In the third I include all the changes in our ways of appreciating our situation; what we notice and what we ignore; what we regard as acceptable or unacceptable, important or unimportant, demanding or not demanding action by us. I regard this appreciative system as no mere derivative of the other two. They interact mutually and determine each other.

Consider one example. For many millennia the River Thames has earned its name as a continuing entity. It is in fact the way in which water from a stable catchment area finds its way to the sea. It expresses the relationships, changing but continuous, between rainfall, contours and porosity of the area, vegetation, and a host of other physical variables.

Throughout this time until very recently its valley provided a habitat for many species, including men, who long ago learned to live above its floodmarks and to cultivate its alluvial soil. Then we began to incorporate this river, once an independent variable, into our own man-made socio-technical system. We controlled its floods with barrages and dykes. We adapted it for transportation. We distributed its water. We used it as a sewer. Our demands rose and began to conflict with each other, making necessary, for example, the control of pollution. Now these demands have begun to conflict in total with the volume of the river. We plan to supplement it by pumping out the deep reservoirs. Soon, unless some other solution appears, we shall be supplementing its flow by pumping desalted water from the sea. By then the Thames as an independent physical system, part of the given environment, will have virtually disappeared within a human socio-technical system, dependent on new physical constructions, new institutions, and a new attitude to the use of water and the regulation of the whole water cycle.

Regarding the content of a political system as the relations which it aspires to regulate, I will describe as its setting the standards by which these relations are deemed acceptable or unacceptable. Such standards are essential to regulation. The problems of the traffic regulator are set by the standard of congestion which is regarded as unacceptable. Without such a standard there would be no problem and nothing to regulate. All regulation depends on setting standards by a process of human valuation.

Many people dislike applying mechanical analogies to human affairs but I find it useful, for contrast as well as for similarity, to compare political governors with engineers before the instrument panel of some mechanical assembly. The engineer watches dials, each of which displays the course of some important variable, showing how closely it approximates to some desired standard or how dangerously it strays towards some critical threshold. These standards and thresholds are the settings of his system; and these signals of match and mismatch alert him to the need for regulative action. The picture serves equally for the political governor. He too watches the course of a limited number of variables – limited by his own interests in them and further limited by the number which he can usefully attempt to watch and regulate; and he too depends on signals of match and mismatch for his guidance.

There are differences also. The indices which the political governor watches are for the most part not mere observations of the present state of critical variables but estimates of their future course, based on his latest knowledge of them (which is usually imperfect) and worked up by a process of mental simulation. A more important difference is that half his skill consists in setting the standards which he shall try to attain. For unlike the engineer, who controls a system designed to be controllable, the politician intervenes in a system not designed by him, with the limited object of making its course even slightly more acceptable or less repugnant to his human values than it would otherwise be.

In our society, as in many others, this setting has changed startlingly in recent years. The content of our political system – the sum of relations which we aspire to regulate – has grown and is growing in volume; and the standards to be attained have risen and are rising. The action needed to attain and hold these standards requires more massive operations supported by greater consensus over far longer periods of time than in the past. On the other hand, the situations which demand regulation arise and change with ever shorter warning and become ever less predictable, as the rate of change accelerates and the interacting variables multiply. Clearly the task of the political regulator becomes ever more exacting.

By contrast, the capacity of political societies for accepting regulation is being eroded by several factors. The capacity for collective response is dulled, when the situation which should evoke it is not present to experience but is a mental construct, based on uncertain predictions. It is further dulled by those policies of collective security which cushion the individual against even such present experience as he might otherwise have. It is further limited by the need for greater consensus and by the increasing vulnerability of that consensus to the resistance of protesting or predatory minorities. Above all, it is limited by the emergence of time thresholds, which deny the opportunity needed for the gestation of innovation. These factors [...] create, as it seems to me, a wild and growing disparity between the least regulation that the situation demands and the most that it permits. This is the dilemma [...] I want now to examine more fully from the two angles which I described earlier – first, as an ecological trap; and, secondly, as a failure of communication.

[...] Many species have perished in ecological traps of their own devising. We may already have passed the point of no return on the road to some such abyss.

A population in a favourable but unfilled habitat normally multiplies at a constant rate until it meets or breeds limitations which slow and in time arrest its further growth. It may then stabilize, at or below its maximum, in the same or an altered form, with oscillations of less or greater amplitude; or it may even disappear, because in its period of expansion it has either unfitted itself for life in a limited environment or unfitted its environment to support even a limited population. These are the ecological traps I mentioned, in their most acute form. We call them traps only because our interest is engaged by the species they ensnare. From other viewpoints, such as an interest in the continuance of organic life, the replacement of one species by another is of no importance or appears as a salutary bit of regulation.[...]

The stability of [traditional] societies results from the fact that their way of life does not of itself disturb either the milieu or the society itself in its physical, its institutional, or its appreciative aspect. Each generation, taking over the skills, the institutions, and the ideas of the one before, finds them as apt as ever to the milieu in which they have been developed and the purposes which they have been designed to serve. [...] [However, we] now seem to be approaching a point at which the changes generated within a single generation may render inept for the future the skills, the institutions, and the ideas which form that generation's main legacy to posterity – and the next generations' principal heritage. If this is true, it looks to me like an ecological trap [...] though the determinants of the trap are social and cultural, rather than biological.

But it is true? The analogy is obviously far from exact. Ecological traps arise because biological evolution works too slowly to adapt some species or population to some environmental change or rate of change. Need we assume any significant limits to the far more rapid processes of cultural and political development?

I think we must. The reasons appear when we define the conditions that make regulation possible. They are, I suggest, four:

First, the regulator must be able to discriminate those variables that are involved in the relations it seeks to regulate and to predict – or control – their future course over a period at least as long as the time needed to make an effective response.

Secondly, it must be able to preserve sufficient constancy among its standards and priorities to make a coherent response possible.

Thirdly, it must have in its repertory or be able to discover some response which has a better than random chance of being successful.

Fourthly, it must be able to give effect to this response within the time which the first and second condition allow.

[These] four conditions are limiting [...]. The most obvious disparity is between the 'lead times' needed to mount any regulative action and the future span over which any reliable prediction can be made. The first grows ever longer; [...]. The second grows ever shorter; [...]. [This situation is due largely to] the limitations of human communication. The long lead times which intervene between emergent need for action and its achievement are partly due to the delays inherent in the processes of generating a sufficiently agreed view of the situation, a sufficient consensus on the course to pursue, and sufficient common action to achieve it; and all these are collective processes, mediated by communication. Even the confusion and loss which rapid technological innovation produces by its unplanned impact on other parts of the process only express a human failure to achieve, at that level, that phasing of complex activities which, at simpler levels, is recognized as a proper technological necessity and a proper technological skill. The far more difficult conflicts between nations, classes and cultures [...] remain insoluble so long as they reflect the lack of any common basis for communication. Technology has made this lack into a threat, by reducing the distance between cultures and increasing the distance between generations; but it did not cause the lack and it cannot abate the threat.

[...] Since we depend absolutely on communication, within societies, between societies, and between the generations, developments which threaten these communications with failure are a lethal form of trap. By failure of communication I do not mean failure in the means to transmit, store, and process information. Of that we have already more than we can use. I mean failure to maintain, within and between political societies, appropriate shared ways of distinguishing the situations in which we act, the relations we want to regulate, the standards we need to apply, and the repertory of actions which are available to us. This fabric, on which communication depends, is itself largely the product of communication. Demands on it are rising. We need to consider what chance there is of meeting them and at what cost; especially at a time when new techniques for handling information are finding their way into the regulative process at all levels, based on assumptions about how that process works which are not, I think, well validated and at the same time changing the process more deeply than we realize. [...]

(Source: Vickers, 1970, pp. 89–98. © Sir Geoffrey Vickers Archives)

References

Checkland, P. 1994, Systems theory and management thinking. *American Behavioural Scientist* 38, p. 83.

Checkland, P.B. and Casar, A. 1986, Vickers concept of an appreciative system: a systemic account. *Journal of Applied Systems Analysis* 13, pp. 3–17.

Vickers, G. 1970, *Value systems and social process*. Penguin Books: London (First published by Tavistock Publications in 1968).

Vickers, G. 1972, *Freedom in a rocking boat*. Penguin Books: London (First published by Penguin: Harmondsworth in 1970).

Vickers, G. 1973, *Making institutions work*. Associated Business Programmes: London.

Vickers, G. 1987, *Policymaking, communication and social learning: essays of Sir Geoffrey Vickers*. Adams, G., Forester, J., Catron, B. Eds. Transaction Publishers: New Brunswick.

Part II
Critical Social Learning Systems – The Hawkesbury Tradition

This part of the book describes a tradition of social learning systems developed in Australia which has informed thousands of practitioners around the world in life-changing yet subtle ways that have enabled them to improve their practices. The approach associated with this tradition has been used, mainly, in development contexts that involve managing human and natural resources in more sustainable ways.

At first sight this description might sound like a contradiction in terms. How can ideas that have the potential to affect and change lives remain subtle? My impression is that these qualities come from an approach that builds on the learners' experiences to the extent that those who engage with it are encouraged to integrate the many different dimensions of their learning. Integration here is in the sense that, for instance, a learner's existing worldviews are accommodated while other worldviews are appreciated. West Churchman (1971), the American philosopher, referred to the ability to hold different, preferably conflicting, worldviews together at the same time with others as 'maturity'. This implies viewing the world from as many different perspectives as possible and from a systemic perspective to use those different worldviews to inform the other. Few approaches to learning appear to me to address this worldview aspect of learning as well as that developed by the group of academics and other practitioners at Hawkesbury. The impact of their work has not been limited to their part of Australia, as those involved have moved on to other contexts. In the way that this group of practitioners synthesised many systems-related ideas and practices from different domains and locations around the world, their work has also influenced others elsewhere. Two of the chapters in this book have been written by Richard Bawden who had a leading position in the Hawkesbury group over many years. Jim Woodhill and Ray Ison's times at Hawkesbury were shorter but influential to their subsequent work. All three, and others from the group, have worked in many different locations and with many other people around the world.

Before reviewing what distinguishes the Hawkesbury approach from others, I first consider some of the contextual factors that prompted development of this critical social learning systems perspective. Land and water catchment degradation, desertification, use of 'natural' resources more generally and failure to manage for climate variability (including floods and drought) have become major issues in rural

Australia, with many effects to and from urban areas, including issues around, for instance, water supply and bush fires. There have also been major efforts to involve local communities in land conservation and integrated natural resource management, many of them successful at a local level. But, as in many parts of the world, the capacity and ability to take account of interconnections among people and their environments have been limited by the nature of institutions at local, national and international levels. It is against this kind of background that the authors of the chapters in this part of the book deliberate and make their recommendations for more systemic praxis.

Two distinguishing factors of the Hawkesbury approach are that *epistemology* and *ethics* are valued, alongside other dimensions, as important to learning. The epistemic dimension deals with valuing different kinds of knowledge and ways of knowing, explicitly, and with the idea that we each have an individual episteme that can change and develop over time, indeed so that our worldviews can mature as Churchman suggests. The ethical dimension is manifest in the 'critical' focus of the Hawkesbury work which, in common with other critical systems traditions (e.g. critical systems heuristics), has been influenced by critical theory.

A third factor that distinguishes the Hawkesbury work is its focus on *systemic praxis* and it was largely for this reason that I selected it as a case study for this book. From my experience of working with people associated with Hawkesbury, through my own teaching, research and scholarship, I got a sense of people not just using systems theories or immersed in systemic practice but blending both together. Also in the process of practising what they teach they appeared to develop understanding of what it means to *be* systemic. To capture this aspect in the written word is, I think, quite difficult. Some aspects of the following chapters focus on theory that might be unfamiliar to readers, in which case there might seem to be a lot to take in. From past experiences of reading this material I recommend in that case a second read through along with some further exploration of the contexts described.

In Chapter 3 Richard Bawden presents the story of the Hawkesbury group, its ideas and practices as seen in 1997. The chapter is a written version of a presentation made at an international conference concerning community development and includes a range of diagrams representing critical learning systems. Key points are drawn out in boxes.

Chapter 4 was written by Jim Woodhill in 2002, adapted from part of his 1999 PhD thesis and based on his research and other experiences with a community-based land conservation movement called 'Landcare'. He is particularly concerned with institutional and political dimensions of multi-level social learning and draws on the themes of 'risk society' and 'reflexive modernisation' after Ulrich Beck and Anthony Giddens.

Chapter 5, written in 2005, describes Ray Ison's perspective on social learning systems. It emphasises the need to be aware of our 'traditions of understanding' and frames these traditions in terms of language, dialogue and experience. He makes links with other systems traditions such as soft systems methodology and grounds the chapter in research on social learning in the implementation of new European legislation for managing water resources and other examples.

Chapter 6 was written in 2009 by Richard Bawden, specifically for this book. The chapter continues the story begun in Chapter 3 giving an overview of praxis associated with critical social learning systems. He focuses specifically on worldviews and their influence and systemic competencies. Among the influences of Hawkesbury some of the work of Vickers (as discussed in Chapter 2) is included. Descriptions of the Australian contexts appear in the second half of the chapter, which ends with some challenging questions regarding our collective behaviour and what we do and do not seem to appreciate.

References

Churchman, C.W. (1971) *The Way of Inquiring Systems: The Design of Inquiring Systems.* Basic Books, New York.

Suggested Further Reading

Several 'special issues' of academic journals have documented the experiences of the Hawkesbury group. Details of two of these publications are given below. There is also a lot of online material (available through using a search tool such as 'Google' on the Internet) that documents contemporary issues in Australia that might usefully be informed by critical social learning systems approaches.

1. *Cybernetics & Human Knowing*, Vol. 7, No. 4, 2000.
   The editors of this special issue on reflective practice in learning and research, that includes articles from Hawkesbury were Nadarajah Sriskandarajah and Søren Brier.
2. *Systems Research and Behavioral Science*, Vol. 22, No. 2., 2005.
   This issue published papers from the Hawkesbury group that were presented at the 47th Meeting of the International Society for Systems Sciences held in Crete in 2003. This meeting celebrated the achievements of the group on the 25 year anniversary of the launch of its work in 'systems education'. The guest editorial was written by Richard Bawden.

Chapter 3
The Community Challenge: The Learning Response

Richard Bawden

Genesis

In this presentation I intend to narrate a story that has its particular origins in three strategic decisions collectively taken, almost 20 years ago now, by a small group of educators within a small agricultural polytechnic located on the urban/rural fringe of Australia's largest city. It is a story which arises out of the integrated thoughts and actions of an academic community, which, tired of its marginal status, decided in the late 1970s, to profoundly and concurrently transform itself as a School of Agriculture in three fundamental ways: (a) to change its own focus from production agriculture to responsible rural development, (b) to change its own emphasis from a teaching approach based on courses to one of learning based on projects, and (c) to change its own prevailing reductionist paradigm to embrace an holistic one. The mission became one of helping people in rural communities across the state, to learn their way forward to better futures, in the face of the immensely complex, dynamic, and slowly degrading environments – socio-economic, politico-cultural and bio-physical – in which they increasingly recognised they were deeply embedded. The intent would thus become that of helping people to see their worlds differently as a prelude for doing things differently – essentially more systemically. The context for this grand enterprise is captured in the aphorism 'if we always see how we've always seen, we'll always be who we've always been'! Changing the way we collectively construe ourselves means collectively changing the way we think about ourselves, to lead in turn, to changing the way we collectively act.

In this manner, we, as faculty at Hawkesbury Agricultural College, committed ourselves to helping in the facilitation of the development of learning communities across rural Australia, through the direct involvement of our students and ourselves, in collaborative learning projects with members of rural families and communities. As faculty and students alike, we would learn how to become a learning community

---

Source: Bawden (1999). Reproduced with permission. Originally this chapter was an Invited Plenary Paper: 29th Annual International Meeting of the Community Development Society. Athens Georgia 27–30th July 1997.

C. Blackmore (ed.), *Social Learning Systems and Communities of Practice*,
DOI 10.1007/978-1-84996-133-2_3, © The Open University 2010.
Published in Association with Springer-Verlag London Limited.

of scholar practitioners, through our active participation in other emerging learning communities, and critical reflection upon those engagements.

> Together we would learn how to see the world differently, and in the process, discover just how difficult a transformation this is, for individuals and the community both.

Many of the details of the journey which has ensued to date at Hawkesbury following those essential decisions, including both theoretical and practical details of the evolution of the processes of curriculum reform, of community outreach, of research, and of the organisation itself, have already been told elsewhere (cf. Bawden et al., 1984; Bawden, 1992; Bawden and Packham, 1993). What has not yet been clearly described or explained however, are recent developments in the model of the learning process which is central to the whole endeavour of what can now be referred to as, systemic development. This is the praxis involved in bringing abstract 'systems ideas' to bear to help inform actions to deal with events which are being experienced in the concrete world; and vice-versa, with systems ideas being generated out of the process of critical reflections on both the events themselves, and the actions which are being used to deal with them, which includes the process itself – the systemic development of systemic development, if you will, in which the metaphor of the community as a critical learning system is privileged.

This presentation provides an opportunity then not just to give an update on the model of critical learning systems, but more importantly, to illustrate the manner by which that model is being both generated and used in practice in the creation of learning communities.

A Word About Systems

It is important to emphasise here that the word system as it is used in the present context, has a particular conceptual meaning, which is distinct from the rather woolly way that the word is often used in everyday conversation. Thus in contrast to the loose metaphoric images which are conjured up with talk of transport systems or information systems or health systems, critical learning systems reflect the notion of formal entities with particular structures and properties. To the systems theorist, a system is an organised, coherent, whole entity, which has, or can be assumed to have, properties which are unique to it as a whole entity. More formally stated 'a system is a group of interacting components' (subsystems) that conserves some identifiable set of relations with the sum of the components plus their relations (i.e., the system itself) conserving some identifiable set of relations to other entities (including other systems) (Laszlo and Laszlo, 1997). In other words, when the component parts of a system interact together within the boundary of that system, the process results in the emergence of properties which are different from the mere additive effects of those parts and unique to that particular system – the system is different from the sum of its parts. Moreover, as each component part of a system is also a 'lower order' (sub)system itself, and each system is, in turn, a subsystem of a 'higher order' (supra)system, unique and quite unpredictable properties emerge at a number of different levels of order within what is envisaged as a hierarchy of systems embedded within other systems. When we talk of the environment of a system, we are actually talking of a higher order system in which it is embedded. Systems are systems within systems within systems etc.

It also follows from this logic that each subsystem within a system must be different from all of the others in that system; so different indeed, that a 'tension of difference' exists between them. Subsystems not only influence each other through their interactions, but it is these interactions which create the whole. The whole is different from the sum of its parts because of what von Bertalanffy (1968) termed 'the glorious unity of opposites'.

> The notion of wholeness through 'tensions of difference' is absolutely central to the usefulness of the critical learning systems approach to community development.

From this it is clear that each subsystem must also be significantly different from the system as whole, yet have the potential to influence and be influenced by it. As Ackoff (1981) sees this: each subsystem has an effect on the functioning of the whole, while each is also affected by at least one other subsystem within the whole. These principles of diversity and what is termed 'requisite variety', are also central to the concept of critical learning systems. Finally, systems can only retain their coherence within and across these embedded hierarchies through cybernetic networks of feedback communication and control. The stability of systems is maintained through what is termed 'negative' (or deviation attenuating) feedback, while 'positive' (or deviation amplifying) feedback tends to provoke system into unstable states. Typically these two types of forces are working concurrently; adding further to the 'tensions of difference'. Under certain circumstances, these tensions reach such a level that the whole system suddenly succumbs. As a consequence, it becomes destabilised and for a while acts quite 'chaotically'. This phase is often followed by an equally sudden re-stabilisation in a new and frequently more complex form (Gleick, 1988). These 'chaotic' transformations in organisation are also associated with emergent properties which are therefore also quite unpredictable from knowledge about the previous state of the system before its chaotic change.

Such 'higher order' re-stabilisation does not always occur of course, in which case the system might either revert to its previous position or collapse altogether, following a chaotic episode.

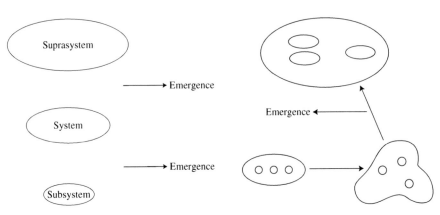

Fig. 3.1a Emergence between levels of a
stable systems hierarchy

Fig. 3.1b Emergence as a function of
chaotic disorganisation

From this discussion it is apparent that there are two sources of emergence in systems dynamics: Firstly between different levels within a 'stable' hierarchy (Fig. 3.1a) and secondly, following a chaotic reorganisation to a higher order of complexity (Fig. 3.1b).

While these theories have been constructed from studies of physical systems, strong parallels can also be drawn with the behaviour of so-called social systems, whether they are viewed as such either 'in actuality' or metaphorically. In any event, all of these principles are of considerable significance to the concept and indeed model of a critical learning system, and they are also crucial elements in the notion of any learning community which is viewed from the perspective of systemic development. To view the world systemically is to view it from the perspective of systems, just outlined. Systemic worldviews are a prerequisite for treating the world in a systemic (holistic) way, and the ability to adopt such worldviews and transpose them into practice is not easy, as 20 years of experience at Hawkesbury has confirmed.

A Justification for Critical Learning Systems:
The Community Challenge

A primary context for the work on critical learning systems at Hawkesbury, has been the growing concern that prevailing models of non-systemic development are significantly inadequate in the face of the dynamics, complexities and uncertainties of contemporary life. Early concerns about these models now find justification in the considerable empirical evidence of such matters as the increasing maldistribution of wealth (George and Sabelli, 1994), the gross degradation of the bio-physical environment (Brown, 1989), the loss of both cultural and biological diversity (Milbraith, 1989), and a host of other factors reflecting the inadequacies of the prevailing theoretical paradigm which is characterised by 'reductionism, deter-minism and autonomous individualism, all undergirded by a stringent material-ism' (Vitz, 1996). The force of these collective worldviews has been such as to contribute fundamentally to the often bemoaned 'loss of community' (Fukuyama, 1995), with the lack of trust that has grown from this situation, now acting as a serious impediment to its restoration.

This lack of trust is even beginning to extend to the way development 'is done'. Worse, we are in grave danger of falling victim to our own development 'successes' achieved through the technoscientific applications which reflect these prevailing worldviews. These have had widespread negative impacts as well as positive ones, and yet the process of development based on them, continues to remain relatively free from critique. We must now have a new focus, and there are those who believe that a new era is dawning: As the sociologist Ulrich Beck (1992) reminds us, 'we are therefore concerned no longer exclusively with making nature useful, or with releasing mankind from traditional constraints, but also and essentially with problems resulting from techno-economic development itself'. 'Modernisation' he claims 'is becoming *reflexive*; it is becoming its own theme'. Technoscience has got to learn how to confront itself in a world where the risks flowing from technology-in-action have become global, and paradoxically, only knowable through the very same process through which they were generated. To be self-confrontational however, in the sense that Beck suggests, we will need to approach matters very differently. As Bruce Wilshire (1990) has stated, 'we have powerful means of altering the earth and ourselves, but only a fix on goodness could give our means their aim, support and meaning'. All of the major problematic issues raised above have ethical and aesthetic dimensions as well as instrumental ones, and the need for 'fixes on goodness', or moral judgements, thus becomes an imperative, in the face of a fundamental paradigmatic inadequacy: 'Moral judgement has been eliminated from our concepts of rationality as far as they are actually built into existent scientific and systems paradigms' (Ulrich, 1988).

The challenge then is to re-foster what might be a lost competency for what Edgar Dunn called 'social learning', and a second aspect of reflexivity is indicated here as: 'the process of social learning has not understood itself sufficiently well to rationalise itself as an efficient process with a coherent purpose' (Dunn, 1971). The quest for systemic development is essentially a learning process, which appreciates and accommodates its own complexity, in addition to that of the main problematical matters (of development) to hand. The central feature of the approach is therefore the design, establishment, maintenance and development of self-referential, or critical, learning systems.

In the terms of our critical learning system approach then, we need to facilitate the transformation of communities into learning systems which are sufficiently self-referential that they will be able to learn about their own learning.

Meaning as an Emergent Property

Important cues for the basic form and process of the Hawkesbury critical learning systems model are provided by the work of Victor Frankl (1963), Gregory Bateson (1978), and C. West Chuchman (1971), with ideas from Aristotle, the medieval cleric Bonaventure and Ken Wilber (1990) also as foundational.

> The central notion here is that *meaning* is a property which is emergent in both individuals and communities, through the interactions of different 'ways of knowing'.

As we see it at Hawkesbury, meaning emerges as the result of 'interactions' between the process of *experiential learning* on the one hand, and what we have termed *inspirational learning* on the other with these processes in turn involving the concrete world of experience, the spiritual world of insights, and the abstract world of concepts at the interface (Fig. 3.2).

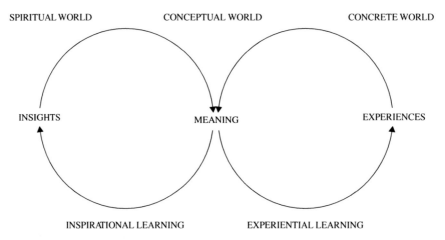

Fig. 3.2 Meaning as an emergent property of two ways of learning

These ideas of the *spiritual*, the *conceptual* and the *concrete* are not that far removed from those mooted by Bonaventura, who, as Ken Wilber (1990) records, distinguished between an *eye of contemplation* ('by which we rise to a knowledge of transcendent realities'), an *eye of reason* ('by which we obtain a knowledge of philosophy, logic and the mind itself'), and an *eye of flesh* ('by which we perceive the external world of space, time, and objects'). Wilber himself distinguishes between transcendelia, intelligibilia and sensibilia (Wilber, 1990).

A key concept from Hawkesbury is that this process can be represented in systems terms: Thus the experiential learning process can be envisaged as one subsystem within a learning system of two subsystems, with inspirational learning as the

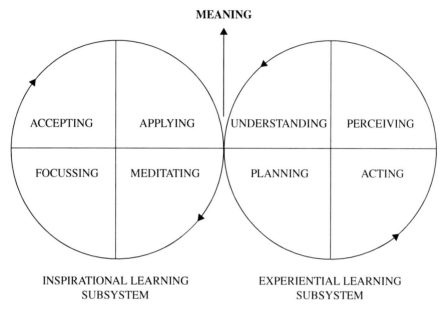

MEANING

| ACCEPTING | APPLYING | UNDERSTANDING | PERCEIVING |
| FOCUSSING | MEDITATING | PLANNING | ACTING |

INSPIRATIONAL LEARNING
SUBSYSTEM

EXPERIENTIAL LEARNING
SUBSYSTEM

Fig. 3.3 The sub(sub)systems of a learning system for generating meaning for actions

second. Each learning subsystem is itself a system with its own subsystems, and the model can be further expanded to illustrate the four sub(sub)systems in each (sub)system in a learning system, as illustrated in Fig. 3.3.

As this model illustrates, a dynamic is established between the processes of experiential and inspirational learning, through which concepts derived from the transformation of experience are qualified by insights derived from inspirational learning in the creation of meaning as a prerequisite for responsible, systemic action.

The Experiential Subsystem

To understand the dynamics of such a system, and how it might be used as a model in practice, we need to explore these processes in more detail, and to do this, we turn first to the process of experiential learning, and to the work of David Kolb in particular.

Kolb (1984) suggests that learning is the creation of knowledge through the transformation of experience. He posits that the process occurs as a result of our need to reconcile two dialectic tensions that we feel as a result of two different ways through which we 'grasp' reality (through *concrete experience* or through *abstract conceptualisation*), and two ways through which we transform what we have grasped (through *reflective observation* or through *active experimentation*). He expresses these two dialectics as polar positions on a matrix, which he then converts into a cycle to illustrate the dynamics of the dialectic resolution (Fig. 3.4).

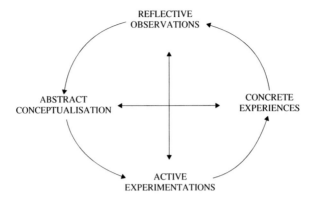

Fig. 3.4 An experiential learning 'cycle'

Kolb went on to argue that the complete experiential learning process thus involves the learner, in resolving the dialectical tensions between these two pairs of polar opposites, in four basic activities which he termed *divergence*, *assimilation*, *convergence* and *accommodation* respectively:

- *divergence* involves the learner moving from concrete experiences to reflective observations
- *assimilation* from reflective observations to abstract conceptualisation
- *convergence* from abstract conceptualisation to active experimentations, and
- *accommodation* from active experimentations to concrete experiences

The essence of these four activities can be captured with the notions of perceiving as the act of divergence, understanding as assimilation, planning as convergence, and acting as accommodation (Fig. 3.5).

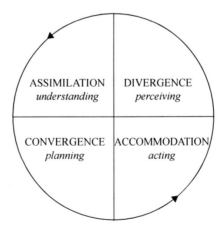

Fig. 3.5 The four basic activities in an experiential learning process

Following Kolb, but using the language we have introduced, the process of experiential learning can be described in a highly simplified manner, in the following terms: The process of learning starts with the immersion of the learner in a concrete experience from which as many observations as possible are gathered and perceptions recorded. This stage of information gathering is then followed by a phase of thinking, during which attempts are made to understand what has been experienced – and sense is made out what has been sensed! This stage is followed, in turn, with plans for action based on the understanding achieved. Finally, the planned action is taken, and as this changes the situation, the whole process is repeated, and more knowledge created.

> Experiential learning is thus a recurrent process of adaptation to change, based on a rigorous process of transformation.

In reality of course, this learning process is far less systematic than is being inferred here. Rarely do we conduct our learning with such discipline and rigour, and nor does all of learning start with 'immersion in a concrete experience'. Much of our learning (and virtually all of our formal education!) starts at the opposite pole, as we are immersed not in concrete realities but in preformed abstract conceptualisations. Rarely do we therefore get the chance to test those ideas back in the concrete world, nor plan or take action as a consequence of what we have learned (save perhaps to feedback our understanding to the 'teacher' for a grading of our ability to understand, or at least remember).

The first step towards the creation of a learning community – a critical learning system – is therefore the facilitation of consciousness of the process of learning itself: learning to learn about learning. And this need for what has been termed meta-learning (Kitchener, 1983), immediately adds a new and vital dimension to the learning systems model, which becomes a 'higher order' system within the learning systems hierarchy. Finally in this regard, a third 'level of learning', referred to as epistemic learning (Kitchener, 1983), must now be added to provide the dimension of learning about the worldviews which contextualise what is being learned (Fig. 3.6).

Speaking in terms of 'levels of cognitive processing', Kitchener herself describes these three levels as (a) cognition, which deals with knowing, (b) meta-cognition, which deals with knowing about knowing, and (c) epistemic cognition, which deals with knowing about the nature of knowledge. It is through epistemic learning that we learn to appreciate the nature of the worldviews and paradigms which we hold as the contexts for what and how we know, and also that we learn how to both challenge and, if appropriate, change them. It is at this level that we learn the implications of the prevalence of the worldview identified earlier as being based on the 'reductionism, determinism, autonomous individualism, and materialism' (Vitz, 1996).

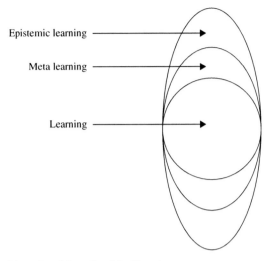

Epistemic learning

Meta learning

Learning

Fig. 3.6 A systems hierarchy of three 'levels' of learning

Worldviews

To help us help learners to explore this domain, we have, introduced an icon to depict worldviews, again in the form of dialectics. Drawing on ideas introduced by Burrell and Morgan (1979) and Miller (1983), we have developed the notion of a worldview matrix composed of an ontological dimension (as the polar positions of holism on the one hand and reductionism on the other) and an epistemological dimension (with the polar positions of objectivism on the one hand and relativism on the other). As we see it, where ontologies are concerned with beliefs about the 'nature of nature', epistemologies concern themselves with the 'nature of knowledge' (about the nature of nature!). The distinctions in ontology recognised here, reflect the idea that one either accepts the irreducible wholeness of nature and other systems (holism), or one does not (reductionism). With respect to the epistemological distinctions one either accepts that there is 'a permanent, ahistoric matrix or framework to which we can ultimately appeal in determining the nature of rationality, knowledge, truth, goodness or rightness' (objectivism) – as Bernstein (1983) put it – or we do not (relativism). We present each of the four quadrants as particular worldviews or paradigmatic positions, and have labelled them according to the idea of the specific focus or 'centricity' of each (Fig. 3.7).

Given that our worldviews, as represented here at least, reflect our most fundamental belief positions, it is not at all surprising that we hold to them with such conviction. It is equally understandable that communication between people with different worldviews, is typically so distorted.

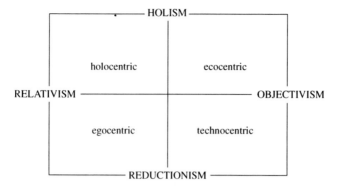

Fig. 3.7 Four worldviews as functions of differing ontological/epistemological positions

The *technocentric* view of the world, which from the earlier comments can be taken as representing the prevailing paradigm of modernisation, is as far removed from the *holocentric view* as is conceivable to imagine, on this model. It is not surprising that the discourse about what constitutes responsible community development, for instance, is so difficult, given the tensions that exist between different belief positions and thus worldviews. A critical learning process must therefore include discourse about the nature and influence of worldviews on the process of learning – and ultimately, on development itself?

Ourworldviews are not limited to cognitive belief positions but also extend to include normative positions, which are grounded in values frameworks. A similar form of matrix to the cognitive worldview framework can also be used to express different normative positions, although in this instance the situation is more complex as a function of the very nature of values. To illustrate the possible dimensions of a 'value framework', we have chosen two dimensions of the 'good society' that many claim to be at the core of our civilisation: Following James O'Toole (1993) we can thus discriminate between *libertarianism* and *egalitarianism* as one dialectic tension, and between *corporatism* and *communitarianism*, as the other (Fig. 3.8).

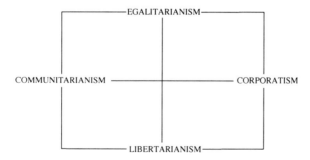

Fig. 3.8 A normative worldview window

These normative dialectics are of course different from their cognitive counterparts in that they only express themselves as 'polar opposites' when taken as extreme positions. The four cells furthermore, remain unlabelled, as the notion of centricity is also less apposite here. The point remains however that we do hold views which are markedly influenced by the particular normative positions we take on matters related to our respective dreams of the 'good society' and on liberty, equality, efficiency and community, which, as O'Toole (1993) submits 'tug like polar forces . . . at the society as a whole' and where 'these four great themes of political argument are tradeoffs with each other, zero-sum positions in which an increment of one value leads to a consequent equivalent loss of its opposite'. Again it must be emphasised that these dimensions, fundamental that they are, represent but a fraction of the total value positions which we bring to bear in any discourse about development.

> The issue here is that normative elements are as basic to the worldviews that we hold as are cognitive elements, and that awareness and critical consciousness of them are necessary perquisites for the 'emergence of meaning' from any learning system.

And it is through talking about values that we are inevitably led from the *experiential* focus to what we can sensibly call the *inspirational* focus.

The Inspirational Subsystem

While the British science writer Snow (1959) certainly popularised the notion of the 'two cultures', with the reason of the sciences on the one hand and the aesthetics of the arts on the other, the recognition that being human is much more than being objectively rational, stretches back at least to the time of the ancient Greek civilisation. The clear distinction which Aristotle made between the *episteme* on the one hand, and *nous* on the other, was a theme which persisted to the eighteenth century of Immanuel Kant – with his concern for the relationships between the facts and principles of science, and ethics and moral discourse – and beyond. Indeed today, there persists a distinction within philosophy between those who judge right from wrong solely on the consequences of actions, and those who focus on the theory of natural law or on notions of natural rights (Singer, 1994).

The principle of inspirational learning draws its logic from the time-honoured distinction between learning from 'outer experiences' on the one hand, and from 'inner insights' on the other: The spirit of being human if you will – hence the use of the word *spiritual* below. It is accepted that just as experiential learning draws its dynamics from the dialectics of two opposing ways of grasping reality and two opposing ways of transforming it, so a similar proposition can be raised concerning

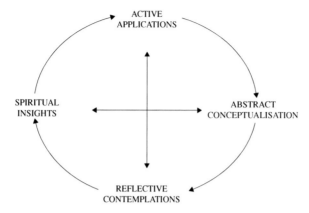

Fig. 3.9 An inspirational learning 'cycle'

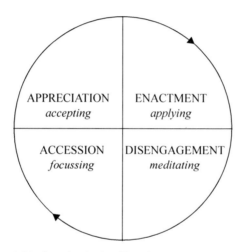

Fig. 3.10 Four basic activities in an inspirational learning process

two opposing sources of understanding (concepts and insights) and two opposing ways of transforming them (contemplation and application) (Fig. 3.9).

In a manner analogous to the experiential process of Kolb (1984), and drawing on notions developed by Francisco Varela and his colleagues (1992), Ken Wilber (1990), and a lifetime's reading of poetry and listening to great music, the following four domains can be tentatively proposed as appropriate to a process of inspirational learning: *disengagement, accession, appreciation,* and *enactment* (Fig. 3.10).

- *disengagement* involves the learner moving from abstract conceptualisation's to reflective contemplations
- *accession* from reflective contemplations to spiritual insights
- *appreciation* from spiritual insights to active applications, and
- *enactment* from active applications to abstract conceptualizations

Again following Kolb, but using the new language just introduced, the process of inspirational learning can be described in the following way:

The process of learning starts with the disengagement of the learner from the conceptual world through some process akin to meditation, in order to allow the mind to free itself from thoughts and enter a state of self-awareness with compassion. This stage is then followed by an attempt to 'focus' on one's innermost being and on the insights that are either 'held' there or are created through the process of introspective contemplation. The third stage involves the learner in accepting the insights that have been revealed during the previous stage, while the final phase sees the application of these insights into the process of meaning-making.

> Meaning emerges from the 'systemic' interaction of insights gained through inspirational learning with abstract concepts learned through experiential learning.

Earlier it was submitted that the experiential process, when regarded as a learning system, could be envisaged as a system within a three 'level' systems hierarchy which also involved meta and epistemic dimensions. Following the same logic, it is tempting to suggest a similar situation with respect to inspirational learning. However, given the deliberate rejection of 'rational' analysis within the latter process, it is probably not relevant to speak in these hierarchical and rational terms with reference to the inspirational learning process. It is appropriate however, to incorporate the values-based worldview into the process, reflecting the notion that just as there is an important relationship between the cognitive framework and the generation of meaning in the experiential learning system, so too can one defend the probability of the significance of a normative framework influencing the process of insight 'creation' or 'revelation'.

The Integrated System

We are now almost in a position to integrate all that as been discussed into a complete model of a critical learning system, which has, in turn, practical application as a 'road-map' for the design, maintenance, development and evaluation of 'learning communities'. There are just two further aspects to the system that require addition and explanation, and they relate to the matters of emotion and of power. It has long been recognised that emotions not only affect the process of learning, but can be harnessed by it; to advantage. Aristotle put it this way: 'anyone can become angry – that is easy. But to be angry with the right person, to the right degree, at the right time, for the right person, and in the right way – this is not easy.' The source of this quotation is a recent book by Goleman (1996) on what he terms emotional intelligence. The point that he makes and both defends and extends, is that as emotions very significantly influence the way we learn, it is sensible to learn how to use them to our advantage. From the perspective of a learning system, we

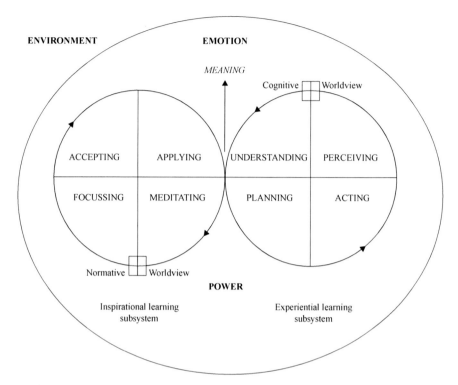

Fig. 3.11 The integrated critical learning system

might envisage emotions such as anger, sadness, fear, enjoyment etc, as constituting important environmental 'elements' both within the system (as its ambience), and beyond it, in the environment at large. The intelligent learner both recognises and manipulates these environments to advantage in the construction of meaning.

And this brings us to the final issue of power, and its influence, as Habermas (1984) has emphasised, as a potential source of distortions in communication, and thus on learning. This is not the place to elaborate on this complex matter, save to recognise that it too, needs to be a focus of critical reflection, and central to any self-referential learning system (Fig. 3.11).

Practical Application

As with any conceptual model it is vital to remember that the 'map is not the territory'. The image of the critical learning system above is just that: An image, a mental construct, which has been generated through the application of theory and insights to help create meaning from real world experiences, which have in turn, helped in the modification of those theories and the creation of fresh insights. So this is as much an illustration of what some of us see as the process of community learning that has characterised initiatives at Hawkesbury over the past two decades, as it is an idealised image of what we believe describes a generalised model of a critical learning system.

In its application, it suggests a series of important factors to consider whenever the establishment, development and evaluation of a learning community is being mooted. It illustrates a number of key aspects of 'social learning' indicating some of the domains and dynamics that need to be considered. These are worthy of review under the rubric of an effective learning community as one which:

- Has achieved a sense of its own coherence and integrity.
- Contains a requisite level of variety and diverse tensions of difference which are essential for its own dynamic.
- Is clear about its purpose and the influence of this on the boundary of its concerns and indeed its structure.
- Combines both experiential and inspirational learning processes in its quest for meaning for responsible action.
- Is conscious of meta and epistemic cognition, and of the influence of both cognitive and normative worldviews as frameworks for the way meaning is created.
- Is critically aware of its own emotional ambience, and competent at the intelligent management of those emotions.
- Is aware of the emergence of properties unique to different levels of its own systemic organisation, just as it is to the dynamics of chaotic change and the potential of property emergence following reorganisation.
- Appreciates the nature of the environments (suprasystems) in which it operates, and is conscious of both constraining and driving 'forces' in that environment.
- Is critically conscious of its own power relationships and those which exist between it and the environment about it, and knows what influence this has as a potential distorter of communication.
- Is self-referential, critical of its own processes and dynamics, and capable of self-organisation in the face of continual challenge from its environment.
- Exhibits leadership as well as meaning as an emergent property.

This 'checklist' of systems' characteristics provides a framework for the sort of conversations and discourse which guide a community which is intent on improving its own capacities for learning its way into better futures.

It is a map for systemic development which has its own continuing systemic development.

Dedications and acknowledgement

This presentation is dedicated to the memory of Diane, who, in learning how to die, provided an infinite source of insights into learning how to live.

As always it is a privilege to acknowledge the generations of learners who have been, as many continue to be, participants in Hawkesbury's grand enterprise, whose experiences, concepts and insights have both helped in the evolution of the model, and been informed by it in their own extensive activities in the facilitation of learning communities. Among my academic colleagues, I would specifically like to acknowledge the support of Bruce McKenzie, Roger Packham and Bob Macadam as together we attempt to create a new critical learning system at the Centre for Systemic Development.

References

Ackoff, R.L. (1981) *"Creating the Corporate Future"* Wiley, New York.

Bateson, G. (1978) *"Steps to an Ecology of Mind"* Paladine, London.

Bawden, R.J. (1992) "Systems Approaches to Agricultural Development: The Hawkesbury Experience" *Agricultural Systems* 40: 153–176.

Bawden, R. (1999) "The Community Challenge: The Learning Response" *New Horizons in Education* 99 (October): 40–59.

Bawden, R.J. and Packham, R.G. (1993) "Systemic Praxis in the Education of the Agricultural Practitioner" *Systems Practice* 6: 7–19.

Bawden, R.J., Macadam, R.M., Packham, R.G., and Valentine, I (1984) "Systems Thinking and Practices in the Education of Agriculturalists" *Agricultural Systems* 13: 205–225.

Beck, U. (1992) *"Risk Society: Towards a New Modernity"* Sage Publications, London.

Bernstein, R.J. (1983) *"Beyond Objectivism and Relativism"* University of Pennsylvania Press, Philadelphia.

Bertalanffy, L. von (1968) *"General Systems Theory"* Braziller, New York.

Brown, L. (1989) *"State of the World"* (series) Worldwatch Institute Allen and Unwin, London.

Burrell, W.G. and Morgan, G. (1979) *"Sociological Paradigms and Organisational Analysis"* Heinemann, London.

Churchman, C.W. (1971) *"The Way of Inquiring Systems"* Basic Books, New York.

Dunn, E.S. (1971) *"Economic and Social Development: A Process of Social Learning"* John Hopkins University Press, Baltimore.

Frankl, V. (1963) *"Man's Search for Meaning"* Simon and Schuster, New York.

Fukuyama, F. (1995) *"Trust"* The Free Press, New York.

George, S. and Sabelli, F. (1994) *"Faith and Credit: The World Bank's Secular Empire"* Westview Press, Boulder.

Gleick, J. (1988) *"Chaos: Making a New Science"* Heinemann, London.

Goleman, D. (1996) *"Emotional Intelligence"* Bloomsbury, London.

Habermas, J. (1984) *"The Theory of Communicative Action"* Vol 1 Heinemann, London.

Kitchener, K. (1983) "Cognition, Metacognition, and Epistemic Cognition: A Three Level Model of Cognitive Processing" *Human Development* 26: 222–232.

Kolb, D.A. (1984) *"Experiential Learning: Experience as the Source of Learning and Development"* Prentice Hall, New Jersey.

Laszlo, E. and Laszlo, A. (1997) "The Contribution of the Systems Sciences to the Humanities" *Systems Research and Behavioural Science* 14: 5–19.

Milbraith, L. (1989) *"Envisioning a Sustainable Society"* SUNY Press, New York.

Miller, A. (1983) "The Influence of Personal Biases on Environmental Problem-Solving" *Journal of Environmental Management* 17: 133–142.

O'Toole, J. (1993) *"The Executive's Compass: Business and the Good Society"* Oxford University Press, Oxford.

Singer, P. (ed) (1994) *"Ethics"* Oxford University Press, Oxford.

Snow, C.P. (1959) *"The Two Cultures and the Scientific Revolution"* Cambridge University Press, Cambridge.

Ulrich, W. (1988) "Systems Thinking, Systems Practice and Practical Philosophy: A Program of Research" *Systems Practice* 1: 137–163.

Varela, F.J., Thompson, E. and Rosch, E. (1992) "*The Embodied Mind*" MIT Press Cambridge.
Vitz, P.C. (1996) "Back to Human Dignity: From Modern to Postmodern Psychology" *The Intercollegiate Review* 31: 15–23.
Wilber, K. (1990) "*Eye to Eye: The Quest for the New Paradigm*" 2nd edition Anchor/Doubleday, New York.
Wilshire, B. (1990) "*The Moral Collapse of the University: Professionalism, Purity and Alienation*" State University of New York Press, New York.

Chapter 4
Sustainability, Social Learning and the Democratic Imperative: Lessons from the Australian Landcare Movement

Jim Woodhill

Drawing on the experience of community based land conservation in Australia, this chapter examines the deeper structural and institutional causes of the unsustainability of modern industrialised society. Social learning is presented as a potential paradigm for engaging with these broader institutional dilemmas. Such a perspective locates the concept of social learning at the heart of current debates about the tensions between sustainable development, democracy and free market ideology. The chapter introduces the themes of risk society and reflexive modernisation as a perspective that can help explain why modern institutions are structurally biased against the ideals of sustainable development. This provides a brief political economic context for then outlining a perspective on social learning that gives particular attention to questions of how to facilitate the design of institutions more supportive of sustainable development.

> The themes of the future, which are now on every-one's lips, have not originated from the foresightedness of the rulers or from the struggle in parliament – and certainly not from the cathedrals of power in business, science and the state. They have been put on the social agenda against the concentrated resistance of this institutionalised ignorance by entangled, moralising groups and splinter groups fighting each other over the proper way, split and plagued by doubts. Sub-politics has won a quite improbable thematic victory.
>
> (Source: Beck, 1994, p. 19)

Introduction

From the mid-1980s and in response to massive problems of land degradation, a community-based land conservation movement called Landcare evolved in Australia. Landcare now involves some 4,000 local level groups working to overcome land degradation. The system of land conservation in Australia also involves catchment or regional scale mechanisms for integrated natural resource management. Both these initiatives have been underpinned by a philosophy of community participation with claims that they are empowering landholders and local commu-

---

Source: Woodhill (2002), which was adapted from Woodhill (1999).

nities to deal with the problems of land degradation. The idea of local level community action with an emphasis on stakeholder participation and empowerment is not unique to Australia, rather, it has become a corner stone of natural resource management and development programmes the world over.

There is little doubt that Australia's recent approaches to natural resources management (NRM) are in many ways world leading, particularly in terms of the effectiveness with which they have engaged the community. However, the harsh reality is that these approaches are not leading to the scale of on-ground change necessary to overcome land degradation and achieve widespread ecologically sustainable land use. Farmers have been furnished neither with the resources nor the incentives to make the changes or to take the risks, that achieving sustainable agriculture demands.

The problem of unsustainable land use continues largely unabated, despite these current initiatives, I argue, because of a lack of attention to the deeper structural causes of the problem. There has been an over simplified assumption that development of a 'landcare ethic' along with the right knowledge and skills will enable farmers to tackle land degradation. Further, it has been assumed that land conservation can be achieved by following an essentially voluntary approach to action by individual farmers. In reality, a combination of cultural, legal, and particularly, economic factors results in an environment that provides farmers neither with the incentives nor the financial capacity to invest at the level required to make a significant difference to land degradation. Understanding these factors leads to exposing the deeper structural causes of the problem which are embedded in the dominant scientific, political, economic and normative institutions of modern industrial society. Consequently, an understanding of the relationship between land degradation, the wider ecological crisis and contemporary political economic change becomes fundamental to overcoming the emerging impasse in Australia's capacity to protect its land resources.

Again, this is a phenomenon not unique to Australia. Everywhere in the world, environment and development work that focuses on local level participation and empowerment eventually runs up against constraints that have to do with broader scale institutional arrangements. These constraints, for example, range from a global economic system that does not adequately value natural capital to dwindling investments in public services, inequitable land and resource tenure, institutionalised corruption and the inability of global governance mechanisms to keep pace with the ramifications of globalisation.

Recognition of this situation has led to a growing focus on the institutional aspects of environment and development work. Only a decade or two ago, environmental and development issues were seen predominantly as a technical problem requiring technical solutions, developed and imposed, or 'extended' by government. What could be called a 'technocentric era' [...]. Over time it was realised that local communities and key stakeholders needed to be more actively involved and committed if there were to be much hope of change. Consequently, during the 1980s, community participation became accepted as fundamental to effective environment and development work. Along with this came notions of facilitation, community empowerment and community learning, informed, at least in part, by insights from sociology and psychology. The importance of the social dimension of the problem became common rhetoric. The rationale for community participation was supposedly to empower local people with an understanding of their problems and with the knowledge and skills to tackle them in a self-reliant fashion.

After a decade of experience with such 'localist' approaches, there is now a rapidly growing realisation that much wider forces are at play that hinder the resolution of many environment and development problems solely via the local level. Ultimately, if the often remarkable efforts of local communities are not supported by broader scale institutional change, such efforts end up being in vain. In response, environment and development work can be seen as entering a new 'institutionalist era'. The sociology of community action of the 'localist era' now needs to be complemented by political economic insights and theory and coordinated action at meso- and macro-scales.

My intention in this chapter is to present social learning as a potential paradigm for engaging with these broader institutional dilemmas. Such a perspective locates the concept of social learning at the heart of current debates about the tensions between sustainable development, democracy and free market ideology. In the chapter I shall first introduce the themes of risk society and reflexive modernisation as a perspective on modern industrialised society (modernity) that can help explain why modern institutions are structurally biased against the ideals of sustainable development. This provides an albeit brief political economic context for then outlining my perspective on the meaning of social learning as it has emerged from a critique of the Australian Landcare movement.

Risk Society and the Democrative Imperative

In the late twentieth century, there is a dynamic of intellectual, cultural and political economic change that can be seen as shaking the foundations of modernity. Beck et al. (1994) refer to this as *reflexive modernisation*. They argue that in simple or early modernity, the driving motor is instrumental reason applied to the transformation of nature and traditional society for the creation of material and economic wealth. The major concerns for society are on how this wealth is to be distributed and how to avoid exploitation of less fortunate people in its production. In an era of reflexive modernisation, the driving motor begins to change to risk. The institutions of modernity are confronted with risks that are their own side effects; for example, ecological collapse, global warming, nuclear war, social dislocation, effects of pollution on health, or economic system collapse. This is modernity turned back on itself. In simple modernity, an external environment is being transformed. In late modernity, the question is how to transform a manufactured environment to avoid its own internal risks. This is the reflexive nature of late modernity.

In simple modernity, all that was required of government was overseeing technological and industrial progress. The direction and goals of this progress had been set
by the Enlightenment and were largely accepted. Over time the techno-economic
decisions that really impact on society have come to rest predominantly with scientists, bankers and corporate managers – and not with elected governments. Globalisation, it can be argued, relegates democratic and parliamentary decision making to
a pawn on the global economic chessboard. The structural transformation of modernity, driven by risk, does not erupt, as Marx had predicted, as a class revolution.
Rather, as Beck (1994) comments, it creeps in through the back door on cat's paws.
But ultimately the political ramifications may be no less significant.

The argument of reflexive modernisation is that sooner or later the escalating
risks of modernity start to become unacceptable to the polity, and indeed a problem for the techno-economic sphere itself. Questions of coordination, control and
democracy open up. The old lines of political dissent between left and right lose
their meaning and there is no Enlightenment ideal to guide society into a new or
post modernity. The structures and processes of democracy, and their capacity to
cope with the risks of late modernity, emerge as a central concern and the necessity
of a collective response prompts a surge of interest in democratisation and concepts such as social learning. 'Development' can be seen as being dominated by
a globalised capitalist economic system that is largely disconnected from democratic control and has no heart, soul or ethical concern for the direction it takes.
However, as the risks mount a dialectic of control comes into play, questions begin
to get asked, assumptions are challenged and alternatives are sought. Nevertheless,
uncertainty abounds, science is no longer seen as having all the answers for modern
society, and religious beliefs have become pluralistic and unacceptable as a basis
for political decisions. All may not be well with current forms of democratic governance, but monarchies, aristocracies, dictatorships, or anarchy are hardly desirable
alternatives. Significantly, Giddens, Habermas and Beck 'all make the case, in one
way or another, that more democracy and more radical democracy is an essential
precondition of creating environmental sustainability.' (Goldblatt, 1996, p. 201)
These are the circumstances that propel society towards a reformulation of the role
that dialogue, discourse and social learning should play in shaping the future – a
democratic imperative for restructuring core institutions.

I wish to make three propositions regarding the connection between greater participation in democratic processes and sustainability:

1. Power structures in current forms of liberal democracy have biased decision
   making against sustainability. In other words, our current political systems tend
   to appease powerful economic interests at the expense of the overall well-being
   of the majority and the environment. Goldblatt (1996, p. 188) concludes that;

   > The kinds of changes in consumption and definition of well-being required to bring
   > Western societies within the orbit of sustainability are both extensive in their coverage
   > and intensive in their consequence. Everyone will be affected in such a transition. Nego-
   > tiated social change of this form is an enormous political task. At the same time, the
   > political and legal systems of capitalist societies are not neutral but structurally biased
   > in their allocation of power to environmentally problematic interests.

2. Sustainability is a substantively different problem from the problems for which the current political and policy system has evolved to cope (Dovers, 1997). Modern institutions have evolved to enable economic growth, technological progress and individual liberty. They were never designed to cope with an unsustainable relationship between human kind and the natural environment. Genuinely reorienting institutions towards the sustainability (and poverty) problem requires open and informed debate across society about the likely consequences of unsustainability and, given these, what values ought to underpin society's decisions. Greater participation in democratic processes is required to ensure: (a) a society-wide understanding of the issues; (b) the contribution of society's best intellectual resources; (c) the debate is not biased by short term economic interests; and (d) the debate is not biased by the short term political interests of governments.
3. Scale is a critical consideration for democratic participation and in this regard local and sub-national (regional) remain critically important. While sustainability requires a sophisticated balancing of agency from local to global levels (Conti, 1997; Gallopin, 1991), enhanced local and regional action is critical for three reasons. One, it is the scale at which much direct action needs to be taken and coordinated. This local level implementation is likely to be more effective if a high degree of responsibility and ownership is felt, which presupposes a high level of community participation. Two, it is through activities at the local or regional level that individuals can engage in a meaningful political discourse about sustainability. Three, it is from this level that any counterbalancing and political opposition to the power of purely economic interests, global corporations, or the state has to be mobilised and sustained.

Against this discussion of politics and democracy, it is interesting to reflect on the often-stated desire within the Landcare movement to 'keep politics out'. At one level, this is an understandable desire to ensure that people of all political persuasions can feel at ease within the Landcare movement and to avoid the polarisation associated with party politics. At another level, however, it reflects a curious and disturbing dismissal of politics altogether and a naïvety about power relations in social interaction. To claim to be apolitical is, in effect, to accept the status quo of social and political relations, which in itself is political. This is a theme picked up by Held (1996, pp. 296–297):

> Politics is frequently associated today with self seeking behaviour, hypocrisy and 'public relations' activity geared to selling policy packages. The problem with this view is that, while it is quite understandable, the difficulties of the modern world will not be solved by surrendering politics, but only by the development and transformation of 'politics' in ways that will enable us more effectively to shape and organise human life. We do not have the option of 'no politics'.

People are becoming disillusioned with politics. Giddens (1994, p. 116) claims, because 'key areas of social life – some of them areas they are able reflexively to master, others of them areas which are sources of threat – no longer correspond to any accessible domains of political authority.' Further, and critically, 'nor does consumer power, as the neoliberals suppose, substitute for such absent authority'

(1994, p. 116). In a similar vein of criticism, Dryzek (1996, p. 9) claims that capitalist democracies 'are home to gathering forces either sceptical of or hostile to any deeper democratisation.' Anti-democratic constraints are, he argues, of a structural, ideological and intellectual nature and need to be comprehended in terms of the capitalist state, the international system, economic rationality and ideology.

> All these antidemocratic constraints are associated with the idea that liberal democracy in a capitalist economic context is the pinnacle of feasible democratic achievement. This idea has gained considerable support in the wake of the collapse of Soviet-style communism and the crisis of confidence among socialists of all sorts in the West.
>
> (Source: Dryzek, 1996, p. 10)

Authors such as Habermas (1984a, b), Giddens [1984, 1990, 1994, 1998], Beck [1992, 1994, 1997], Dryzek [1987, 1990, 1992, 1996, 1997], Held [1996] and Pepper [1993, 1996] all cast their conceptual analysis of democracy in slightly different ways, with different terminology, and by reference to differing schools of social and political thought. Nevertheless, they all highlight the common themes of: a concern for ecological decay; the anti-democratic consequences of unbridled economic power; the consequences of an unbalanced use of instrumental reason; and the need for forms of democracy that open opportunities for constructive political dialogue between ordinary citizens. It is within this context that I now examine the concept of social learning.

Towards a Paradigm of Social Learning

Why is the articulation of a paradigm of social learning warranted? It is largely because the challenges of sustainable development and a response to the risks of late modernity require a third way of governance (Beck, 1997:132–156; Dryzek, 1997, pp. 197–201; Giddens, 1998). Old style socialist central planning, with its faith in experts, has been proven ineffective and incapable of responding to the dynamics of late modernity. But the alternative, unfettered free market capitalism, as discussed above, equally has many fault lines and internal contradictions that become all too clear when set against the backdrop of the quest for sustainability.

In this context, I argue that social learning should seek to build on local level processes of community participation, such as Landcare, to involve a wider citizenry in the dialogue about and decision making over higher order political economic life. Social learning requires attention to the processes and structures necessary to involve a heterogeneous set of actors in analysing and making decisions about complex, multifaceted and value-laden problem situations, such as NRM. Dryzek (1997, p.198) concludes that environmental issues demand 'the capacity to facilitate and engage in social learning in an ecological context.'

Social learning has parallels with the evolving discourse on adaptive management (Dovers and Mobbs, 1997; Gunderson et al. , 1995; Holling, 1995; Lee, 1993).

However, having emerged essentially from the application of the natural sciences to problems of environmental management, adaptive management, in my assessment, does not yet deal adequately with the sort of institutional, political economic and democratic constraints to NRM that I have raised above. In this regard it is interesting that Lee (1993, p. 8) defines social learning as a combination of adaptive management and political change.

We should recognise that the concept of social learning is not new. In 1971 Dunn, driven by a concern for an improved practice in economic and social development, argued for social learning as a new paradigm for the social sciences. However, although the term has become commonly used in the environment and development literature (cf. Dryzek, 1997; Dunn, 1984; Francis and Lerner, 1996; Friedmann, 1984, 1992; Glasbergen, 1996; Irwin, 1995; Lee, 1993; Milbrath, 1989; Parson and Clark, 1995; Princen and Finger, 1994; Weale, 1992; Woodhill and Röling, 1998; World Bank, 1996) there have been few attempts to articulate its meaning in detail. The works of Milbrath (1989), Parson and Clark (1995) and Dunn (1971, 1984) are the notable exceptions.

Social learning is concerned with the ways in which different individuals, or groups (actors) within society engage with each other to understand, contest and influence the direction of social change. It looks at how society understands both itself and its relation to the external environment, and then adapts its assumptions, belief systems, approaches to problem solving, and systems of social organisation, either to achieve particular ambitions or cope with external and internal threats. A society that is unable to do this effectively runs the risk of annihilation either because of the internal collapse of its social organisation, or because of an inability to respond to external threats such as ecological collapse. These ideas are akin to what Maturana and Varela (1987, pp. 75–80, 181–192) refer to as 'the structural coupling' between an organism and its environment and what Giddens (1984) refers to as the process of 'structuration' in social change.

At one extreme, social change can be dictated by tradition, existing institutional structures, brute economic or political power, vested interests, technocratic and instrumental thinking, political expediency or ambivalent resignation to the status quo. At the other, it can be facilitated and engendered by open dialogue, democratic constraint of inequality, investment in education and social capital, the establishment of mediating forums, open policy processes, questioning of basic assumptions, and greater democratisation of politics and the techno-economic sphere.

Social learning, then, I define as: *Processes by which society democratically adapts its core institutions to cope with social and ecological change in ways that will optimise the collective well-being of current and future generations.*

Four aspects of this definition warrant clarification. First, is the democratic and cognitive process of social learning. By this I mean that foundations of social learning must be drawn from the theories of individual and collective cognition and democratic participation.

Second is the notion of adaptation. Social learning does not imply grand plans or blueprints for the future. Nor is it premised on the Enlightenment idea that through rational and instrumental human ingenuity, the shape of the future can be directly determined. Social life and the dynamics of the earth's ecosystem are far too complex for this. Instead, social learning fosters a critical awareness of social and ecological trends and the relationship between these trends and efficacy of existing social institutions. However, taking a constructivist epistemological perspective, while we may not be able to control the future directly, how we think and act in our current circumstances will most certainly have consequences for the future (Giddens, 1990, pp. 154–158; Maturana and Varela, 1987, pp. 244–250).

Giddens (1994, 1998), Beck (1997), Dryzek (1996) and Hutton (1995, 1997) all agree that one of the more dangerous ideas of modern times is that we can have no purposeful influence over the future shape of society save what is brought about by the fate of the market. The consciously adaptive and reflexive character of social learning potentially offers an alternative to such fatalism.

The third critical aspect of social learning is its concern with institutions. Over the last two decades there has been a surge of interest in the psychology of learning and its application, in particular, to the fields of education, organisational development and community development (Bawden and Packham, 1991; Kolb, 1984: Mabey and Isles, 1994; Pretty et al., 1995; Senge, 1992). For a summary of these ideas see Parson and Clark (1995). But learning conceived in this way has focused primarily on individual cognition and micro-level processes within teams, organisations and communities. Far less attention has been given to the role of learning in shaping social institutions or in the way institutions and organisations interact. Here I am being inclusive of social norms and values, public, private, and civic sector organisations and political and economic structures. Of vital importance to this institutional perspective is the critique of economic and political power and how it impacts upon institutional design.

The fourth and final aspect of the definition I wish to emphasise is its reference to a purpose. The higher order reasons for improving and facilitating social learning, in general and in specific situations, need to be clear and explicit. Consideration of what constitutes optimising the collective well-being[1] for the majority, and the ethics, values and assumptions that justify this, must be an integral part of social learning.

Social learning requires conscious design and facilitation – it does not happen by accident. But what principles should underpin the design of systems to facilitate social learning? What is required to develop a paradigm of social learning to the point that it could guide improved practice in NRM? I wish to consider three elements for facilitating the development of social learning: philosophical reflection, methodological pluralism and institutional design. These elements can be considered the three defining features of a paradigm, as a paradigm is itself defined by its philosophical assumptions, methodological approaches and institutionalised social practices.

---

[1] For a discussion on the context of well-being see Dodds (1995) and Quizilbash (1996).

Philosophical Reflection

In today's world of technical specialisation, and particularly in areas such as NRM where training in the biophysical sciences is the norm, philosophy is more often than not seen as an esoteric and academic irrelevance. Education systems, at both secondary and tertiary levels, and particularly in the sciences, have taught the methods of science and the specialist knowledge and techniques of disciplines with little regard for critique of underlying assumptions and the place of specialist knowledge in a broader picture of society and social values. This has resulted in a whole cadre of professionals who are largely uninterested and certainly intellectually ill equipped to deal with the more fundamental questions of human existence, knowledge and action. As a consequence, this philosophical ignorance becomes endemic within wider society, a situation that is antithetical to the aspirations of the original Enlightenment thinkers 'for whom critical philosophy was the basic instrument of human enlightenment' (Maxwell, 1992a, p. 23). It is this philosophical ignorance that enables the more extreme neoliberal ideologies to be peddled with relative impunity. While as a society we have little difficulty in mastering the concepts and language (or jargon) of technological change, the same cannot be said for our ability to master the concepts and language required to think deeply about our social ecological predicaments. This is potentially catastrophic if, as Maturana and Varela (1987, p. 248) argue, '. . . at the core of all the troubles we face today is our very ignorance of knowing.'

If, following the constructivist turn in philosophy, it is accepted that there are no absolute or metaphysical foundations for knowledge or morality, then the values and principles around which social life is organised need to be socially negotiated. This should be the task of philosophy, in a broader sense, in late modernity (Maxwell, 1992b). Philosophical reflection, or what might be called action philosophy, involves equipping the facilitators and actors in processes of social learning with the intellectual resources to think critically and deeply about what they are doing and to be able to cope with the concept of learning at meta and epistemic levels.

Social learning involves different actors with different interests being able to engage in dialogue. For this to occur individuals need to be aware, or be assisted to become aware of the underlying assumptions and values that lead them to take a particular position. It is well-recognised that conflict resolution and negotiation require individuals or groups to seek out common values, which requires being explicit about their assumptions. In other words, philosophical reflection becomes a key tool in working through problem situations where values are in conflict and need to be reassessed. One of the failings of many of the facilitation techniques and methodologies adopted by participatory approaches to NRM is that they are used without any philosophical understanding. Thus they are reduced to little more than an instrumental technique, while the reasons for involving people in the first place become lost.

The key point about philosophical reflection in relation to social learning is that it is a task that cannot be left to academics alone. If NRM professionals, community leaders and activists, and politicians are to engage with facilitating social learning there is a necessity and a responsibility for them to be conscious and critical of the assumptions that underpin their praxis.

Methodological Pluralism

The problems to be faced in managing natural resources range from understanding fundamental biophysical processes through to negotiating conflicts associated with controversial political decisions. NRM requires an integration of the social and bio-physical sciences, holistic and systemic thinking, a capacity to deal with risk and uncertainty and a capacity for wise political decision making. The classical methods of science, based on empiricism, objectivism, reductionism and quantification are, on their own, wholly inadequate for the complex and multi-dimensional nature of the task (Dryzek, 1987; Funtowicz and Ravetz, 1993; Irwin, 1995, pp. 37–80; Miller, 1985; Pepper, 1996, pp. 239–294).

By methodological pluralism I mean the capacity to develop and utilise a diversity of methodologies that may range from highly reductionist basic scientific research at one extreme, through to creative artistic expression as a means of developing community understanding at the other. But methodological pluralism also means more than simply an ad hoc application of diverse and potentially incommensurable methods and approaches. What is fundamental is a critical consciousness of why a particular methodological approach is being followed in a particular situation and what the underlying epistemological assumptions are, as well as an understanding of the alternative methodological options. Bawden (1989, pp. 33–45) discusses epistemic learning in terms of a critical awareness of the underlying assumptions of a particular paradigm, which is particularly important to methodological pluralism.

The last decade or two has seen something of a swing in the methodological pendulum. In a reaction to the highly technical expert oriented approaches that characterised NRM and rural development from the post-war period through to the late 1970s, the 1980s saw increasing emphasis being placed on community participation and local knowledge. In many ways, Participatory Rural Appraisal (PRA) has been the icon for this change. But with issues as complex as NRM and sustainable development there is nothing sacred about community perspectives or local knowledge. Ignorance and uncertainty about environmental problems are not overcome by recourse to participatory methodologies alone. Rather creative dialectics between science and art, science and politics, experts and lay people, reductionism and holism, local perspectives and global perspectives need to be actively constructed.

Institutional Design

The focal question in relation to institutional design is quite simple. What types of institutions would facilitate social learning and participatory democracy? There are numerous examples that could be given, for example, an independent well-funded government broadcaster, a strong non-governmental organisation sector supported by government funding, forums for open policy debate, and education systems that expose students to philosophical and political ideas. However, the degree to which institutions can be designed – as opposed to accidentally or automatically evolve – is a complex question that is enjoying renewed interest in several disciplines under the banner of the 'new institutionalism' (Goodin, 1996).

Institutionsare both the means to, and the outcome of, social learning. For example, the development of an incentive framework to drive sustainability in rural Australia can be seen as depending on a process of social learning, but this process of social learning itself depends on a set of supportive institutional arrangements. In other words, there is a two-stage process at work in that institutions are needed to support social learning so that institutions to achieve sustainability can be developed. The institutional dimension of social learning is further illustrated by the evolution of Landcare groups. These groups provide an organisational context that has made it possible for farmers to come together to learn about land degradation on their farms in their local area. The structure, practice and culture of these groups is heavily oriented towards learning. At one level, Landcare represents a good example of institutional design for social learning. At another level, it does not. Landcare, as I have argued, has failed to engage with the structural causes of land degradation and has not facilitated any significant learning about them.

Facilitating Institutional Design

To conclude I propose a set of eight principles for facilitating institutional design:

Self-organisation

One of the great appeals of market systems is their self-organising nature, while one of the great failures of socialist states, large bureaucracies and large corporations is the ineffectiveness of centralised hierarchical command and control systems. However, markets do not operate independently of boundaries, guidelines and rules that are socially established. The negative impacts of free markets are not due to the idea of markets themselves but due to the particular set of assumptions and rules by which they operate. One of the principles of organisational learning is establishing a culture in which individuals, or units within an organisation, are self-organising in that they understand and contribute to the overall goals of the organisation in a relatively autonomous fashion. In terms of the institutional and organisational structure of society, there is still an enormous amount to learn about the idea of self-organisation and self-organising systems (Capra, 1997, pp. 75–111). However, it is clearly a principle of institutional design that needs to be developed if the problems of cumbersome state intervention, on the one hand, and down sides of unfettered free markets, on the other, are to be surpassed (see Conti, 1997).

Cultivation of Social Capital

To function, any society needs institutions that build trust and enable people to have a sense of place, a sense of responsibility and a sense of belonging. Individuals need opportunities for personal growth and education. When society shifts its investment towards building institutions of the economic system while starving those that foster the social capital of resources, the whole fabric of society is threatened.

Facilitated Coordination

One of the major problems for society is the lack of coordination between different spheres of specialisation, different disciplines and different arms and levels of government. Institutions are required to overcome these coordination difficulties. It is necessary to invest intellectually and financially in this difficulty. Simply requesting that existing organisations and specialisations 'communicate' and bemoaning the fact that they do not, is far from adequate.

Institutional Diversity

Social learning is enhanced by the interplay of a diverse range of smaller organisations with a balance between government sector, business sector, and public sector organisations. Large, all-powerful organisations, whether state or corporate in nature threaten processes of both social learning and democracy. Social learning is particularly dependent on non-governmental organisations and other institutions that emerge from civil society. Institutions that are funded by government but which operate independently from it are also particularly important for supporting the activities of civil society.

Local – Global Dialectics

Social learning depends greatly on responsibilities and decision-making processes occurring at the appropriate scale. Ecological problems, in particular, depend on a concurrence between the scale of the problem and the scale at which decisions are made. The tension between local autonomy and globalised control needs to be recognised as a creative force in institutional design.

Multi-layered Democratic Participation

Following this principle there are many ways in which participation in political processes can be enhanced at all levels. The basic idea is for increased participation by the community and different interest groups in the dialogue over policy matters. Part of the objective is for political processes to be dominated less by professional politicians with allegiance to one of two main parties and the opaque dealings of bureaucracy.

Autonomous and Integrative Knowledge Systems

The wisdom of society's decisions is inevitably dependant on the quality of knowledge and the degree to which experts, decision makers and the wider public are well informed. Institutions involved in the creating of society's knowledge base need to be redesigned to cope better with complexity, uncertainty and the social nature of contemporary problems. It is also critical that these institutions and institutions associated with the media and public education are autonomous. They should not become dominated and manipulated by particular interests, as is currently the case with much of the world's media.

Meta-Reflexiveness

Possibly one of the greatest failings of modernity has been the limited degree to which meta-level reflection on knowledge, learning and institutions has occurred. Institutions need to be designed that encourage and enable learning about learning. Those institutions that are organisations need to be critically conscious of their own institutional order and have built-in mechanisms for review and adaptation. Where, for example, is the ministry responsible for institutional design to ensure that the processes of government are commensurate with the dynamics of late modernity? All too often it is not until institutions demonstrably fail that they receive attention – and then it is a reactionary, crisis-driven response.

Conclusion

Only a decade or two ago, NRM was seen predominantly as a technical problem requiring technical solutions, developed and imposed, or 'extended' by government. What could be called a 'technocentric era of NRM' [. . .]. Over time, government realised that local landholders and local communities needed to be more actively involved and committed for there to be much hope of change. Consequently, during the 1980s community participation became accepted as fundamental to effective resource management. Along with this came notions of facilitation, community empowerment and community learning, informed, at least in part, by insights from sociology and psychology. The importance of the social dimension of the problem became common rhetoric. NRM was no longer seen purely as a technical field and to a large extent the problem was redefined in terms of society at large lacking a 'landcare ethic' and farmers lacking the knowledge and skills to manage land in a sustainable way. The rationale for community participation was supposedly to empower local people with an understanding of resource degradation problems and the knowledge and skills to tackle them. Government provided catalytic funding to encourage the formation of groups, support facilitation and awareness raising and assist farm and catchment planning. I am referring to this as the 'localist era' because it was essentially about local change.

After a decade of experience with a 'localist' approach, there is now a rapidly growing realisation that much wider forces are at play that hinder the resolution of many NRM problems solely via the local or catchment levels. These forces include: market forces of a global economy that does not adequately value natural capital; conflict, confusion and poor coordination between (and within) Australia's three tiered system of government; cutbacks to the technical support provided by government agencies; inappropriate legal frameworks; and grossly inadequate resource management information systems. In the long run, if the often remarkable community efforts at local and catchment scales are not supported by broader scale institutional change, this effort may well end up being in vain. NRM can now be seen as entering an 'institutionalist era'. The sociology of community action that entered the resource management field in the 'localist era' now needs to be complemented by political economic insights and theory. The development, articulation and implementation of a paradigm of social learning is, I believe, central to overcoming such institutional constraints and engaging with the deeper structural causes of the ecological unsustainability of modern society.

References

Bawden, R. (1989) Towards action researching systems. In: Zuber-Skerritt, O. (ed.), *Action research for change and development*. Griffith University, Brisbane.

Bawden, R. J. and R. G. Packham (1991) Systemic praxis in the education of the agricultural systems practitioner. Proceedings of the *35th Meeting of International Society for Systems Sciences*, 1991, at Ostersund, Sweden. Also published as: Systemic praxis in the education of the agricultural systems practitioner. By Bawden and Packham. *Systems Practice* 6 (1): 7–19.

Beck, U. (1992) *Risk society: Towards a new modernity*. Sage, London.

Beck, U. (1994) The reinvention of politics: towards a theory of reflexive modernization. In: Beck, U., Giddens, A., and Lash, S. (eds.), *Reflexive modernization: Politics, tradition and aesthetics in the modern social order*. Polity Press, Cambridge.

Beck, U. (1997) *The reinvention of politics: rethinking modernity in the global social order*. Polity Press, Cambridge.

Beck, U., A. Giddens, and S. Lash (1994) *Reflexive modernisation: Politics, tradition and aesthetics in the modern social order*. Polity Press, Cambridge.

Capra, F. (1997) *The web of life: A new synthesis of mind and matter*. Flamingo, London.

Conti, S. (1997) Interdependent and uneven development: A systemic view of the global-local dialectic. *International Geographic Union* 27 (2):195–205.

Dodds, S. (1995) Towards a science of sustainability: The need for a better understanding of human well-being in ecological economics. Proceedings of the *Ecological Economics Conference*, Coffs Harbour, November 19–23, 1995. Australia New Zealand Society for Ecological Economics, University of New England.

Dovers, S. (1997) Sustainability: Demands on policy. *Journal of Public Policy* 16 (3):303–318.

Dovers, S. R. and C. D. Mobbs (1997) An alluring prospect? Ecology, and the requirements of adaptive management. In: Klomp, N. and I. Lunt (eds.), *Frontiers in ecology: Building the links*. Elsevier Science, Oxford.

Dryzek, J. S. (1987) Complexity and rationality in public life. *Political Studies* XXXV:424–442.

Dryzek, J. (1990) *Discursive democracy: Politics, policy and political science*. Cambridge University Press, New York.

Dryzek, J. (1992) Ecology and discursive democracy: Beyond liberal capitalism and the administrative state. *Capitalism, Nature and Society* 3 (2):394–418.

Dryzek, J. S. (1996) *Democracy in capitalist times.* Oxford University Press, Oxford.

Dryzek, J. S. (1997) *The politics of the earth: Environmental discourses.* Oxford University Press, Oxford.

Dunn, E. S. (1971) *Economic and social development: A process of social learning.* John Hopkins University Press, Baltimore.

Dunn, E. S. (1984) The nature of social learning. In: Korten, D. C. and R. Klauss (eds.), *People centred development: Contributions toward theory and planning frameworks.* Kumarian, Connecticut.

Francis, G. and S. Lerner (1996) Making sustainable development happen: Institutional transformation. In: Dale, A. and J. Robinson (eds.), *Achieving sustainable development.* UBC Press, Vancouver.

Friedmann, J. (1984) Planning as social learning. In: Korten, D. C. and R. Klauss (eds.), *People centred development: Contributions toward theory and planning frameworks.* Kumarian, Connecticut.

Friedmann, J. (1992) *Empowerment: The politics of alternative development.* Blackwell, Oxford.

Funtowicz, S. O. and J. R. Ravetz (1993) Science for the post-normal age. *Futures* 25 (7): 739–755.

Gallopin (1991) Human dimensions of global change: Linking the global and the local processes. *International Social Science Journal* 130:707–718.

Giddens, A. (1984) *The constitution of society. Outline of the theory of structuration.* Polity Press, Cambridge.

Giddens, A. (1990) *The consequences of modernity.* Polity Press, Cambridge.

Giddens, A. (1994) *Beyond left and right: The future of radical politics.* Polity Press, Cambridge.

Giddens, A. (1998) *The third way: The renewal of social democracy.* Polity Press, Cambridge.

Glasbergen, P. (1996) Learning to manage environment. In: Lafferty, W. M. and J. Meadowcroft (eds.), *Democracy and the environment: Problems and perspectives.* Edward Elgar, Cheltenham.

Goldblatt, D. (1996) *Social theory and the environment.* Polity Press, Cambridge.

Goodin, R. (1996) Institutions and their design. In: Goodin, R. (ed.), *Institutional design.* Polity Press, Cambridge.

Gunderson, L. H., C. S. Holling, and S. S. Light (1995) Barriers broken and bridges built: A synthesis. In: Gunderson, L. H., C. S. Holling, and S. S. Light (eds.), *Barriers and bridges to the renewal of ecosystems and institutions.* Columbia University Press, New York.

Habermas, J. (1984a) *The theory of communicative action: Volume 1 – Reason and the rationalisation of society.* Polity Press, Cambridge.

Habermas, J. (1984b) *The theory of communicative action: Volume 2 – The critique of functionalist reason.* Polity Press, Cambridge.

Held, D. (1996) *Models of democracy.* Polity Press, Cambridge.

Holling, C. S. (1995) What are barriers and bridges? In: Gunderson, L. H., C. S. Holling, and S. S. Light (eds.), *Barriers and bridges to the renewal of ecosystems and institutions.* Columbia University Press, New York.

Hutton, W. (1995) *The state we're in.* Vintage, London.

Hutton, W. (1997) *The state to come.* Vintage, London.

Irwin, A. (1995) *Citizen science: A study of people, expertise and sustainable development.* Routledge, London.

Kolb, D. A. (1984) *Experiential learning.* Prentice-Hall, New Jersey.

Lee, K. N. (1993) *Compass and gyroscope: Integrating science and politics for the environment.* Island Press, Washington, DC.

Mabey, C. and P. Lies (eds.). (1994) *Managing learning.* Open University Press, London.

Maturana, H. R. and F. J. Varela (1987) *The tree of knowledge – The biological roots of human understanding.* New Science Library, Boston.

Maxwell, N. (1992a) Science, reason, knowledge, and wisdom: A citique of specialism. *Inquiry* 23:19–81.

Maxwell, N. (1992b) What kind of inquiry can best help us create a good world? *Science, Technology, & Human Values* 17 (2): 205–227.

Milbrath, L. W. (1989) *Envisioning a sustainable society: Learning our way out*. State University of New York Press, New York.

Miller, A. (1985) Technological thinking: Its impact on environmental management. *Environmental Management* 9 (3): 179–190.

Parson, A. and W. Clark (1995) Sustainable development as social learning: Theoretical perspectives and practical challenges for the design of a research program. In: Gunderson, L. H., C. S. Holling, and S. S. Light (eds.), *Barriers and bridges to the renewal of ecosystems and institutions*. Columbia University Press, New York.

Pepper, D. (1993) *Eco-socialism*. Routledge, London.

Pepper, D. (1996) *Modern environmentalism*. Routledge, London.

Pretty, J., I. Guijt, J. Thompson, and I. Scoones (1995) *Participatory learning and action: A trainer's guide*. International Institute for Environment and Development, London.

Princen, T. and M. Finger (1994) *Environmental NGO's in world politics*. Routledge, London.

Quizilbash, M. (1996) Capabilities, well-being and human development: A survey. *Journal of Development Studies* 33 (2): 143–162.

Senge, P. M. (1992) *The fifth discipline: The art and practice of the learning organisation*. Random House, Sydney.

Weale, A. (1992) *The new politics of pollution*. Manchester University Press, Manchester.

Woodhill, J. and N. G. Röling (1998) The second wing of the eagle: How soft science can help us to learn our way to more sustainable futures. In: Röling, N. G. and M. A. E. Wagemakers (eds.), *Facilitating sustainable agriculture: Participatory learning and adaptive management in times of environmental uncertainty*. Cambridge University Press, Cambridge.

Woodhill, J. (1999) *Sustaining rural Australia: A political economic critique of natural resources management*, thesis submitted for PhD, Australian National University, Canberra.

Woodhill, J. (2002) Sustainability, social learning and the democratic imperative. Lessons from the Australian landcare movement. In: Leeuwis, C. and R. Pyburn (eds.), *Wheelbarrows full of frogs – Social learning in rural resource management*, pp. 317–331. Assen: Koninklijke Van Gorcum BV.

World Bank. (1996) *The World Bank participation source book*. World Bank, Washington, DC.

Chapter 5
Traditions of Understanding: Language, Dialogue and Experience

Ray Ison

At a Glance

- The reader is invited to reflect on how understanding arises in relation to language, metaphor and dialogue; and how, as environmental managers, we use these to interpret our learning and experience.
- This chapter provides reflections on how particular understandings can become institutionalised and on the different ways 'institution', 'organisation' and 'structure' can be understood in the practice of environmental management.
- Together, these reflections open up ideas of how we can become aware of our own understandings when working to incorporate social learning in environmental management.
- Research on social learning in the implementation of the European water framework directive is used to ground the ideas discussed in this chapter.

Creating the Contexts to Foster Social Learning

I am writing this chapter from the context of coordinating a research project on Social Learning for the Integrated Management and Sustainable Use of Water at Catchment Scale, funded by the European Union (SLIM – Contract No EVK1-CT-2000-00064 SLIM; see http://slim.open.ac.uk). It involves 30 researchers from six countries, with backgrounds spanning the social and biophysical sciences. English is used as the operational language and the research group has worked hard to engage in social learning in their research practice, as well as studying social learning using case studies and action research.

The project runs in parallel with the implementation of the European water framework directive by all European Union member states. The water framework directive has significant elements for social learning. These include the mandatory nature of public participation and demands for transparency in decision making,

Source: Ison (2005). Reproduced with permission of Earthscan Ltd., www.earthscan.co.uk

C. Blackmore (ed.), *Social Learning Systems and Communities of Practice*,
DOI 10.1007/978-1-84996-133-2_5, © The Open University 2010.
Published in Association with Springer-Verlag London Limited.

necessitating what Williams (2001) terms 'a joined up strategy' to bring together all those affected. Preliminary research findings suggest that in the great majority of cases studied or encountered there is little or no:

- systems orientation providing strategic and systemic thinking of the sort that might facilitate the further development of an interactive approach (that is, social learning)
- integration and synthesis creating awareness among policy-makers and catchment managers of the opportunities afforded by an interactive approach or the growing experience of these approaches in contexts outside Europe
- participation and engagement generating capacity in terms of extant skills, to engage with and enact interactive approaches (especially facilitation skills).

Water management and implementation of the water framework directive and associated legislation are happening mainly in a technical and instrumental context. Research and practice are radically separated and only a very limited range of knowledge sources are deemed 'legitimate' (Schön, 1995). Ends, or goals, are being pursued at the expense of any consideration of the process by which the ends are expressed and met. In the water management 'industry', goals are mainly technical, at the expense of the social and ecological context (Sterling, 2001). So long as these technical and instrumental approaches dominate, many of the demands of the water framework directive that require stakeholder participation are unlikely to be met. Thus opportunities for enabling social learning and building citizen ecological literacy are being squandered.

The long-term outcomes of enhanced water quality and its management are also threatened because, at the end of the day, achieving ecological and technical goals involves changes in the behaviour of a diverse array of stakeholders. Lack of understanding of the importance of taking social factors into account constrains the development of policies based on fostering social learning. The alternatives are not promising since regulation is expensive and economic incentives are not always appropriate.

How can this loss of opportunity be explained? I start with the traditions of understanding within which policy-makers, water engineers, ecologists and other stakeholders in water management think and act. Thus, in the first instance it is a crisis of how we claim to know what we know. This rests, in turn, on widely entrenched distortions in what we understand as human communication, and a lack of awareness of the biological basis of language. From both of these come practices that have been conserved over time, even when the circumstances that made them necessary are no longer relevant. That is, not only do practices become institutionalised, but institutions also shape practices. Institutions and institutionalised behaviours are thus self-justifying. Here I am using North's (1990) idea of institutions as 'any form of constraint that human beings devise to shape interaction'. This could be formal arrangements such as promotion procedures or organisational cultures, or informal arrangements such as the rules of a weekly touch football game.

Becoming Aware of Our Traditions of Understanding

In a book based on their fieldwork in the semi-arid rangelands of New South Wales (NSW), Ison and Russell (2000a) present a wide-ranging critique of the understandings that have dominated rural research and agricultural extension practice for most of the second half of the twentieth century. From their co-research with pastoralists, they present an alternative model for research and development (R&D) based on understandings that come from systems theory. Their work deconstructs widespread understandings about knowledge, information, learning, extension, technology transfer and communication. However, they also offer conceptual tools and a framework for reconstruction.

The work can also be seen as a model for systemic inquiry of any set of complex issues; Fig. 5.1 models one way a systemic inquiry might be conducted based on enacting soft systems methodology (see Checkland, 2001). Ison and Russell set up a structured exploration of how our understanding of R&D is developed and our understanding of change constructed. This leads to an exploration, using experiential, narrative, historical and theoretical sources, of the research context in the semi-arid rangelands of NSW, where technology was perceived to have failed (Ison, 2000a). Central to this part of their inquiry was a critical distinction based on the perceptions and actions of the researcher.

In first-order research and development, which is still the most common, the researcher remains outside the system being studied. The espoused stance by researchers is that of objectivity and, while the system being studied is often spoken of in open system terms, intervention is performed as though it were a closed system. Perception and action by researchers and those who manage and maintain the R&D system are based on a belief in a real world; a world of discrete entities that have meaning in and of themselves (Russell and Ison, 2000a, p. 10).

In contrast to this tradition, Russell and Ison (2000a, b) stress the need for a second-order R&D in which the espoused role and action of the researcher or practitioner are very much part of the interactions being studied. In this framework, how the researcher/participant perceives the situation is critical to the system being studied. Responsibility replaces objectivity as the central ethic, and perception and action are based on one's own experiential world, rather than on a belief in a single external real world. Any move towards second-order R&D has implications for the behaviour and practice of researchers and other stakeholders in environmental issues. I propose that it is the lack of capacity to move to a second-order perspective with its associated social learning practices of reflection, systems orientation and negotiation with the self and others, that threatens the successful implementation of the water framework directive.

As unique human beings, we are part of a lineage and our history is a product of both biological and social development, which I will call a tradition. Perhaps another way to describe this is that a tradition is the history of our being in the world. Traditions are important because our models of understanding grow out of traditions. I further define a tradition as a network of prejudices or pre-understandings that

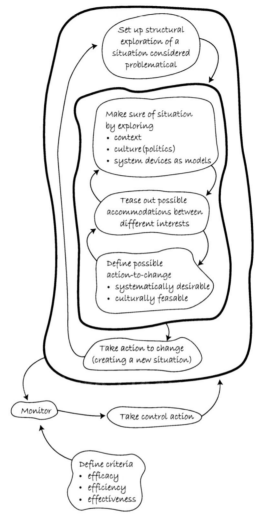

Fig. 5.1 A model of implementing soft systems methodology.
Source: Checkland (2001)

provides possible answers and strategies for action. Traditions are not only ways to see and act, but also ways to conceal (see Russell and Ison, 2000a).

Traditions in a culture embed what has been judged to be useful practice. The risk for any culture is that a tradition can become a blind spot when it evolves into practice that lacks any avenue for critical reflection. The effects of blind spots can be observed at the level of the individual, the group, the organisation, the nation or culture, and in the metaphors and discourses in which we are immersed. This explication of traditions of understanding and learning is built on Maturana and Varela's (1979) biological theory of cognition, particularly that of structural coupling. Structural coupling explains how as living organisms we can never escape acting according to our context, and being acted upon by it. At one and the same time we are both independent (maintaining our own organisation as a living system) and related (coupled) to our external world. This explanation challenges the common idea that we adapt to an environment, and replaces it with the idea of organisms and environments co-evolving.

A period of fieldwork in the semi-arid rangelands of NSW was one of growing awareness of this different way of understanding on my own part. I now find that the following questions posed by von Foerster (1992) best capture the choices I can make:

- Am I apart from the universe? That is, whenever I look, am I looking through a peephole upon an unfolding universe (the first-order tradition)?
- Am I part of the universe? That is, whenever I act, am I changing myself and the universe as well (the second-order tradition)?

It is these two questions I must consider when reflecting on what it is that I do. And the choice is not just one of principle, as in articulating an ethical code to be followed. For von Foerster, the answer to these questions unfolds in our living as we do what we do – it is how we experience others and ourselves. It is important to emphasise that both first-order and second-order traditions are different modes of doing R&D.

First-order Research and Development

The ethos and achievements of first-order R&D are characterised by disciplinary knowledge, a 'fix' mentality, and the belief that generating new knowledge is a good thing in itself (Russell and Ison, 2000a). Explicitly, it is a tradition based on a belief in an increasingly knowable world: a world capable of being understood without the need to take into account our actions as participants in creating that very world we experience. There is a basic assumption that a fixed reality is out there and that, by applying rational understanding, we will increasingly gain accurate knowledge of its elements and the laws of its functioning. In addition, most often there is no distinction between phenomena that are observable to the senses (such as sounds, sight and touch) and phenomena that are the products of the intellect (such as thoughts, beliefs and memories). The development of this approach has had its own phases, outlined next, all of which exemplify the fix mentality:

1. The problem is seen as a mismatch between what is scientifically known and technically feasible, and current practice. The new technology is designed by research scientists and then transferred to the end users, who put it into action to address the problem
2. Built into the belief of a technological solution is a conception of the benefits that could be derived from better farming systems or, in the case of rangelands

a return to the 'natural ecosystem' state, without considering who participates in defining 'better' or how what is perceived as 'natural' has come to be constructed
3. Social and political insights are specifically added to the R&D equation (for example most multidisciplinary research).

At its simplest, the first-order view accepts the existence of an objective reality, made up of things bearing properties and entering into relations. Such has been the success and prestige of modern science that many accept it as the best framework available for understanding how we think, which delivers a powerful social and political role to science, as understood in this form. The point of departure from the first-order view in the SLIM project saw social learning as part of an interactive approach that acknowledges we are actors in our environment and thus all our actions, including those of scientific inquiry, inevitably act on our environment.

The original SLIM project proposal argued that water catchments are conventionally understood as biophysical 'hard' systems and that problems are addressed through instrumental interventions, typically through engineering works. However, in recent years, another approach has emerged in response to the frequent failure of the instrumental and strategic reasoning of the first-order perspective. This approach is based on the idea that sustainable and regenerated water catchments are the emergent property of systems practice, of systemic inquiry (see, for example, King and Jiggins, 2002; Röling, 1994, 2002; Röling and Woodhill, 2001). That is, desirable water catchment properties arise from interactions among multiple interdependent stakeholders in the catchments and between those stakeholders and the catchments themselves. Where such an interactive approach applies, centralised policy provides a context for a dynamic local decentralised process and, in the case of large watersheds, for concerted parallel local processes. In seeking to move away from taking only a first-order approach the SLIM project has no intention of fostering irrationality or fuzzy thinking. Rather, along with Winograd and Flores (1987), the commitment is to developing a new ground of rationality – one that is as rigorous as the first – order tradition in its aspirations, but does not share the technical and instrumental presuppositions underlying it.

Second-order Research and Development

Awareness of the distinctions between first- and second-order R&D traditions has important implications for how social learning is understood, fostered and researched. In the context of the SLIM project, an interactive second-order approach has three important implications.

Firstly, it emphasises social learning as an emergent property of collaboration. Stakeholders are considered intelligent, responsible agents who are willing to act in the collective interest. It is taken as given that they are learning about their domain of existence and are creating reciprocal arrangements. Typically, such social learning is facilitated by helping stakeholders see the water catchment (in its social and biophysical dimensions) as one system, in which they are interdependent with others.

Secondly, for social learning to emerge, stakeholders must develop shared plat-forms for decision making and action. A capacity for communication, shared learn-ing processes and concerted action must be created at the water catchment level. A water catchment managing system must be developed, often within an already complex social context of existing organisations, vested interests and institutional arrangements.

Thirdly, the interactive approach has important consequences for policy. It implies a different policy basis from the customary biophysical and economic models of the catchment, one that calls for totally different instruments and practices.

At the heart of a social learning approach is some form of communicative action, so one needs to understand how human communication occurs. My concern is to provide a biological explanation, though others may find inspiration in Habermas's work (1984, 1987) on communicative action and reason or in other traditions.

Learning Through Language and Dialogue

Living in Language

The Santiago school of cognition (see Capra, 1996) suggests that all knowing is derived from doing. Our capacity as individuals to respond is inextricably linked to the interaction between our language and emotions. This interaction is what we call conversation. This is central to our reflections on what it is we do as practitioners of one sort or another in the name of sustainability. What is not clear, however, is what practices we need to engage in, individually and collectively, to address the quality of our relationship (as a species) with our environment (including other species).

Talbott (2002) sets out to chart a pathway between the advocates of scientific management and radical conservationists. Responding to the claim that 'the limits of our knowledge should define the limits of our practice', Talbott asks (p. 23): 'By what practice can we extend our knowledge, if we may never act without already possessing perfect knowledge?' The answer he offers is that 'We conduct an ecological conversation'. Talbott suggests three main features of an ecological conversation:

1. putting cautious questions to the other
2. compensating for past inadequacies – in the sense that in a conversation later words modify the meaning attributed to earlier words
3. recognising that at any stage of a conversation there is never a single right or wrong response – nor is it an act of making a choice from something predeter-mined.

As a species, conversation is our unique selling point! To converse is to turn together, to dance – and thus an ecological conversation is a tango of responsibility. A conversation is inventive, unpredictable and always particularising to place and people (see, for example, Shaw, 2002). Engaging with this metaphor is not to turn away from the doing of science or ecology, or any other practice. This experiential activity opens up new possibilities. It entails the responsibility of reflection, of making other distinctions and considering their consequences. It provides the basis of conducting an ecological conversation.

The Role of Metaphor

Metaphors provide a way to understand our understandings and how we use language. Our ordinary conceptual system, in terms of which we think and act, is metaphorical in nature. Paying attention to metaphors-in-use is one way we can reflect on our own traditions of understanding (McClintock et al., 2003a, 2003b).

Metaphors both reveal and conceal, but because we live in language it is sometimes difficult to reflect on our metaphors-in-use. The strategy of mirroring particular metaphors or metaphor clusters thus holds open the possibility for reflection and learning. For example, as outlined by McClintock (2000), the metaphor 'countryside as a tapestry' reveals the experience of countryside as a visually pleasing pattern, of local character and diversity and of what is lost when landscapes are dominated by monocultures. However, the metaphor conceals the smell, danger, noise and activity of people making a living. By exploring metaphors, we can make part of our language use 'picturable' and thus rationally visible, publicly discussable and debatable, as well as socially useful as a practical resource 'with which and through which we can think and act' (Shotter, 1993).

McClintock's (1996) conclusions contribute to an agenda for meeting demands for increased transparency and participation in environmental decision making. This, in turn, requires building social and relational capital through processes of social learning. Exploring metaphors-in-use and what they may reveal or conceal is one of many ways to explore the context of issues in the process of environmental decision making. It may also be used to explore and trigger enthusiasms – where enthusiasm is a predisposition to action (Russell and Ison, 2000b).

McClintock (1996) identified two parallel ways of working with metaphor: acting as practitioner – narrator and practitioner – facilitator. (Practitioner here can be translated as researcher, manager, community worker or government agent.) The role of practitioner – narrator includes the following steps:

1. Make initial distinctions around the metaphors-in-use (for example for landscapes, lifestyles, products, events).
2. Bring forth metaphors of the practice context.
3. Explore the metaphors by considering revealed and concealed aspects.
4. Judge enabling and disabling metaphors and identify alternatives.
5. Iterate, involving different people, different sources of metaphors or different issues.

The role of a practitioner – facilitator is to use metaphors to create a space for understandings to emerge. A six-step process has been proposed:

1. Propose initial distinctions around metaphors and anticipate ways in which the distinctions can be meaningful.
2. Consider activities for jointly bringing forth and exploring metaphors (in workshops or on farm walks).
3. Consider activities to jointly juxtapose metaphors and consider what each metaphor implies and does not imply (a proxy for revealed and concealed aspects).
4. Revisit the distinctions around metaphors and propose further distinctions around judging metaphors, choosing between metaphors, and dominant and reified metaphors.
5. Consider activities to facilitate processes of moving between metaphors.
6. Iterate steps 1–5.

Fostering Dialogue

Debate-based communication is often grounded in situations of conflict. Dialogue differs from and contrasts with debate. The roots of the word 'dialogue' can be translated as meaning 'flowing through', while the roots of the word 'debate' mean 'to beat down' (Isaacs, 1993). Isaacs' (p. 45) definition of dialogue is 'a sustained collective inquiry into the processes, assumptions, and certainties that compose everyday experiences'.

Dialogue is a process that does not seek consensus, but to provide an environment for learning, to think together. This does not refer only to analysing a problem, but to sharing understandings and assumptions and the reasoning behind these assumptions in order to build richer pictures and act jointly. With these distinctions as background Kersten (1995) devised a research process based on listening to and exploring the local context with the aid of local people. [...][1] Her research showed that dialogue meetings have to be situated in a broader approach if dialogue is to emerge.

As part of her research, Kersten set out to design dialogue workshops between scientists (mainly ecologists) and pastoralists. Her subsequent experience reflects a flaw in the overall R&D system – the ecologists were concerned only with formulating research problems from within their 'system of doing ecology'. In effect, what they tried to do was to impose their system of interest on the context, rather than allow a jointly conceived system of interest to emerge from the dialogue. This process of using dialogue to resolve conflicts and support social learning is consistent with [a] negotiation 'strand' of social learning [...]. Both [ideas] view conflict as an opportunity to support social interactions and learning through problem definition and resolution.

---

[1]A two-part figure showing 'schemas for iterative cycles of listening and allowing interpretation by stakeholders' that appeared in the original chapter has been edited out of this chapter.

Table 5.1 Issues arising from meetings between pastoralists and scientists that enhanced or restricted dialogue

Enhancing dialogue	Restricting dialogue
Participants come to a meeting as individuals	Participants come as representatives of a group
Participants articulate their personal understanding at the meeting	Participants are at the meeting as groups and act as part of that group
Time has been spent on building relationships before the meeting and during the meeting	Little time has been spent on building relationships
Participants are prepared to relax preconceived ideas about other participants at the meeting	Participants have fixed general or stereotyped ideas about other participants
Participants do not know each other beforehand	Participants know each other beforehand and are not prepared to relax preconceived ideas about each other
Participants listen actively to other participants with an open mind that is not blocked by preconceived ideas	Participants listen to re-establish preconceived ideas
Participants are open to ideas and ask for suggestions from other participants	Participants are defending or attacking statements made
Participants respect other meanings and understandings. Multiple realities are acknowledged	Participants do not respect meanings and understandings other than their own. They believe in one reality
Participants feel they can benefit from a good discussion with people who see the same issue from different perspectives	People have the feeling they are 'being participated'

Source: Kersten and Ison (1998)

Kersten found that the context and history of participants have a major influence on the possibilities for dialogue to emerge. She identified a set of nine factors that either enhanced or constrained dialogue (see Table 5.1). When situated in an overall research approach that values multiple realities, techniques such as mind-mapping and matrix ranking were found to break down the cultural barriers between the individual as 'pastoralist' or 'researcher'. These techniques opened up the possibility of each genuinely hearing the other.

Facilitating Learning and Dialogue: Institutional Directions

Institutional Factors

In recent years, I have moved my research focus from practices directly associated with biophysical phenomena to a concern with how our institutional and organisational practices mediate our relationships with the biophysical world (for example through dialogue, social learning and exploring metaphor). This shift of attention has been prompted by my experience that how humans think, learn and act in relation to the biophysical world (and other species) is the arena in most need of attention. However, there is much confusion in the literature and in everyday conversation about what is meant by organisation, institution and structure (see Ison, 1994, 1996, 2000b).

North's (1990) distinctions between 'organisation' and 'institution' are initially helpful but, from a systems perspective do not go far enough. I suggest the need to recognise a further set of distinctions between the organisation and structure of a system. The organisation of a system is defined as a particular set of relationships, whether static or dynamic between components that constitute a recognisable whole – a recognisable unity as distinguished by an observer. Organisational relationships have to be maintained to maintain the system – if they change, the system either 'dies' or becomes something else.

On the other hand, the structure of a system is defined as the set of current concrete components and relationships through which the organisation of a system is manifest in particular surroundings. Thus for a particular R&D organisation like NSW Agriculture, the key organisational relationships might be those between politicians, researchers, administrators, extension officers and agricultural/horticultural producers (experience suggests that consumers are often excluded). If these relationships cease to exist, then that which is unique to a particular organisation ceases to exist. If it were a biological organism, this would mean the death of the organism. But because organisations are not biological organisms, those involved can choose to become some other organisation – remember that the same organisation can realise or manifest itself through different structures. Structures in this example might include particular divisions, programmes or practices.

Social Learning Systems in Practice

In many ways the water framework directive in Europe is a unique piece of legislation and presents many opportunities for creative implementation. In the main, however, it is not being grasped creatively. The systems of interest that are beginning to be enacted in some circles can be characterised as:

- a system to ensure our minister does not face infraction (court) proceedings by Brussels (from the perspective of ministry and senior line agency staff)
- a system to establish the best possible scientific basis for water quality (from the perspective of scientists and engineers in the environment agencies)
- a system to cause minimum disruption to our current procedures and so avoid additional costs (from the perspective of English water policy-makers and ministers)
- a system to engender duplication and conflict with planning and land use management practices and legislation (from the perspective of professional planners).

Many other possible systems of interest could be formulated in the current context. None of them is right or wrong, but merely different ways of thinking systemically about the situation and beginning a process of systemic inquiry. However, this systems orientation is not much in evidence. For example, in Scotland the baseline status for the water framework directive established in-house by the Scottish Environmental Protection Agency is based on existing technical data and professional judgement. For them, the goal was to meet the reporting deadline without considering:

- who learns or could learn in the process of developing the baseline data (that is, who might relevant stakeholders be and how might they be involved?)
- who, apart from professionals may have relevant data to contribute (for example anglers, gillies, estate managers, school children)
- whether how they are enacting the water framework directive will deliver what it aspires to deliver in, say, 2020. There has been no backcasting, for example, and little consideration of whether their implementation model is sustainable in terms of human resource and transaction costs. Participation is seen as a luxury that can wait until later.

In contrast, from a second-order perspective, the creative implementation of the water framework directive could be likened to the design of a learning system (Ison, 1994; Ison and Russell, 2000b). Table 5.2 shows some considerations for designing particular learning systems.

The elements of Table 5.2 are not prescriptions, but considerations for design that must be adapted in space and time. But adapting for design requires an opening up to our traditions of understanding. The same is true of designing for or facilitating social learning.

When applied to good environmental management or even the broader concept of sustainability, social learning has been described as the process of collective action and reflection among different actors directed towards improving the management of human and environmental interrelations. The SLIM project originally proposed that the research would focus on social learning as a combination of (a) stakeholders' shared learning about the biophysical nature of the watershed (ecological parameters) and (b) stakeholders' shared learning about human collective agency. In this sense, we argued for the need for reflection, that is, learning about learning and its facilitation. Further, because social learning has remained a rather vague concept, we proposed to use the theory of partnership as collective cognitive agency, with its emphasis on structural coupling and consistency among perception, emotion and action, as the basis for an alternative policy framework.

Despite committing from the outset to build a community of practice engaged in its own social learning, the members of SLIM have still found it difficult to articulate and reflect on existing deeply held theoretical commitments. What is more, we have found it difficult to explore and honour our differences. Recognising this dilemma, we set up an international midterm review of our project built around each partner's articulation of social learning and their reflections on it. This has helped and enabled us to move on [. . .].

Table 5.2 Two independent sets of design considerations for the design of learning systems

Nine design features of systems courses at The Open University	Ten design considerations from the SWARD project[a], including some key starting conditions
1. Ground concepts and action as much as possible in the student's own experience	1. A perceived issue or need that has local identity
2. Learn from case studies of failure	2. Active listening to stakeholder perceptions of the issue/need
3. Develop diagramming (and other modelling) skills as a means for students to engage with and learn about complexity	3. Good staff – in this case, young, motivated and proactive women
4. Take responsibility as authors (or researchers) for what we say and do (epistemological awareness)	4. No, or very limited forms of, control
5. Recognise that learning involves an interplay between our emotional and rational selves	5. Proper resourcing, particularly in the early stages
6. Develop skills in iterating – understanding learning as emerging from processes that are not deterministic	6. A minimum number of initial group leaders who acted as 'key attractors'
7. Introduce systems concepts, tools, methods and methodological approaches to develop skills in formulating systems of interest . . . for purposeful action (an example would be an exploration based on metaphors)	7. Scope for self-organisation around particular enthusiasms
8. Use verbs not nouns! Verbs denote relationships and activity and are key to the process of activity modelling, one of the main features of soft systems methodology	8. An appropriately experienced participant to conceptualise systems
9. Make assessment relevant to action in the personal and professional lives of students	9. Some small 'carrots' for participants at the beginning
	10. A supportive local press creating a positive publicity network

[a] 'A community-based R&D project in the southwest of England'. Source: Ison (2002)

Conclusions

My intention has been to invite and trigger the reader's reflections on their own traditions of understanding, particularly how that understanding arises in relation to language, metaphor and dialogue, and how they might choose to understand learning. These reflections are designed to recognise that 'my world is different to your world and this must always be so. The common ground, which is the basis of our ability to communicate with one another, comes through the use of common processes of perceiving and conceptualizing' (Russell, 1986, p. 54).

I have also invited reflection on how particular understandings can become institutionalised. These reflections invite the use of a systems orientation and consideration of emergent properties (practices) that might arise from this perspective. In my experience, many line agencies, government ministry staff and expert advisers are not prepared to relinquish their perceived power and control. To engage or participate fully in a social dialogue, an emergent property of a social learning strategy for sustainability may well be enhanced citizen ecological literacy.

Acknowledgements The support of the European Union and members of the SLIM Contract No. EVK1-CT-2000-00064 SLIM (website: http://slim.open.ac.uk) is gratefully acknowledged. David Russell is, as ever, a source of inspiration. My thanks to the editors for the invitation to contribute and the hard work they put into the original manuscript.

References

Capra, F. (1996) *The Web of Life*, Harper Collins, London.
Checkland, R. B. (2001) 'Presentation to a joint meeting of UKSS/OUSys', OU Systems Society Newsletter, February. See also www.spmc.org.uk
Habermas, J. (1984) *The Theory of Communicative Action, Vol 1, Reason and the Rationalization of Society*, Beacon Press, Boston.
Habermas, J. (1987) *The Theory of Communicative Action, Vol 2, Lifeworld and System, A Critique of Functionalist Reason*, Beacon Press, Boston.
Isaacs, W. N. (1993) 'Taking flight: Dialogue, collective thinking and organisational learning', *Organizational Dynamics*, Vol 22, pp. 24–39.
Ison, R. L. (1994) 'Designing learning systems: How can systems approaches be applied in the training of research workers and development actors?', In *Lectures and Debates*, Proceedings, International Symposium on Systems-oriented Research in Agriculture and Rural Development, Vol 2, pp. 369–394.
Ison, R. L. (1996) *Facilitating Institutional Change*, Proceedings, ANU/IIED/OFI Sustainable Forest Policy Short Course, Oxford.
Ison, R. L. (2000a) 'Technology: Transforming Grazier Experience'. In: Ison, R. L. and Russell, D. B. (eds.) *Agricultural Extension and Rural Development: Breaking Out of Traditions*. Cambridge University Press, Cambridge.
Ison, R. L. (2000b) 'Experience, tradition and service? Institutionalised R&D in the rangelands', In Ison, R. L. and Russell, D. B. (eds) *Agricultural Extension and Rural Development: Breaking Out of Traditions*, Cambridge University Press, Cambridge.
Ison, R. L. (2002) 'Systems practice and the design of learning systems: Orchestrating an ecological conversation', In *An Interdisciplinary Dialogue: Agricultural Production and Integrated Ecosystem Management of Soil and Water*, Proceedings, Ballina, NSW, Australia, 12–16 November.
Ison, R. L. (2005) 'Traditions of understanding: Language, dialogue and experience.' In Keen, M., Brown, V. A., and Dyball, R.(eds) *Social Learning in Environmental Management*, pp. 22–40, Earthscan, London. Reproduced with permission of Earthscan Ltd., www.earthscan.co.uk.
Ison, R. L. and Russell, D. B. (eds) (2000a) *Agricultural Extension and Rural Development: Breaking Out of Traditions*, Cambridge University Press, Cambridge.
Ison, R. L. and Russell, D. B. (2000b) 'Exploring some distinctions for the design of learning systems', *Cybernetics and Human Knowing*, Vol 7, No 4, pp. 43–56.
Kersten, S. (1995) 'In search of dialogue: Vegetation management in western New South Wales, Australia', Unpublished PhD thesis, University of Sydney.
Kersten, S. and Ison, R. L. (1998) 'Listening, interpretative cycles and dialogue: Process design for collaborative research and development', *The Journal of Agricultural Education & Extension*, Vol 5, pp. 163–178.

King, C. and Jiggins, J. (2002) 'A systemic model and theory for facilitating social learning', In Leeuwis, C. and Pyburn, R. (eds) *Wheelbarrows Full of Frogs. Social Learning in Rural Resource Management*, Koninklijke van Gorcum, Assen, the Netherlands.

Maturana, H. R. and Varela, F. G. (1979) *The Tree of Knowledge. The Biological Roots of Human Understanding*, New Science Library, Boston.

McClintock, D. (1996) 'Metaphors that inspire " researching with people" : UK farming, countrysides and diverse stakeholder contexts', PhD thesis, Systems Department, The Open University, Milton Keynes, UK.

McClintock, D. (2000) 'Considering metaphors of countrysides in the United Kingdom', In Cerf, M., Gibbon, D., Hubert, B., Ison, R., Jiggins, J., Paine, M., Proost, J., and Roling, N. (eds) *Cow Up a Tree. Knowing and Learning for Change in Agriculture, Case Studies from Industrialised Countries*, INRA (Institut National de la Recherche Agronomique) editions, Paris.

McClintock, D., Ison, R. L., and Armson, R. (2003a) 'Metaphors and understandings: Building systems practice', *Cybernetics and Human Knowing*, Vol 11, pp. 25–47

McClintock, D., Ison, R. L., and Armson, R. (2003b) 'Metaphors of research and researching with people', *Journal of Environmental Planning and Management*, Vol 46, No 5, pp. 715–731.

North, D. (1990) *Institutions, Institutional Change and Economic Performance*, Cambridge University Press, Cambridge.

Röling, N. (1994) 'Platforms for decision making about eco-systems', In Fresco, L. O., Stroosnijder, L., Bourn, J., and Van Keulen, H. (eds) *Future of the Land: Mobilising and Integrating Knowledge for Land Use Options*, Wiley, Chichester, UK.

Röling, N. (2002) 'Beyond the aggregation of individual preferences. Moving from multiple to distributed cognition in resource dilemmas', In Leeuwis, C. and Pyburn, R. (eds) *Wheelbarrows Full of Frogs. Social Learning in Rural Resource Management*, Koninklijke van Gorcum, Assen, The Netherlands.

Röling, N. and Woodhill, J. (2001) 'From paradigm to practice: Foundations, principles and elements for dialogue on water, food and environment', Background document, National and Basin Dialogue Design Workshop, Bonn, December.

Russell, D. B. (1986) 'How we see the world determines what we do in the world: Preparing the ground for action research', Mimeo, University of Western Sydney (Hawkesbury) Richmond.

Russell, D. B. and Ison, R. L. (2000a) 'The research-development relationship in rural communities: An opportunity for contextual science', In Ison, R. L. and Russell, D. B. (eds) *Agricultural Extension and Rural Development: Breaking Out of Traditions*, Cambridge University Press, Cambridge.

Russell, D. B. and Ison, R. L. (2000b) 'Enthusiasm: Developing critical action for second-order R&D', In Ison, R. L. and Russell, D. B. (eds) *Agricultural Extension and Rural Development: Breaking Out of Traditions*, Cambridge University Press, Cambridge.

Schon, D. (1995) 'The new scholarship requires a new epistemology', *Change*, November/December, pp. 27–34.

Shaw, P. (2002) *Changing Conversations in Organizations. A Complexity Approach to Change*, Routledge, London.

Shotter, J. (1993) *Conversational Realities: Constructing Life through Language*, Sage, London.

Sterling, S. (2001) *Sustainable Education. Re-visioning Learning and Change*, Schumacher Briefings No 6, Green Books, Totnes, UK.

Talbott, S. (2002) 'Ecological conversation. Wildness, anthropocentrism and deep ecology', Netfuture, www.netfuture.org/2002/Jan!002_127.html/accessed in January 2002.

von Foerster, H. (1992) 'Ethics and second-order cybernetics', *Cybernetics and Human Knowing*, Vol 1, pp. 9–19.

Williams, K. (2001) 'The impact of the water framework directive on catchment-management planning in the British Isles', *Chartered Institution of Water and Environmental Management Journal*, Vol 15, pp. 97–102.

Winograd, T. and Flores, F. (1987) *Understanding Computers and Cognition: A New Foundation for Design*, Addison Wesley, New York.

Chapter 6
Messy Issues, Worldviews and Systemic Competencies

Richard Bawden

Introduction

This chapter continues the story of the tradition of systemic praxis that emerged from Hawkesbury Agricultural College in Australia from the late 1970s. While *critical social learning systems* (CSLS) best describes this ongoing tradition at this present time of writing (2009), the concept of a critical learning system did not appear explicitly in the Hawkesbury literature until the mid nineties (Bawden, 1994). The seeds of this powerful notion however can be traced right back to the seminal papers describing the logic and organisation of the foundations of the initiatives in systems education at that institution (Bawden et al., 1984; Macadam and Bawden, 1985). Details of developments of the Hawkesbury initiatives over subsequent years appear in Bawden (2005) in which an extensive list of references to other publications that trace and describe intermediate developmental stages of the Hawkesbury endeavours, can also be found. While the word 'social' is not explicitly included in descriptions of the nature and development of critical learning systems in this endeavour, a strong emphasis on social or collective learning has been an essential feature of the initiative from the outset.

For instance, five particular aspects of the developments of the Hawkesbury initiatives – that are well worth noting at this stage – can be stated as a set of beliefs or tenets that came to be held collectively by the Faculty as a whole:

- Experience is a critical source of human learning and development
- Such experiential learning is essentially a multi-dimensional, developmental system of cognitive processing by which we make sense out of the world around us as the foundation for the actions that we take as we live our lives in it
- What we learn about the world is markedly influenced both by the way we go about that learning and by the limitations that are imposed by the particular intellectual and moral perspectives (worldviews) that each of us (usually tacitly) adopts through which we 'filter' our 'sense-making'
- Worldview perspectives are themselves capable of development as reflected in transformations of basic value and belief assumptions which are achieved essentially through 'higher order', critical cognitive processing

C. Blackmore (ed.), *Social Learning Systems and Communities of Practice*,
DOI 10.1007/978-1-84996-133-2_6, © The Open University 2010.
Published in Association with Springer-Verlag London Limited.

- The ability to act systemically in the world, with an acute appreciation of 'whole-ness', 'inter-connectedness' and 'emergence', is a function of particular intellec-tual and value assumptions concerning the nature of reality, the nature of knowl-edge and of knowing, and the nature of human nature.

The significance of these five key assumptions to the emergence and character of Critical Learning Systems as they have evolved at Hawkesbury will become appar-ent as the narrative of this chapter unfolds.

Learning Systems Creating Systems of Learning

A most compelling aspect of the emergence of the principles and practices of CSLS at Hawkesbury has been the sustained commitment, over many years, of some forty educators or so, to an enterprise which has led to the evolution of a radically unconventional system of learning: one which has been characterised by a systemic, experiential approach to social learning for collective development. The insights and practices that have come to characterise this enterprise have emerged over the years through the experiences, thinking, reflections and actions of those academics and through their co-engagement with hundreds of their students and scores of other stakeholder actors in the events and ideas of the times. In other words this has been a developmental project characterised by the social experiential learning and collective action of the academics that has led, in turn, to the development of their theory-informed practices as facilitators of social experiential learning and collec-tive action. In essence, these academics have persistently walked their own talk on a path of social learning for change that they have been laying down even as they have walked! And as circumstances have unfolded, that path has taken many different twists and turns and developed many branches with many individuals eventually leaving Hawkesbury and going their own way while creating their own paths of systemic development.

Incredibly, what started out as a relatively circumscribed project to reform the curriculum at one of Australia's oldest agricultural institutions of higher education, eventually evolved into something a great deal more comprehensive, assuming as it did, a much greater degree of messy complexity itself (see Bawden, 1990, 1999, 2005).

Perhaps the most significant overall insight to emerge from this work in critical social learning systems as they relate to transformative development is captured by the following claim (Bawden, 2005): 'Every systemic act of development in the material and social worlds demands the development of particular ways of "seeing" the world from a systems perspective along with a set of practical skills that reflect this particular systemic view of the world.' At first sight, there would seem to be nothing particularly challenging about approaching matters from a perspective that appreciates the nature of wholeness and of the inter-connectedness of parts; or of a practice that continually places problems into their wider, more complex contexts as a key aspect of the problem-solving process. Nor would it seem to be that difficult, to approach changing problematic situations in such a manner that those changes would reflect an appreciation of the 'whole picture', as it were, with respect to moral concerns as well as to the facts of the matter. We all know that each of us has certain moral principles and aesthetic ideals that we like to see played out in practice, just as we like to believe that we are rational in the ways that we come to decisions. And yet in actuality, such systemic appreciation either of ourselves as integrated knowing valuing persons or of the world about us in all of its 'big picture' complexity, is far from common in our society. Indeed it might be said that the prevailing approach to problem-solving and situation improving across the entire globe, remains very un-systemic even when the issues under review are messy and complex and the inadequacies of conventional problem-solving approaches are there for all to see.

As it turns out, the ability to adopt a systems (or systemic) perspective to some issue or another in the 'real' world, and to use systemic practices to achieve changes to it, are not at all a straightforward matter, of simply learning systems theories or learning to use systems methods in practice. Rather, as the Hawkesbury initiatives have revealed, the transformation of complex situations in the world in a systemic manner will only effectively happen if those who need to act to achieve those transformations are themselves transformed in the way that they 'see' that world and 'act' in it. This self-transformation involves challenges and changes to those profound sets of beliefs and values that constitute the perspectives that we each use to make sense out of the worlds about us. These are our worldviews, or our *epistemes* as Michel Foucault (1970) called them, from which word the notion of *epistemic development* is derived as an expression meaning the transformation of worldviews. This transformation of our abilities to view the world systemically and to act accordingly – the development of our systemic competencies as it were – is thus a function of our epistemic development (see Bawden 2002). This process involves profound changes to the beliefs that we hold about a whole lot of aspects to do with the world about us, as well as to the values that we cherish, that together constitute our intellectual and moral 'sense-making' frameworks – also often referred to as paradigms.

It would appear that the essential reason for our intransigence in changing our prevailing ways of 'seeing' and 'doing', is fundamentally an expression of our prevailing unwillingness to even explore the character of the worldviews that we hold – as individuals and as whole cultures alike – to say nothing about our lack of preparedness to challenge and change them. Worse yet, we are, by and large, all abysmally ignorant of the fact that we even hold to particular epistemes or worldviews, and accordingly assume specific intellectual, aesthetic, moral and even spiritual perspectives. Let alone are we aware of the specific characteristics of these worldviews or conscious of the extent to which they influence the way we live our lives. If, for instance, we accept the word of the Bible that we have been granted dominion over the earth, then we will accept without question that we can do all that we can to control nature herself in every way possible to meet our own ends.

Yet raise awareness of, and mount challenges to prevailing worldviews is precisely what the Hawkesbury group set out to do: to first explore and challenge their own worldviews – both as individuals and collectively as an entire Faculty; and then, where appropriate, commit themselves to epistemic transformations where they would set out deliberately to develop their worldviews in a manner that allowed them to embrace systemic perspectives and effectively use systemic practices. Group members would then come to embed this practice of worldview review and development into their educational practices with a clear focus on learning to learn as a process of 'cognitive processing'.

This issue of facilitation of worldview transformation as a prerequisite for the development of systemic competencies became so important to the Hawkesbury Faculty that it was extended from its application to formal curricula, to a much broader endeavour that would come to embrace a much more inclusive range of stakeholders beyond the campus. In essence the group would introduce a new focus for development in shifting their primary concerns from concrete events in the world to processes of the mind that allowed systemic exploration of those events. This entailed a shift in emphasis from landscapes to mindscapes as it were, from 'systems in the world' to those 'systems of cognition'. These latter systems are learning systems or knowing systems that are responsible for the recognition of systems in the 'concrete world' as well as the construction of systemic abstractions, such as 'human activity systems' or 'thought systems' or 'value systems' or indeed 'learning systems' themselves.

The Faculty came to adopt two vital conceptual models related to learning and cognition which they integrated together to create the organisational structure (and hence dynamic and disparate functions) of a critical learning system:

1. An experiential model of learning developed by the American organisational psychologist David Kolb which portrayed learning as a perpetual cycle between the four cognitive activities that fluxed between the concrete and the abstract, and between reflection and action (Kolb, 1984).
2. A three-level model of cognitive processing developed by another American researcher, Karen Kitchener, that discriminated between cognition, meta-cognition and epistemic cognition (Kitchener, 1983). The integration of these two models together led to a framework for developing learning practices that focused in turn on:

   (a) learning about the matter to hand and how to transform that for the better,
   (b) learning about the learning processes that are brought to bear to learn about the matter to hand (meta-learning), and how to improve them, and
   (c) learning about the limitations to learning that are imposed by prevailing worldviews (epistemes) (epistemic learning), and how these can be appropriately characterised, challenged and, where indicated, transformed.

So, in marked contrast to a number of other contemporaneous initiatives in systems education around the world, where the emphasis was being placed on mastery of particular systems methodologies or the development of systemic competencies with a range of different methodologies, the Hawkesbury approach focussed very specifically on the nature and development of systems of learning. The model of a critical learning system as a social, critically reflexive, developmental process emerged through such a focus. Learning was not seen an outcome from the use of any systems methodology to explore particular messy complex issues, but was the key system of interest itself.

The Hawkesbury project thus developed into a major intellectual and moral assault on conventional approaches to dealing with complex, multi-dimensional, messy issues – especially those at the interface between people and their bio-physical environments. The particular relevance of this project is that such messy complexity has come to characterise life in general these days. There are a whole host of messy problematic issues emerging that are truly global in their character and impact as exemplified by such phenomena as climate change, infectious disease pandemics, biodiversity reduction, deforestation and so on. While they go by many names – 'wicked problems', hybrid matters of concern, complex situations, mixed-up affairs, imbroglios, or just sheer messy issues – they are everywhere we look while increasingly becoming the major concerns of scientists, policy-makers, and the citizenry alike. They represent the most pressing of the pressing issues of the day and they demand the urgent and critical attention of all of us acting collaboratively in a systemic manner that reflects our collective yet critical judgements for improvements or 'betterment' based on shared beliefs, shared values and shared interpretations and knowledge of what is happening 'out there'. And while we might not all agree with everything that we are sharing at any given time, we must do all that we can to accommodate our differences in seeking consensus on what needs to be done – and we need to do this urgently and effectively.

There is an urgent imperative that we need to learn how to organise ourselves and to act as critical social learning systems, with each one of the four elements – critical, social, learning, and systems – having very considerable application in the circumstances.

- We need to learn how to be rigorously *critical* of the way that we are currently living our lives and we need to learn how to harness that criticism to achieve constructive changes in our ways of being-in-the-world – our lifeworld as it were.
- We need to learn how to act collectively as families, tribes, communities, organisations and societies, as it is only through such *social* collaboration that our circumstances can be improved on the scale that present circumstances dictate.
- We need to *learn* how to transform our shared new experiences into new knowledge that we can then use as the basis for our collective, consensual judgments about desirable, feasible and defensible actions to take in the name of responsible and sustainable improvements.
- We need to learn how to approach these issues *systemically*, with a sense of their wholeness, their patterns of inter-connectedness, their dynamics, their embeddedness, and their emergent properties.

The Nature of Critical Social Learning Systems

As recently described (Bawden, 2007) a CSLS is a group of people that have decided to collaborate in order to seek systemic improvements to some messy complex situation that together they regard as critically problematic. Rather than thinking of themselves as a group of decision-makers or researchers, or as a task-force or a committee however, they embrace the notion of 'being and behaving as a reflexive system'. In this manner they imagine themselves to be a coherent 'whole' entity in which each individual participates as an embedded inter-connected component of the whole, so contributing to both the organisational form of that system as well as its functions.

The essential function of this system is to seek critical improvements or 'betterment' with respect to:

(i)   the issue that it has identified as critically problematic,
(ii) its own integrity and functions as a critical learning system and its development in these regards, and
(iii) the quality of its relationships with the environment in which it recognises it is embedded.

In other words a CSLS is a collection of individuals who agree to act together as a coherent group of people who are prepared to 'collectively learn their way through' an issue that they all agree is problematic in some way or another to them all. They accept that in addition to learning all they can about that issue as 'the matter to hand' as the prerequisite for taking informed action to improve it, they will also address, and respond to two other 'levels of learning' as they proceed: In essence they will be learning in three dimensions concurrently. So even as they are investigating the matter to hand they will also be critically reflecting on the processes of learning that they are bringing to bear: their 'meta-learning'. These reflections will include (i) their own impressions on the actual processes that they are using to generate shared knowledge and understanding from their experiences, (ii) how they are testing the quality or validity of that knowledge, (iii) how they are designing plans for action in the face of the knowledge that they are generating and decisions that they are beginning to formulate in response, and (iv) how they might actually put those plans into action for change. In this manner, they are seeking improvements in the way that they are learning even as they go about that learning. Most essentially, they go further yet, and engage in the most difficult learning of all – at the epistemic level where they will be exploring the nature of the beliefs and values that each of them bring to bear that have relevance to both of the other two 'levels of learning'. At this level of learning, they are engaging with each other in examination of similarities and differences in the beliefs and values that they hold as individuals, that are relevant to the matter at hand. For it is these differences in epistemes or worldviews that are so often the cause of tensions between people as they seek consensus on understanding and, most particularly, on their judgements with respect to the 'the right and proper thing to do' to change the circumstances in which they find themselves. It is epistemic differences that most frequently test the coherence of any group in the face of the quest for consensual action thus representing the greatest threat to the integrity of the CSLS that they have formed.

Criticality here is vital: A critical social learning system is characteristically critical in three aspects:

(a) It is inherently critical of the conditions of the environments in which it identifies itself as being embedded and to which it seeks improvements.
(b) It is critically reflective (reflexive) about its own structure and functions and is consistently monitoring itself and adapting its behaviours in response to those reflections.
(c) It is critically conscious of the character and implications of each boundary judgment that it makes with particular reference to what and who it includes and excludes from its activities as an improvement-seeking social learning system.

The system is also critically conscious, as already articulated, of the three dimensions of its cognitive processing capabilities: Firstly it sees itself as a sub-system within a 'system of interest' (an institution or a community or any set of human endeavours) that is, in turn, embedded within a higher-order environmental supra-system. It is this learning or 'knowing' sub-system that effectively brings each particular 'system of interest' into being. Secondly because it is a learning (sub)system, it is conscious of the three levels of its own cognitive functions as learning, meta-learning, and epistemic learning.

It is impossible to over-emphasise the significance of worldviews in the context of dealing with messy issues or indeed with any learning for that matter. For the particular worldview perspectives that we hold at any given time, both as individuals and collectively as cultures, have a very profound influence on the way that deal with the world about us – including each other!

Worldviews and their Influence

It has long been accepted that what each of us 'does' in (and to) the world about us in the course of our everyday lived experiences is a reflection of the way that, as individuals and members of particular cultures alike, we 'see' or perceive that world. In other words, our everyday actions in our environments, in the broadest sense of that word, are greatly influenced by the particular mental models or worldview perspectives or mindsets or epistemes that we rely on, to help us make sense out of our day-to-day experiences of what we hold to be the reality about us as well as what we consider to be the right and proper things to be doing. It is our worldviews that act as the 'filters' to our understandings, our frames of mind as the contexts for our judgments, our fundamental beliefs as the foundations for our morality.

Importantly the worldviews that we hold, as individuals and as social collectives, can be transformed to a greater or lesser extent. The so-called Enlightenment

Movement of seventeenth and eighteenth century Europe for instance, where reason trumped tradition, represents such epistemic transformation on a very grand socio-cultural scale indeed. Other, much more modest transformations are represented by individuals 'changing their own minds' about such matters as capital punishment, cigarette smoking, stem cell research, carbon emissions, animal welfare and a host of other epistemic positions that reflect changing beliefs and values. Such changes are often triggered by the arguments of others as well as by the sheer weight of previously ignored or newly generated evidence.

Given their significance, it is quite amazing that worldviews do not attract much attention by educators: Most of the time we are not even aware that our behaviour is a reflection of a particular set of essentially tacit assumptions that each of us holds about the world about us, about the universe, and about our own human characteristics and how we relate to the world and to the greater universe beyond. Succinctly, worldviews – or *Weltanschauungen* to use the German expression which is commonly employed in the systems literature – can be seen to comprise a set of personal presuppositions about:

(a) the nature of nature (or ontology, philosophically speaking),
(b) the nature and origins of the universe, of life itself and, especially, of the spiri-tual essence of mankind (or cosmology),
(c) the nature of knowledge (or epistemology) and
(d) the nature of human nature especially as it relates to motivations, dispositions and values, especially ethics and aesthetics (or axiology).

Interacting together, these constituencies of beliefs greatly shape our personal perceptions and, when reflective of our particular culture, our collective views of the world about us. They are thus the major determinants of the decisions and judgments that we make and the actions that we take. They play a major role in defining the goals that we set for ourselves as well as the goals that we believe we could set for ourselves, and indeed should set for ourselves as expressions of what we hold to be good or bad, right or wrong, virtuous or vicious.

Is it possible that we are ill-equipped to deal the complex messiness of life today because of the perspectives that we hold as a culture. Have we become prisoners of a collective worldview that is proving to be hopelessly inadequate and inappropriate to the circumstances that are unfolding all about us? Are we even aware of the nature and significance of our own individual worldview or epistemic perspectives or conscious of how these are expressed collectively as the prevailing and pervasive set of shared beliefs, values and assumptions that characterise our Western culture with its almost obsessive commitment to economic growth through modernisation?

Appreciation and the Origins of the Hawkesbury Initiatives

Geoffrey Vickers was fond of portraying the march of human history – the his-tory of our lived experiences – as a 'two-stranded braid' of *events* with *ideas* each interacting with, and mutually affecting the other, as time unfolds. As he saw it, in response to some concern or another, more often than not a shared concern, we human beings focus on some issue or another from this binary flux and make two forms of judgements about it – with regards to (a) what seems to be the 'facts' (reality judgments) and (b) what we regard as good or bad (value judgements) – before contributing, if appropriate to the circumstances, both to the stream of ideas and thence to the events through our idea-informed actions. This ever-recurring, iterative and reflexive process Vickers referred to as 'an appreciative system' (Vickers, 1965) which constantly revises or confirms itself by attention to three needs:

  (i) that it should 'correspond with reality sufficiently to guide action',
 (ii) that it should be 'sufficiently shared by our fellows to mediate communication' and
(iii) that it should be 'sufficiently acceptable to ourselves to make life bearable' (Vickers, 1983).

Without being aware of it at the time of their earliest initiatives, which were launched in 1978, the behaviour of the Hawkesbury academics would come to embrace and reflect all of the key characteristics of what Vickers had ascribed to 'appreciative systems' (Vickers, 1965). Somewhat unconventionally, they agreed that rather than following the usual 'rules' for curriculum design which emphasised knowledge and skills long considered to be essential to an agricultural scientist or technologist, they would first experientially explore the conditions prevailing within the Australian rural sector and how those conditions had evolved over recent preceding decades (past and present events). They would also investigate the principles, concepts and theories about agricultural development that were currently in vogue at that time and their intellectual foundations (the *ideas* – again past and present).

Through these a typical experiential observations, the faculty soon came to appreciate that the overall events that were prevailing in rural Australia at that time were cause for very considerable concern: Furthermore they came to appreciate that the conventional ideas about agricultural development in particular, and rural development in general, that were being promulgated in response to the conditions were at best inadequate and at worst, downright counter-productive and even destructive.

Many of the theories and principles that were being used to justify particular actions by the 'experts' of the day – be they concerned with actual farming practices, agendas of research, or policy-formulations – were seen to miss the 'wholeness' and complex messiness of the situation at large. Many of the specific 'factual' details of the nature of the events were well-known to researchers and to policy-makers alike and also, to quite a considerable extent, to the public at large through various media reports on different aspects of the prevailing conditions in rural Australia. However, little to no attention was being given by any institution to what might be termed 'the systemic well-being' of rural Australians and of their environments taken together as a whole; in all of its complex messy entirety. Like the fable of the blind individuals trying to establish the character of an entire elephant through their exposure only to its specific parts, so too were the discipline-based experts missing the whole picture by concentrating their investigations and observations only on particular aspects of it. This situation arose through the limitations of their own specific disciplinary expertise and the different 'worldview perspectives' that characterised each particular discipline in isolation from others.

Furthermore, while 'reality judgements' abounded, voices proposing 'value judgements' especially with respect to ethics and moral positions, were noticeably mute or extremely limited with respect to what constituted improvements to existing circumstances and what actions would be necessary to achieve them in practice.

The impact of different ways of seeing the world on different proposals for actions for change were there for all to see. Yet nobody beyond those of the Hawkesbury group seemed to actually see that.

From economists the unequivocal message to farmers was 'get big (or at least get far more efficient) or get out'. They were urging farmers to adopt intensive production methods to improve the efficiency of their operations in the face of declining economic conditions. Within that spirit, agricultural scientists and technologists of all shades were out and about peddling their wares of scientifically designed technological innovations that 'progressive' farmers could/should adopt as productivity enhancers. As for the laggards – those who were regarded as 'insufficiently scientifically or technologically literate' to grasp the significance of the innovations available – then that was just too bad for them.

On the other hand, a few sociologists were expressing their concern at the negative impacts that many such labour-saving productivity-intensifying technologies were having on employment levels in rural areas. They were also worried at the socio-cultural impact on all affected by the associated outmigration of people from rural communities, as displaced farm workers and their families headed for larger metropolitan areas in search of employment. Social workers, in turn, were having to cope with the ever-increasing levels of stress in those families and individuals who were remaining in the rural areas as unemployment rates began to accelerate, levels of indebtedness began rapidly to increase. Paradoxically, as the level of services to rural areas, by public service institutions and corporations alike, these social workers were being increasingly withdrawn.

All the while, environmental scientists were becoming increasingly vocal about the degrading effects of many agricultural practices on the quality of the natural environments and on the sustainability of resource extraction to support increased production. These observations were, in turn, nurturing support from, and emerging expressions of activism by, a wide range of citizens concerned about the impact of intensive agricultural practices on the integrity of the rural landscape. Consumer groups were also beginning to talk of the potential threat to public health of many of the new farming practices based on chemical pesticides and other biocides. These voices of public protest were further amplifying the objections and actions of other citizens concerned about the lack of attention to the land title rights of the traditional Aboriginal occupiers of the land for instance. There were yet other citizens, who were calling for legislation to protect the welfare of livestock animals not just in the face of increased intensification of housing, handling etc, but also from the perspective of the potential of emerging bio-technologies to cause harm to animals or in other ways to assault their integrity.

It was not all surprising that farmers themselves, as well as the many other rural Australians for whom agriculture was the basis for their livelihoods, were feeling that their integrity as individuals and communities alike, was also under severe assault with high levels of anxiety prevailing across the entire sector.

Deeply impressed and significantly depressed by the messy complexities that their investigative experiences in rural Australia were revealing, the members of the Hawkesbury School of Agriculture took a number of decisions (made a number of both 'reality' and 'value' judgments, in Vickers' terms) that would lead eventually to the principles and practices of what can now be described as Critical Social Learning Systems. Three foundational decisions that were taken were:

(a) to recognise that any education for agriculturists needed to be placed in the broader context of the development of inclusive rural well-being;
(b) to accept that the essential pedagogy for such a focus needed to embrace the concept of personal and shared experience as the basis for learning and development; and
(c) to embrace and further develop the fundamental principles of the so-called 'systems sciences' as the conceptual core for the development of competencies relevant to the complexities and messiness of unfolding events in rural Australia.

These decisions represented a number of key ideas that were generated by what can now be seen as a Critical Social Learning System, as critical reflections on events that the members of that system were experiencing: Subsequent actions by that CSLS in collaboration with other such systems then represented attempts to transform the events that were prevailing in rural Australia. While this is not the occasion to enumerate or evaluate any of these particular actions there is wide and growing acknowledgement of the contributions that the Hawkesbury initiatives in CSLS development have made to the emerging discourse about the sustainability and sustainable development of agri-food systems and of rural livelihoods that is increasingly patent in Australian society.

Some Concluding Remarks

The pressing issues that we currently face as human kind have much in common with each other and, as events, they deserve, in fact demand, the generation of innovative ideas with respect to improvements to the conditions that they reflect. As mentioned earlier, these events are often truly global in their scale and profoundly systemic in the complexity of their inter-connectedness. They are typically hard-to-define in their details and invariably unstructured, multi-causal, and multi-faceted: In sum, they are really, really messy situations. Witness the pervasive complex and unpredictable changes that are happening to the world's climate, or the growing ubiquity of sectarian terrorism throughout the world. Witness too our current experiences with grossly distorting instabilities in world financial systems, and the mysterious dynamics of emergent disease pandemics that are spreading to all corners of the planet. Then there is the looming global energy crisis associated with peak rates of oil discovery and production that soon we must face, a potential planetary catastrophe caused by gross reductions in bio-diversity through deforestation and other human activities. Perhaps above all, there are the impending threats to global security through the relentless demands for non-renewable resources by an ever-burgeoning human population that, by 2050, is estimated to reach a level that, staggeringly, will be almost four times what it was a mere century earlier at the outbreak of the Second World War in Europe.

The tragedy is that the root cause of the majority of these threatening issues lies with much of what we ourselves have been doing in and to the world about us in the name of the development of our Western industrialised civilisation: While they may be classified as the unintended consequences of the process of our quest for modernisation, they have, for the most part, certainly not been unforeseeable to any thinking person.

Yet paradoxically, while we are increasingly aware that we are in large part responsible for fouling our own nest, as it were, we are seemingly fundamentally loathe to do very much about changing our ways of being in any socially coordinated or profoundly necessary manner as citizens of the world. While the global scale and reach of these issues might be new, events of this kind are certainly not unique to our current era. So why is it that we seem to have learned nothing from history? Why is it that we are not moved to change what it is that we are doing as we can clearly foresee what could happen to future generations of our own kind – to say nothing of the myriad of others species on earth – if we do not change our current behaviours and lifestyles? Why is it that we are not collectively 'learning our way forward' out of the mess that we ourselves continue to create? Is it possible that we have not actually learned how to learn in a manner that would allow us to collectively learn our way forward'? Are we so intellectually and morally immature that we don't even recognise (or worse yet, admit) that indeed we tend to be intellectually and morally immature – or at least continue to behave as if we were?

Most seriously of all, are the ways by which we make sense of the world about us and make judgements about the right and proper things to do, limiting our creativity in designing better ways of doing things – and indeed, seeking better things to be doing? Are we victims of our own particular, culturally embedded way of 'seeing' what is happening about us and as a consequence, helpless to grasp the full severity of the matters to hand – or to do anything about them in any coherent, collaborative, cooperative way? Do we appreciate that there is a clearly significant mismatch between the events that are unfolding about us and the ideas that are being generated in response as the frameworks for responsible, systemic, sustainable, and defensible actions for change?

The establishment and conduct of Critical Social Learning Systems would represent a highly appropriate medium for addressing urgent and crucial questions of this kind.

References

Bawden, R.J. (1990) 'Of Agricultural Systems and Systems Agriculture: Systems Methodologies in Agricultural Education.' Chapter 22. In *Systems Theory Applied to Agriculture and the Food Chain*, J. Jones and P. Street (Eds), Elsevier, London, pp. 305–325.

Bawden, R.J. (1994) 'Creating Learning Systems: A Metaphor for Institutional Reform for Development.' Chapter 35. In *Beyond Farmer First: Rural Peoples Knowledge, Agricultural Research and Extension Practice*, I. Scoones and J. Thompson (Eds), Intermediate Technology Publications, London.

Bawden, R.J. (1999) 'A Cautionary Tale: The Hawkesbury Experience.' Chapter 20. In *Integrating Concepts of Sustainability in Education for Agriculture and Rural Development*, W. van der Bor, P. Holen, A.E.J. Wals, and W. Leal Filho (Eds), Peter Lang, Frankfurt am Rhein.

Bawden, R.J. (2002) 'Valuing the Epistemic in the Search for Betterment: The Nature and Role of Critical Learning Systems.' Chapter 12 (Volume 4). In *Systems Thinking*, G. Midgley (Ed) Sage Publications, London (First Published in *Cybernetics and Human Knowing* 7: 5–25, 2000).

Bawden, R.J. (2005) 'Systemic Development at Hawkesbury: Some Personal Lessons from Experience.' *Systems Research and Behavioural Science* 22: 151–164.

Bawden, R. (2007) 'Knowing Systems and the Environment.' In J. Pretty, A. Ball, T. Benton, J. Guivant, D.R. Lee, D. Orr, M. Pfeffer, and H. Ward (Eds) *Handbook of Environment and Society,* Sage, London, pp. 224–234.

Bawden, R.J., Macadam, R.D., Packham, R.G., and Valentine, I. (1984) 'Systems Thinking and Practices in the Education of Agriculturalists.' *Agricultural Systems* 13: 205–225.

Foucault, M. (1970) *The Order of Things: An Archaeology of the Human Sciences*, Pantheon, New York.

Kitchener, K.S. (1983) 'Cognition, Metacognition, and Epistemic Cognition: A Three Level Model of Cognitive Processing.' *Human Development* 26: 222–232.

Kolb, D.A. (1984) *Experiential Learning: Experience as the Source of Learning and Development,* Prentice-Hall, Englewood Cliffs, NJ.

Macadam, R.D. and Bawden, R.J. (1985) 'Challenge and Response: A System for Educating More Effective Agriculturalists.' *Prometheus* 3: 125–137.

Vickers, G. (1965) *The Art of Judgment: A Study of Policy Making*, Chapman and Hall, London.

Vickers, G. (1983) *Human Systems are Different,* Harper and Row, London.

Part III
Communities of Practice

The term 'community of practice' (CoP), coined by Jean Lave and Etienne Wenger, can be found in a range of literature from around 1991 (some of it cited in the following chapters). Etienne's 1998 popular *book Communities of Practice: learning meaning and identity* details his social theory of learning and offers a wide range of concepts that have helped to both inform and structure inquiries about learning and to act as analytical lenses. According to our first chapter in this part, from William Snyder and Etienne Wenger, the recognition of knowledge-based social structures and groupings of people who interact around their practices, with the aim of improving them, goes far back in history.

So perhaps we should consider CoPs as not appearing but *re*-appearing as significant to many at the end of the twentieth century and beginning of the twenty-first. This can be attributed to numerous factors – downsizing of companies in many parts of the western world and increased mobility of people from job to job has led to a need to find other ways to continue in professional relationships. The increased development and use of information and communication technologies, particularly the Internet, has generally made it easier for many to find out about and communicate with others beyond their own geographical areas. In responses to complexity, needs for different kinds of support have arisen – social, professional and personal. Business and industry imperatives have changed with increased globalisation with a range of new economic and ethical dilemmas to be addressed. Calls for sustainable development and concerns about climate change have presented new challenges in doing and learning with others, some of them undoubtedly addressed by CoPs praxis.

The emergence of explanations under the rubric of 'communities of practice' has had widespread appeal and interested many concerned with creating the circumstances for purposeful action in complex situations. The literature on CoPs has mushroomed since Wenger's 1998 book. The idea of a CoP has clearly captured the imagination of many around the world. Many of those writing about CoPs early on identified with academic traditions of knowledge management and organisational learning. But papers and chapters on CoPs can now be found in journals and books relating to much broader traditions ranging from information and computer sciences to health services to social psychology to education to water management and farming systems.

A range of perspectives on CoPs is presented in the following chapters, summarised below. They are all relevant to social learning systems and use a rich array of learning theories and concepts. They also all demonstrate systemic thinking and praxis. However, their conceptualisations of 'systems' vary, ranging from systems as constructs – indicated sometimes by the language of 'as a system' – to systems that appear to be perceived in a fixed way (as for instance when referring to a computer-based course management system). Perhaps this usage is at least in part because the word 'systems' is so much a part of our popular language.

In Chapter 7 William Snyder and Etienne Wenger consider 'our world as a learning system'. They identify examples of transformative, inquiry-oriented learning systems in organisations, many of them in the private sector from which we can learn, particularly concerning the support of self-organising groups of practitioners in their development and use of knowledge. These groups cross sectors and are conceptualised as communities of practice. The chapter concerns CoPs in the civic domain and includes several examples at different levels and in various locations, in relation to cities as learning systems and raises challenges of how they can be supported. The structure of large-scale learning systems is considered and how their design might be addressed.

Chapter 8 consists of extracts from Wenger's (1998) CoPs theory and his early (2000) chapter that linked CoPs and social learning systems explicitly. His explications of concepts of particular relevance to CoPs as social learning systems have been selected for this book as potential tools for systems practitioners. These concepts include boundaries, identity, trajectories and participation. He focuses on 'boundary processes' as crucial to the coherent functioning of social learning systems and argues that the perspective of a social learning system applies to many of our social institutions.

Chapter 9 comes from Mary Gobbi and explores the connections between learning, working and professional communities in nursing. It explores characteristics that these communities have in common with CoPs. In focus are interpersonal relationships, the moral being and the purpose of community and knowledge communicated within it. The chapter uses a series of vignettes from practice to illustrate the complexities of learning in workplace communities.

In Chapter 10 Linda Polin considers how graduate professional education can be re-visioned as an activity that occurs at the intersection of practice, pedagogy and digital culture. She explores how a CoPs model can support shifts in roles for students and faculty by increasing peer-to-peer engagement and opportunities to engage with experts beyond a local level. Social and technical networking tools are viewed as a means of bridging a range of academic communities. Her ideas are illustrated through reference to two blended learning programs that combine online and face-to-face settings.

Chapter 11 is an overview from Etienne Wenger of the 'career' of the CoPs concept written in 2009 for this book. In this overview the author considers what a 'learning view of social systems' and a 'social systems view of learning' illuminate by considering CoPs *as* social learning systems and CoPs *in* social learning systems. The author's perspectives on applications and critiques of the CoPs concept are considered and a social discipline of learning is outlined that takes account of all the perspectives considered in the chapter.

CoPs is arguably the most well-known tradition of social learning systems of current times. Its practitioners are also probably the most diverse in terms of their backgrounds and domains of practice. A range of positions is adopted regarding how theories inform practice and which are most significant to practitioners. Not all of those who are influenced by CoPs theories would count themselves as systems thinkers or practitioners but the chapters in this book illustrate that many have adopted creative and systemic approaches to their work that are supported by drawing on their understandings and experiences of CoPs and learning.

References

Wenger, E. (1998) *Communities of Practice: Learning, Meaning and Identity*. New York: Cambridge University Press.

Wenger, E. (2000) *Communities of Practice and Social Learning Systems*, Sage Publications, 7(2): 225–46.

Chapter 7
Our World as a Learning System: A Communities-of-Practice Approach

William M. Snyder and Etienne Wenger

We live in a small world, where a rural Chinese butcher who contracts a new type of deadly flu virus can infect a visiting international traveller, who later infects attendees at a conference in a Hong Kong hotel, who within weeks spread the disease to Vietnam, Singapore, Canada, and Ireland. Fortunately, the virulence of the Severe Acute Respiratory Syndrome (SARS) was matched by the passion and skill of a worldwide community of scientists, health care workers, and institutional leaders who stewarded a highly successful campaign to quarantine and treat those who were infected while identifying the causes of the disease and ways to prevent its spread. In such a world, we depend on expert practitioners to connect and collaborate on a global scale to solve problems like this one – and to prevent future ones.

Marshall McLuhan's assertion in 1968 that we live in a 'global village' has come of age. During the past century, the world has become considerably smaller not only through the effects of the media – McLuhan's focus – but also through science, transportation, the Internet, migration, and the spread of global commerce. At the same time, there has been a proliferation of global problems: environmental degradation, the population explosion, increasing economic disparities between rich and poor nations, threats of biological and nuclear terrorism, disease pandemics, and breakdowns of financial systems. As the world becomes smaller, the problems we face are growing larger in scope and complexity.

We have survived these threats and, paradoxically, also caused or exacerbated them through dramatic innovations in science, technology, and organisational structures that increase our collective capacity to influence life on earth. Consider our ability to improve harvest yields and control diseases; to alter the genes in plants, animals, and humans; to create city- and world-spanning 'virtual communities'; and to extend corporations around the globe. Whether or not we take responsibility for designing our world, the evidence suggests that we are doing it already. For better or for worse, we are Prometheus unbound.

Yet we have just begun to discover the metaphors and mechanisms for participating in global stewardship and, even among cultural elites, incorporating an identity

Source: Snyder and Wenger (2004). Reproduced with permission.

C. Blackmore (ed.), *Social Learning Systems and Communities of Practice*,
DOI 10.1007/978-1-84996-133-2_7, © The Open University 2010.
Published in Association with Springer-Verlag London Limited.

as global citizens. What does it mean to 'think globally and act locally'? Does global stewardship primarily imply building international organisations that address social and environmental issues to compensate for the economic focus of global corporations? Is such a global perspective sufficient to address issues that are essentially local? How can we connect the power and accessibility of local civic engagement with active stewardship at national and international levels? What are the design criteria for such a system and what might it look like?

Design Requirements for a World Learning System

We believe there are three fundamental design criteria that help specify essential characteristics of a world learning system capable of addressing the scope and scale of the global challenges we face today. Problems such as overpopulation, world hunger, poverty, illiteracy, armed conflict, inequity, disease, and environmental degradation are inextricably interconnected. Moreover, they are complex, dynamic, and globally distributed. To address such challenges, we must increase our global intelligence along several dimensions: cognitive, behavioural, and moral. We must increase, by orders of magnitude, our societal capacity for inquiry; our ability to continuously create, adapt, and transfer solutions (Churchman, 1971). A world learning system that can match the challenges we face must meet three basic specifications:

- *Action-learning capacity* to address problems while continuously reflecting on what approaches are working and why – and then using these insights to guide future actions.
- *Cross-boundary representation* that includes participants from all sectors – private, public, and nonprofit – and from a sufficient range of demographic constituencies and professional disciplines to match the complexity of factors and stakeholders driving the problem.
- *Cross-level linkages* that connect learning-system activities at local, national, and global levels – wherever civic problems and opportunities arise.

Civic development is essentially a social process of action learning, in which practitioners from diverse sectors, disciplines, and organisations work together to share ideas and best practices, create new approaches, and build new capabilities. The full potential of this learning process is only realised when it connects all the players at various levels who can contribute to it.

There are a number of organisations – including the United Nations, the World Bank, and an array of nongovernmental organisations such as Doctors Without Borders, the World Council of Churches, Oxfam International, major foundations, and many others – whose mission is to address worldwide problems. But these organisations typically focus on solving the manifestations of problems – eliminating land mines from war-torn regions or reducing the incidence of AIDS, for instance. Given the urgency of these problems, it is understandable that these organisations do not focus on the underlying learning capacity of a city or country. While it is essential to address these and other urgent problems on their own terms, our society's long-term capacity to solve them at both local and global levels will nevertheless require step-change increases in our foundational capacity for intelligent social action.

What is the nature of large-scale learning systems that can operate at local and global levels? How can we take steps to create such learning systems? To what extent can they be designed and what does design even mean in such a context? These learning challenges are among our world's most urgent as we find ourselves today in a race between learning and self-destruction.

Cultivating Learning Systems

Fortunately, we have examples of transformative, inquiry-oriented learning systems in hundreds of private-sector organisations, with a growing number in public and nonprofit organisations as well – at both organisational and interorganisational levels. Strong, broad-based secular forces are driving this movement. Most organisations today, including domestic firms as well as multinationals, have been forced to confront large-scale learning issues to compete in the knowledge economy.

There is much we can learn from the experience of organisations about how to increase our society's collective intelligence. The most salient lesson is that managing strategic capabilities primarily entails supporting self-organising groups of practitioners who *have* the required knowledge, *use* it, and *need* it. We call these groups 'communities of practice' to reflect the principle that practitioners themselves – in active collaboration with stakeholders – are in the best position to steward knowledge assets related to their work. A well-known private-sector example of such practitioner stewardship is the network of 'tech clubs' that Chrysler engineers formed in the early 1990s (see Wenger et al., 2002, Chapter 1). The company had just reorganised its product-development unit into 'car platforms' focused on vehicle types (small cars, large cars, minivans, etc.). Design engineers with specialties related to the various vehicle components – such as brakes, interior, and windshield wipers – organised communities of practice to foster knowledge sharing across car platforms. The cross-boundary sharing of these communities was a critical success factor for the reorganisation. We are now seeing a proliferation of organisations fostering the development of communities of practice across industry sectors, geographic locations, and various elements of the value chain.

Communities of practice are not new. They have existed since *Homo sapiens* evolved 50,000 years ago,[1] but organisations have now become increasingly explicit about cultivating these communities. Distinctive competencies in today's markets

---

[1] In 1902, in the preface to the second edition of his seminal book *The Division of Labor in Society* (New York: Free Press, 1964), Emile Durkheim traced the history of professional groups-communities of practice-from ancient times through the twentieth century. He argued that these groups would be essential in the twentieth century and beyond for re-weaving the fabric of social capital that would be torn apart as industrialisation took hold in countries worldwide.

depend on knowledge-based structures that are not restricted by formal affiliation and accountability structures. The most distinctive, valuable knowledge in organisations is difficult or impossible to codify and is tightly associated with a professional's personal identity. Developing and disseminating such knowledge depends on informal learning much more than formal – on conversation, storytelling, mentorships, and lessons learned through experience. This informal learning, in turn, depends on collegial relationships with those you trust and who are willing to help when you ask. Informal learning activities and personal relationships among colleagues are the hallmarks of communities of practice. Hence, we see an increasing focus on informal community structures whose aggregate purpose is to steward the learning of an organisation and its invaluable knowledge assets.

Communities of practice have three basic dimensions: domain, community, and practice. A community's effectiveness as a social learning system depends on its strength in all three structural dimensions.

- *Domain*. A community of practice focuses on a specific 'domain,' which defines its identity and what it cares about – whether it is designing brakes, reducing gun violence, or upgrading urban slums. Passion for the domain is crucial. Members' passion for a domain is not an abstract, disinterested experience. It is often a deep part of their personal identity and a means to express what their life's work is about.
- *Community*. The second element is the community itself and the quality of the relationships that bind members. Optimally, the membership mirrors the diversity of perspectives and approaches relevant to leading-edge innovation efforts in the domain. Leadership by an effective 'community coordinator' and core group is a key success factor. The feeling of community is essential. It provides a strong foundation for learning and collaboration among diverse members.
- *Practice*. Each community develops its practice by sharing and developing the knowledge of practitioners in its domain. Elements of a practice include its repertoire of tools, frameworks, methods, and stories – as well as activities related to learning and innovation.

The activities of a community of practice differ along several dimensions – face-to-face to virtual; formal to informal; public to private. Further, activities are orchestrated according to various rhythms – for instance, in one community, listserv announcements come weekly, teleconferences monthly or bi-monthly, projects and visits occur when an opportunity presents itself, back-channel e-mails and phone calls are ongoing; and the whole group gathers once or twice a year face-to-face (See Fig. 7.1). These activities form an ecology of interactions that provide value on multiple levels. Beyond their instrumental purpose of creating and sharing knowledge, they increase the community's 'presence' in members' lives and reinforce the sense of belonging and identity that are the foundation for collective learning and collaborative activities.

Communities of practice do not replace more formal organisational structures such as teams and business units. On the one hand, the purpose of formal units, such as functional departments or cross-functional teams, is to deliver a product or service and to be accountable for quality, cost, and customer service. Communities,

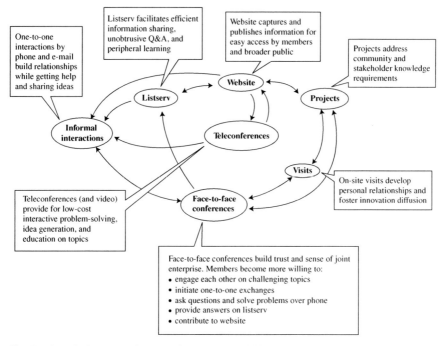

Fig. 7.1 A typical ecology of community learning activities

on the other hand, help ensure that learning and innovation activities occur across formal structural boundaries. Indeed, a salient benefit of communities is to bridge established organisational boundaries in order to increase the collective knowledge, skills, and professional trust of those who serve in these formal units. For instance, at DaimlerChrysler, brake engineers have their primary affiliation with the car platform where they design vehicles. Yet they also belong to a community of practice where they share ideas, lessons learned, and tricks of the trade. By belonging to both types of structure, they can bring the learning of their team to the community so that it is shared through the organisation, and, conversely, they can apply the learning of their community to the work of their team.

Pioneering, knowledge-intensive organisations have recognised that beyond the formal structures designed to run the business lies a learning system whose building blocks are communities of practice that cannot be designed in the same manner as formal, hierarchical structures. Communities of practice function well when they are based on the voluntary engagement of members. They flourish when they build on the passions of their members and allow this passion to guide the community's development. In this sense, communities of practice are fundamentally self-governed.

Our experience suggests, however, that while communities do best with internal leadership and initiative, there is much that organisations can do to cultivate new communities and help current ones thrive. The intentional and systematic cultivation of communities cannot be defined simply in terms of conventional strategy development or organisational design. Rather, sponsors and community leaders must be ready to engage in an evolutionary design process whereby the organisation fosters the development of communities among practitioners, creates structures that provide support and sponsorship for these communities, and finds ways to involve them in the conduct of the business. The design of knowledge organisations entails the active integration of these two systems – the formal system that is accountable for delivering products and services at specified levels of quality and cost, and the community-based learning system that focuses on building and diffusing the capabilities necessary for formal systems to meet performance objectives. It is crucial for organisational sponsors as well as community leaders to recognise the distinct roles of these two systems while ensuring that they function in tandem to promote sustained performance.

The fundamental learning challenges and nature of responses in business and civic contexts are very similar. The size, scope, and assets of many businesses create management challenges that rival those of large cities, or even small countries. In both cases, one needs to connect practitioners across distance, boundaries, and interests in order to solve large-scale problems. Organisations have found that communities of practice are extremely versatile in complementing formal structures. They are known for their ability to divide and subdivide to address hundreds of domains within and across organisations; they lend themselves to applications where scalability, broad scope, and the need for extensive, complex linkages are relevant. Hence there is much we can learn from the early, highly developed business examples. The approaches for building largescale learning systems in organisations – by combining both formal and informal structures – provide a blueprint for thinking about how to build such systems in the messy world of civil society.

Civic Communities of Practice: Local, National, and International

Communities of practice already exist in the civic domain, where they complement place-based communities as well as the ecology of formal organisations, including businesses, schools, churches, and nonprofits. In the civic arena as well as in organisations, our challenge is not to create communities of practice so much as to foster them more systematically.

Our analysis of societal learning systems – whether at local, national, or international levels – focuses on cities (which we define as an entire metropolitan region) as highleverage points of entry for a number of reasons. For one, as of the year 2000, there are more humans on the planet living in cities than outside them. In 2002, there were twenty megalopolises in the world with more than 10 million people, and by 2015 there will be nearly forty. Cities have always been the font of new ideas, new applications of technologies, new cultural movements, and social change. They constitute natural nodes in a network for disseminating innovations. In the problems they face and the opportunities they offer, they also provide a microcosm of the world. Finally, cities possess an organisational infrastructure and established leadership groups with the potential to see the value and to sponsor the design of a local learning system.

In many cities, multisector coalitions or alliances are formed to take on a pressing issue such as improving urban schools, increasing access to low-income housing, cleaning up a business district, or building a stadium, park, or cultural facility (see Grogan and Proscio, 2000). These coalitions, however, generally do not take sustained responsibility for stewarding a civic domain or for bringing together the full array of stakeholder constituencies to identify and address short- and long-term priorities. One way to assess the level of civic stewardship in any city or region is to map the prevalence, inclusiveness, and effectiveness of civic communities of practice (also known as coalitions, associations, partnerships, and alliances, among other terms) who take responsibility for clusters of issues related to particular civic domains, such as education, economic development, health, housing, public safety, infrastructure, culture, recreation, and the environment. The reality is that in many cities these domains have no explicit stewardship, or they are left to public agencies

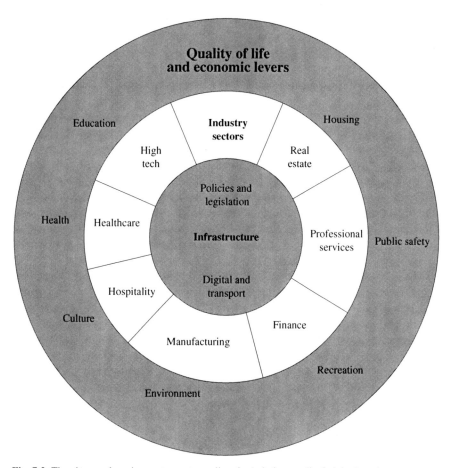

Fig. 7.2 The city as a learning system: stewarding the 'whole round' of civic domains

or to a menagerie of disparate, often competitive and conflicting organisations that carve out small pieces of the puzzle – regarding housing availability, for example – but do not coordinate efforts or leverage a common base of expertise and resources.

The city, re-imagined as a learning system, consists of a constellation of cross-sector groups that provide stewardship for the whole round of civic domains (See Fig. 7.2). Cultivating a learning system at the city level means taking stock of the current stewardship capacity in the city and accounting for the array of civic disciplines and the quality of active communities of practice stewarding them. This city-level assessment provides a template for what a nation can do. At the nation level, leaders might evaluate a representative sample of major cities and regions as a baseline assessment of its civic stewardship capacity. By extension, an evaluation of the top 500 strategic cities in the world could provide a benchmark for our civic learning capacity at a global level. At the national and global levels, the analysis also considers the strength and quality of linkages across cities both within and across nations. Of course, even at the city level, there are subsectors and neighbourhoods that are fractal elements of the city, each with its own whole round of civic practices, and among which neighbourhood-to-neighbourhood linkages are as instrumental as ones that connect cities and nations.

A City-Based Community: Economic Development in Chicago

A city-based initiative to promote economic development in Chicago provides an example of an effort designed to leverage communities as agents of civic development.[2] In 1999, the City of Chicago established a cross-sector coalition, the Mayor's Council of Technology Advisors, to create 40,000 new high-tech jobs in the Chicagoland region. The coalition leaders began by pulling together a group of forty-five civic leaders to brainstorm ways to achieve this goal. According to a study commissioned before the group met, the greatest challenge they faced was encouraging business development in high-tech industries such as telecommunications and biotech. A related challenge was cultivating local sources of seed capital for start-ups in these industries.

The result of the group's first meeting was a slate of long- and short-term initiatives – including the introduction of technology in schools; encouraging young women and minorities to explore technology careers; and building a stronger digital infrastructure in the city, especially in underserved areas. Several of the groups focused on initiatives specific to the industry sectors identified in the initial study: telecommunications, software development, biotech, venture capital, and emerging areas such as nanotechnology. The industry groups were particularly successful in this initiative, largely because they were able to coalesce communities specific to development challenges in each industry sector.

---

[2] For a more extensive review of this initiative see Snyder (2002).

The civic leaders in Chicago understood that coalescing communities of practice – in this case, along industry lines – was the foundation for building relationships, generating ideas, and catalysing business initiatives. As one leader put it, 'Our first objective was to create communities, period. The technology industries were fragmented without a sense of commonality. For example, we have more software developers than in Silicon Valley, but here it's only 9% of the workforce. So we started getting people connected and networked and building a sense of community in our high-tech sectors.'

The Chicago Biotech Network (CBN) is one of the more mature high-tech communities in Chicago and provides an illustration of the influence and stewardship such a community can have over time. CBN started as a grassroots group that held about five seminars a year for diverse constituents interested in biotech developments. At first, it was more for individuals interested in life sciences. Then companies (such as Abbott Laboratories and Baxter, two *Fortune 500* pharmaceuticals located in the Chicago area), started to attend the meetings as well, and they brought different perspectives. Over time, the community came to include scientists, university deans, lawyers, venture capitalists, angel investors, city and state business development staff, and others. Anywhere from twenty-five to two hundred people showed up at the meetings, which were held at various places and sponsored by members. These gatherings provided an opportunity for members to discuss science and industry trends and build relationships. One of the leaders summarised the community's evolution: 'Early on, people mostly came for the personal value of networking and discussing ideas. Now the domain of the community is to promote science and business development in the biotech sector in the Chicago area. We focus on science ideas, business development know-how, and knowledge transfer processes.' Offshoots of community activities include targeted events that link scientists, angel investors, and large pharmaceuticals to fund biotech startups that can commercialise promising innovations coming out of university labs. On a broader level, the community has helped increase biotech lab space in the city, lobbied at state and federal levels for increased research funding, and recruited biotech companies to locate in Chicagoland.

The leader of the Chicago-based biotech community estimated the value of the community's activities for generating start-ups and, by extension, job creation in the region: 'I can't point to anything specific, but our events have brought structure to the interface between R&D scientists and the venture community; and we've gone from very little venture funding to the point where we now have $50 million coming to various biotech companies this year.'

The Chicago Biotech Network illustrates how an industry-based community of practice can serve as a powerful force for civic development. In this case, the focus was on economic development, but the key point is that strong stewardship of civic issues, even in the hard-nosed area of industry development, depends on vital communities of practice. The purpose of the communities was not only to provide professional development and networking opportunities but also to cultivate thriving high-tech industries in Chicagoland. These communities advocated for their domain as a strategic focus for the city, built relationships among community members from various backgrounds, and shared know-how among practitioners. Finally, as one community leader stated, they worked to serve the city they loved, and ultimately their children, who would inherit their civic legacy.

A National Community: SafeCities to Reduce Gun Violence

Communities of practice can also provide powerful stewardship for civic issues at the national level by connecting innovative civic groups across cities. The SafeCities community, for example, was organised in March 1999 by Vice President Al Gore's Reinventing Government initiative to reduce gun violence in the United States. The announcement of the SafeCities community coincided with publication of the FBI's crime-rate statistics, which showed significant variation across cities in injuries and fatalities caused by gun violence. Senior executives in the National Partnership for Reinventing Government (NPR) office began by convening officials from relevant agencies and developing a shared vision for what the network would be about and how they would work together. They sent out an invitation to cities and regions nationwide and selected ten coalitions to participate in the SafeCities community – based on criteria that included multisector collaboration, a track record of innovation, and commitment to improved results. These local coalitions provided stewardship for public safety issues in their cities as did the industry-focused communities in Chicago. A striking characteristic of the initiative was that it offered participants no funding – the value of participation was to get connected, to learn, and to enhance the capacity to reduce gun violence. The scale of the initiative was also distinctive – connecting civic coalitions from across the nation for the purpose of sharing ideas, collaborating on innovation initiatives, and helping to shape policy at local, state, and federal levels.[3]

The SafeCities community can be described in terms of the three structural dimensions of communities of practice. Each of the coalition members was focused, broadly speaking, on issues related to the domain of public safety. Their specific domain targeted a subdomain within this area – defined as reducing injuries and fatalities due to gun violence. The specificity of this domain was crucial for coalescing a community with overlapping interests, focusing its learning activities, and attracting sponsors. The community was composed of members at local and national levels and from various disciplines and constituencies, such as officials from the FBI, the Bureau of Alcohol, Tobacco, Firearms and Explosives, and an assortment of divisions within the Justice Department at the national level; and mayors, police chiefs, faith leaders, hospital and social workers, school principals, neighbourhood activists, and district attorneys at the local level. Finally, the practice of SafeCities members included community policing strategies, after-school programs, crime-mapping methods, prosecutorial strategies, the design of local gun-possession laws,

---

[3] For a more extensive review of the SafeCities initiative and others sponsored by the NPR office and other federal agencies, see Snyder and de Sousa Briggs (2003).

and ways to improve the interaction between at-risk youth and law-enforcement professionals.

After a couple of preliminary teleconferences, SafeCities was launched at a face-to-face meeting in Washington, D.C., explicitly billed as a community-of-practice launch. The sponsors and community coordinating team (based in the NPR office) posed three basic questions for the group to address during the 2-day conference: What is SafeCities about (domain)? Who is part of SafeCities (community)? What does SafeCities do (practice)? The conference included opportunities for members to meet informally, including an evening reception and knowledge-sharing 'fair'. A nationally renowned police chief from Highpoint, North Carolina, gave a talk about his city's success at reducing gun violence through both rehabilitation and enforcement efforts that focused on the city's most violent individuals. (He was so impressed with the gathering that he asked NPR officials if his coalition could join, and they agreed to make his group an honorary member.) During the conference, members outlined a design for how they would learn together – including teleconferences, visits, a website, and other activities. The issues they identified became topics for their biweekly teleconferences. The conference was instrumental in coalescing members around a shared agenda and building trust and reciprocity. The SafeCities teleconferences subsequently became more active and members were more forthcoming about selecting topics and offering to speak to the group about their experiences. Fostering 'community' – a sense of mutual trust, shared identity, and belonging – took on more prominence as an important structural element that made SafeCities successful.

One of the outcomes of the initial conference illustrates the value of network participation for members. After hearing the Highpoint police chief talk about his success, groups from Ft. Wayne, Indiana and Inkster, Michigan – including police chiefs, mayors, and faith leaders from both cities – visited Highpoint and observed programs in action. Both coalitions then adapted the Highpoint model for their own locales with coaching from Highpoint.

SafeCities operated successfully from March 1999 until June 2002, spanning the transition from a Democratic to a Republican administration. Political appointees from both parties, as well as senior civil servants in the Justice and Treasury departments (where the sponsorship was primarily based) believed in the cross-level, cross-sector approach that SafeCities embodied. Sponsors were impressed to see such active participation on the part of senior civic leaders, even though they received no government funding for participating. These local leaders felt strongly about the value SafeCities provided – in terms of ideas, access to expertise, and opportunities for national visibility and influence based on local success.

Agency sponsors ultimately decided to close the SafeCities community in favour of a more conventional federal program. The decision confused many of the participants, given the minimal federal costs associated with the initiative, principally the cost of funding the community's full-time coordinator (a junior staff person, albeit a talented leader) and intermittent attention by agency champions. The coordinator's role was particularly important – arranging speakers for teleconferences, documenting insights on the website, arranging peer-to-peer visits, and coordinating with state and federal officials. The loss of the coordinator and agency attention was a fatal blow to the community. In its place, the US Justice Department enacted a new program, called SafeNeighborhoods, which provided funding for local initiatives such as after-school programs. The program managers intended to build on the SafeCities foundation, but they did not appreciate the distinctive characteristics of the community – opportunities for peer-to-peer learning and collaboration across cities, sectors, and levels of government. While SafeCities members were glad that the government was providing new funds to support local initiatives, they passionately argued that such funding could never substitute or compensate for the value of the SafeCities community.

The SafeCities story thus validates the power of cross-city communities of practice while highlighting a key challenge: how to educate senior leaders with the power to sponsor such initiatives – from public, private, or nonprofit sectors (including foundations). These and other questions about starting, sustaining, and scaling such initiatives must be addressed for communities to succeed at local, national, and international levels.

An International Community: Ayuda Urbana on City Management

At the international level there are a myriad of professional groups and organisations that focus on global civic issues. In recent years a number of these have developed a stronger emphasis on peer-to-peer learning and innovation among members from diverse disciplines. The Ayuda Urbana initiative was started in conversations about developing municipal capabilities between World Bank urban specialists and several mayors of capital cities in the Central American and Caribbean region. They recognised the value of connecting with peers across borders to address problems and challenges that all cities in the region face. A group of ten cities decided to participate in the initiative: Guatemala City, Havana, Managua, Mexico City, Panama City, San José, San Juan, San Salvador, Santo Domingo, and Tegucigalpa. The people involved in the project include the mayors and their staff in each of the ten cities. Additional partners include the World Bank, which provides overall coordination, some regional organisations to provide local legitimacy, and the British and Dutch governments to provide funding.[4]

The project was to create a constellation of communities of practice that would take advantage of the knowledge available in the participating cities. The domains would focus on a challenge of urban development and management the cities shared, including e-government, urban upgrading, environmental sanitation, municipal finances, urban transportation, renovation of historical city centres and poverty alleviation, and disaster prevention and management. The communities would consist of urban specialists in each domain from the participating cities and from local organisations. Together they would build their practice by comparing experiences

---

[4] For a more extensive review of this initiative see: Wenger (2003).

and sharing resources across cities, with input from World Bank experts about what had been learned elsewhere.

The communities of practice were officially launched through a series of 2-day workshops, each focused on one of the topics. Each workshop brought together specialists from the participating cities as well as a few World Bank experts. The purpose of the workshops was to

- create an initial forum to develop relationships and trust through face-to-face interactions among participants
- provide an opportunity for each participating city to share its experience
- engage participants in a discussion of lessons learned based on presentations by World Bank experts
- establish a prioritised list of the most pressing issues and most frequently asked questions
- introduce Web-based tools for use in facilitating an ongoing learning process and train participants to use the system
- choose a person to coordinate the collection of resources to be shared via e-mail and the Web site.

The project has created an interactive website, available to the public, which serves as a repository for the various communities of practice. The site includes a library of resources, downloadable manuals, bibliographic references, and proceedings of meetings. In addition, the site hosts an online forum to give participants the opportunity to discuss issues, ask questions, share relevant information, and stay in touch. For example, a community member asked how to price waste management services. Another member from San Salvador responded with a posting that explained how his city determined the price of such services.

The Ayuda Urbana initiative illustrates the value of collaboration across borders to address urgent issues in urban development, and it raises salient issues common to international communities. Creating communities of practice among cities from different countries is not all that different from similar efforts within a country, but there is additional complexity. The regional focus of Ayuda Urbana meant that participants spoke the same language and shared a cultural context. The situation would have been more complex if the project had expanded beyond the region. Another issue is the role of the convener when members do not share the same national government. Sponsorship has to come from an organisation like the World Bank, which can appreciate the vision of cross-border communities and the subtleties involved in cultivating such communities. Indeed, Ayuda Urbana represents the latest development of a broader initiative at the World Bank to focus on knowledge as a key lever in the fight against poverty. The Bank started an initiative in 1998 to support the development of communities internally, and since then the number of communities has grown from twenty-five to more than a hundred – and the influence of several has been considerable. An external study of the communities found that they were the 'heart and soul' of the Bank's new strategy to serve its clients as a 'knowledge bank.'

The Ayuda Urbana initiative highlights the importance of a skilled convener who is committed to a community-based approach as a way to address societal challenges. In this case, the World Bank is applying the same knowledge strategy with client countries that it has been applying internally. Indeed, the Bank's experience in cultivating communities of practice was critical to the success of the Ayuda Urbana project. The result is a new model for facilitating knowledge development among countries. Experts at the Bank consider it their task not just to provide their knowledge to clients but to build communities of practice among them as a way to develop their capabilities. The Bank experts still have a role to play, but not in a one-way transfer. Instead, their contribution takes place in the context of a community of practice that emphasises peer-to-peer learning. This approach models a shift in the traditional relationship between sources and recipients of knowledge.

The Fractal Structure of Large-Scale Learning Systems

Cultivating civic learning systems involves many of the challenges that organisations face in cultivating internal learning systems, but many of these become amplified in the civic context. The domains are especially complex; the communities tend to be very diverse; and the practices involve different disciplines, varied local conditions, and less well-defined opportunities to work together on projects. But perhaps the greatest challenge is the scale required for civic learning systems to leverage their full potential and match the scale of the problems they address.

How do you significantly increase the scale of a community-based learning system without losing core elements of its success – identification with a well-defined domain, close personal relationships, and direct access to practitioners for mutual learning? The principle to apply is that of a fractal structure (see Gleich, 1987; Wheatley, 1994). In such a structure, each level of substructure shares the characteristics of the other levels. Applying such a design principle, it is possible to preserve a small-community feeling while extending a system from the local to the international level. Local coalitions such as the Chicago Biotech Network and each of the SafeCities partners created a local focus of engagement that made it possible for members to participate in broader networks at national and international levels. The idea is to grow a 'community of communities' in which each level of sub-communities shares basic characteristics: focal issues, values, and a practice repertoire. Each dimension of a community of practice provides opportunities for the constitution of a fractal learning system.

Fractal domain. In many cases, domains may start more broadly and eventually subdivide as members discover nuances and opportunities to focus on different subtopics or to apply a topic to different localities. Ayuda Urbana, for example, is spawning subdomains related to particular civic practices and engaging members with particular expertise and interest in those areas. The city-based coalitions of SafeCities focused on the same issues but within the context of their situations. All these subdivisions retain a global coherence that gives the entire system a recognisable identity and allows members to see themselves as belonging to an overall community even as they focus on local issues.

Fractal community. Topical and geographic subgroups help create local intimacy, but they must be connected in ways that strengthen the overall fabric of the network. A key to this process is multimembership. Members such as those in the SafeCities network join at the local level but end up participating in multiple communities in ways that help interweave relationships in the broader community. As a result, they become brokers of relationships between levels in equivalent types of communities. This works because trust relationships have a transitive character: I trust people trusted by those I trust. The police chief in Highpoint, for example, had developed strong relationships with FBI officials, which in turn encouraged his peers to work more closely with federal agents.

Fractal practice. Useful knowledge is not of the cookie-cutter variety. Local conditions require adaptability and intelligent application. A fractal community is useful in this regard because it allows people to explore the principles that underlie a successful local practice and discuss ideas and methods in ways that make them relevant to circumstances elsewhere. A fractal community can create a shared repertoire and develop global principles while remaining true to local knowledge and idiosyncrasies. Moreover, if one locality has a problem or an idea, the broader community provides an extraordinary learning laboratory to test proposals in practice with motivated sites. In the SafeCities community, local coalition members were ready and willing to share results quickly and convincingly with peers and then translate these into action. A SafeCities member from Michigan reported, for example, that a visit to meet with innovating colleagues in Highpoint 'added ideas and motivation to an initiative that we had been planning for a year. Once our mayor visited, he wanted to do it.' Highpoint members then helped the Michigan coalition adapt their model successfully.

Each locality constitutes a local learning experiment that benefits from and contributes to the overall learning system. The key insight of a fractal structure is that crucial features of communities of practice can be maintained no matter how many participants join – as long as the basic configuration, organising principles, and opportunities for local engagement are the same. At scale, in fact, the learning potential of the overall network and the influence at local levels can increase significantly. The key challenge of a large-scale learning system is not whether people can learn from each other without direct contact but whether they can trust a broader community of communities to serve their local goals as well as a global purpose. This depends on the communities at all levels – local, state, national, and international – to establish a culture of trust, reciprocity, and shared values. Developing this social capital across all levels is the critical success factor for going to scale. The evolution of a learning system must therefore be paced at the time-scale of social relationships, not according to an externally imposed objective to achieve short-term results. Organisers need be careful not to scale up too fast. They need to establish trust and shared values at different levels of aggregation through various mechanisms, including a network of trusted brokers across localities.

Challenges for Supporting Civic Learning Systems

In the civic domain, the institutional context can be fragmented and the issues politically charged. This presents particular challenges for finding sponsorship, organising support, and managing potentially conflicting constituencies.

Sponsorship. All three communities depended on sponsorship from executives such as the Mayor of Chicago, the Vice President of the United States, or representatives of the World Bank and funding governments. Sponsorship is especially important for large-scale learning systems that will require additional activities to connect localities. It can be difficult, however, to identify the 'client' who benefits when a learning system is so dispersed. When you try to engage a city to sponsor a constellation of cross-sector communities of practice to address an array of civic domains, where do you start? A civic community of practice is such an innovative approach that leaders typically do not have enough context to see its value. Sustained sponsorship, furthermore, requires community members to make the value visible enough to demonstrate the payoff of sponsor and stakeholder investments. Finally, the legitimacy of sponsorship can be contested in a politically fractious context, where the role of institutions such as the World Bank or the federal government in orchestrating local affairs is not universally welcome.

Support. Process support was key to the communities we have described. They needed help with local event planning, finding resources, coordinating projects across levels, finding others to connect with, and designing ways to connect. All three communities needed facilitation at meetings, and SafeCities and Ayuda Urbana both required moderation for their online interactions. A challenge for civic learning systems is that there may be no clearly defined institutional context or financing model for process support. The Ayuda Urbana experience also suggests that one must be ready to provide a lot of support at the start to help develop members' local capabilities and prepare the group to operate more independently. Civic communities of practice also need help to build a technology infrastructure for communicating across geographies and time zones, and for building accessible knowledge repositories. This can be particularly difficult when communities span multiple organisational contexts.

Conflict management and collaborative inquiry. Civic communities of practice organised around contentious issues such as housing, education, and health will face considerable obstacles from formal and informal groups with entrenched and opposing views and interests. There are good reasons these basic conflicts have been so intractable: views and values are divergent and trust among players is often low. Moreover, businesses, nonprofits, governments, and universities have reasons to resist the development of communities of practice. These formal organisations and their leaders have developed established, privileged positions in society, and changes initiated by community members may not be welcomed. Inevitable mistakes early on could further diminish low trust levels and reduce the low-to-medium public readiness to invest time in these unfamiliar social commitments. Communities that face such tensions will have to develop expertise in collaborative inquiry and conflict management and learn to build trust over time through activities that enable members to find common ground.

Where Do We Go from Here?

There is an emerging, global zeitgeist about community and learning. These issues have become commonplace in multinational organisations – private, public, and nonprofit. Still, when one looks at the learning requirements of the world, the complexity of the required learning system may seem so overwhelming as to discourage action. But the advantage of a community-of-practice approach is that it can be evolutionary – starting small and building up progressively, one community at a time. It is not necessary to have broad alignment of the kind required for designing or changing formal structures. We can start wherever there is opportunity, energy, and existing connections. We can build on what already exists. Indeed, we have found successful examples of initiatives to cultivate learning systems: within cities, across cities at a national level, and across cities internationally. Taken together, these early examples paint a picture of what a mature world learning system may look like, and they give some indication of what it will take to cultivate such a system.

We now need to develop frameworks for describing the organisational nature of civil society as a community-based action-learning system – and tools and methods for cultivating such systems. This chapter is thus not only a call to action and a proposal for what is possible. It also calls for a new discipline. A discipline that expands the field of organisation design and applies analogous principles at the world level. A discipline that promotes the development of strategic social learning systems to steward civic practices at local, national, and global levels. A discipline whose scope is the world and whose focus is our ability to design the world as a learning system – a discipline of *world design*.

This chapter is only a beginning. There are many established and emerging disciplines – political science, economic sociology, social network analysis – that can inform the work in this domain. A community-based approach to world design is not a silver bullet for solving the problems of the world. While the emphasis here has been on community, a complete discipline of world design would address how the power of communities can be most fully realised by aligning community activities within a broader ecology of formal and informal structures – institutions, cultural groups, laws, and social networks.

To steward such a discipline, we need a community of practice ourselves – or indeed a constellation of communities on the topic of world design, at local, national, and global levels. For instance, a small group of people passionate about civic development may gather to outline an approach to cultivating the city as a learning system. They might connect with various civic leaders and extant initiatives, and organise a gathering for the purpose of assessing the implicit structure of the city today as a practice-based learning system. Which practices have active stewardship? What groups are providing it with what sorts of initiatives and results? Who is represented? Where is the focus of sponsors – such as local government, corporations, universities, the media, and foundations? To what degree is there a shared language and understanding across constituencies of the nature of cross-sector civic governance and how to participate effectively? These questions become the concerns of 'meta-communities' at various levels, which can link together – as a community of meta-communities – and build their own practice to support the development, effectiveness, and influence of civic communities at all levels.

The complexity and intelligence of such a social learning system must match the complexity of world-design challenges and the knowledge requirements associated with them. The messy problems of civil society require a commensurate capacity for learning, innovation, and collaboration across diverse constituencies and levels. The challenge to intentionally and systematically design and develop the world as a learning system must be a global, diverse, interwoven social movement. This social movement is not simply about advocacy; nor is it a political revolution. Rather, it is about the transformation of civic consciousness – a way of thinking about governance as an action-learning process, as a role for civic actors across sectors, as a process that links the local and global in clear and concrete ways. And it depends, fundamentally, on individuals finding a way to participate locally – whether that means a community of place or practice, or both – a way that gives them access to the entire learning system. Let us begin.

References

Churchman, C.W. 1971, *The Design of Inquiring Systems*, New York: Basic Books.

Durkheim, E., 1964, *The Division of Labor in Society*, New York: Free Press.

Gleich, J., 1987, *Chaos: Making a New Science*. New York: Penguin Books, pp. 81–118.

Grogan, P.S. and Proscio, T., 2000, *Comeback Cities*, Boulder, Colorado: Westview Press.

Snyder, W.M., 2002, *Organizing for Economic Development in Chicago: A Case Study of Strategy, Structure, and Leadership Practices*, Boston: CEO's for Cities, www.socialcapital.com

Snyder, W.M. and de Sousa Briggs, X., 2003, 'Communities of Practice: A New Tool for Managers,' *IBM Endowment for the Business of Government*, www.businessofgovernment.org

Snyder, W.M. and Wenger, E., 2004, 'Our world as a learning system: A communities-of-practice approach' In Conner, M.L. and Clawson, J.G. (eds) *Creating a Learning Culture: Strategy, Technology and Practice*, Cambridge: Cambridge University Press, pp. 35–58.

Wenger, E., 2003, *Ayuda Urbana: A constellation of communities of practice focused on urban issues and challenges in Central America, Mexico, and the Caribbean region*. Written for the BEEP Project of the European Union, www.beep-eu.org, Case 333.

Wenger, E., McDermott, R., and Snyder, W.M., 2002, *Cultivating Communities of Practice*, Boston: Harvard Business School Press.

Wheatley, M.J., 1994, *Leadership and the New Science*, San Fransisco: Berrett-Koehler, pp. 80–86.

Chapter 8
Conceptual Tools for CoPs as Social Learning Systems: Boundaries, Identity, Trajectories and Participation

Etienne Wenger

Editor's Note: This chapter comprises a series of five extracts from two works by the author (Wenger, 1998; Wenger, 2000). They concern *boundaries, identity, trajectories* and *participation*. These concepts play important parts in Wenger's Communities of Practice (CoPs) – based theory i.e. his social theory of learning. In the context of this book these extracts have been selected for scrutiny (i) because of their relevance to CoPs as social learning systems and (ii) to highlight the conceptual tools described for use in understanding and managing systemic change. Extracts 2, 3 and 4 make occasional references to 'a community of claims processors'. This example of a community of practice is detailed at the start of Wenger's 1998 book and is not reproduced here. Also, detailed footnotes from the original works are not given here.

Extract 1 Boundaries

The term boundary often has negative connotations because it conveys limitation and lack of access. But the very notion of community of practice implies the existence of boundary. Unlike the boundaries of organizational units, which are usually well defined because affiliation is officially sanctioned, the boundaries of communities of practice are usually rather fluid. They arise from different enterprises; different ways of engaging with one another; different histories, repertoires, ways of communicating, and capabilities. That these boundaries are often unspoken does not make them less significant. Sit for lunch by a group of high energy particle physicists and you know about boundary, not because they intend to exclude you, but because you cannot figure out what they are talking about. Shared practice by its very nature creates boundaries.

Yet, if you are like me, you will actually enjoy this experience of boundary. There is something disquieting, humbling at times, yet exciting and attractive about such close encounters with the unknown, with the mystery of 'otherness': a chance to

---

Source: Extracts 1 and 5 come from Wenger (2000). Extracts 2–4 come from Wenger (1998) reproduced with permission.
The sources of these extracts are indicated at the end of each extract and in the references.

C. Blackmore (ed.), *Social Learning Systems and Communities of Practice*,
DOI 10.1007/978-1-84996-133-2_8, © The Open University 2010.
Published in Association with Springer-Verlag London Limited.

explore the edge of your competence, learn something entirely new, revisit your little truths, and perhaps expand your horizon.

Why Focus on Boundaries?

Boundaries are important to learning systems for two reasons. They connect communities and they offer learning opportunities in their own right. These learning opportunities are of a different kind from the ones offered by communities. Inside a community, learning takes place because competence and experience need to converge for a community to exist. At the boundaries, competence and experience tend to diverge: a boundary interaction is usually an experience of being exposed to a foreign competence. Such reconfigurations of the relation between competence and experience are an important aspect of learning. If competence and experience are too close, if they always match, not much learning is likely to take place. There are no challenges; the community is losing its dynamism and the practice is in danger of becoming stale. Conversely, if experience and competence are too disconnected, if the distance is too great, not much learning is likely to take place either. Sitting by that group of high-energy particle physicists, you might not learn much because the distance between your own experience and the competence you are confronting is just too great. Mostly what you are learning is that you do not belong.

Learning at boundaries is likely to be maximized for individuals and for communities when experience and competence are in close tension. Achieving a generative tension between them requires:

- something to interact about, some intersection of interest, some activity;
- open engagement with real differences as well as common ground;
- commitment to suspend judgment in order to see the competence of a community in its terms;
- ways to translate between repertoires so that experience and competence actually interact.

Boundaries are sources of new opportunities as well as potential difficulties. In a learning system, communities and boundaries can be learning assets (and liabilities) in complementary ways.

- Communities of practice can steward a critical competence, but they can also become hostage to their history, insular, defensive, closed in, and oriented to their own focus.
- Boundaries can create divisions and be a source of separation, fragmentation, disconnection, and misunderstanding. Yet, they can also be areas of unusual learning, places where perspectives meet and new possibilities arise. Radically new insights often arise at the boundaries between communities. Think of a specialization like psychoneuroimmunology: its very name reflects its birth at the intersection of multiple practices.

In social learning systems, the value of communities and their boundaries are complementary. Deep expertise depends on a convergence between experience and competence, but innovative learning requires their divergence. In either case, you need strong competences to anchor the process. But these competences also need to interact. The learning and innovation potential of a social learning system lies in its configuration of strong core practices and active boundary processes (Wenger, 1998).

Which Way Is Up?

Not all boundary processes create bridges that actually connect practices in deep ways. The actual boundary effects of these processes can be assessed along the following dimensions.

- *Coordination* Can boundary processes and objects be interpreted in different practices in a way that enables coordinated action? For instance, an elegant design may delight designers but say little to those concerned with manufacturability. Across boundaries, effective actions and use of objects require new levels of coordination. They must accommodate the practices involved without burdening others with the details of one practice and provide enough standardization for people to know how to deal with them locally.
- *Transparency* Do boundary processes give access to the meanings they have in various practices? Coordination does not imply that boundary processes provide an understanding of the practices involved. For instance, forms like US tax returns enable coordination across boundaries (you know how to fill them out by following instructions line by line), but often afford no windows into the logic they are meant to enforce (following instructions often tells you little about why these calculations are 'fair').
- *Negotiability* Do boundary processes provide a one-way or a two-way connection? For instance, a business process reengineering plan may be very detailed about implementation (coordination) and explicit about its intentions (transparency), but reflect or allow little negotiation between the perspectives involved. Boundary processes can merely reflect relations of power among practices, in which case they are likely to reinforce the boundary rather than bridge it. They will bridge practices to the extent that they make room for multiple voices.[...]

What Is Doable?

Boundary processes are crucial to the coherent functioning of social learning systems. A number of elements can be intentionally promoted in an effort to weave these systems more tightly together. Here, I will talk about three types of bridges across boundaries: *people* who act as 'brokers' between communities, *artifacts* (things, tools, terms, representations, etc.) that serve as what Star and

Griesemer (1989) call 'boundary objects', and a variety of forms of *interactions* among people from different communities of practice.

Brokering

Some people act as brokers between communities. They can introduce elements of one practice into another. Although we all do some brokering, my experience is that certain individuals seem to thrive on being brokers: they love to create connections and engage in 'import–export', and so would rather stay at the boundaries of many practices than move to the core of any one practice. Brokering can take various forms, including:

- *boundary spanners*: taking care of one specific boundary over time;
- *roamers*: going from place to place, creating connections, moving knowledge;
- *outposts*: bringing back news from the forefront, exploring new territories;
- *pairs*: often brokering is done through a personal relationship between two people from different communities and it is really the relationship that acts as a brokering device.

Brokering knowledge is delicate. It requires enough legitimacy to be listened to and enough distance to bring something really new. Because brokers often do not fully belong anywhere and may not contribute directly to any specific outcome, the value they bring can easily be overlooked. Uprootedness, homelessness, marginalization, and organizational invisibility are all occupational hazards of brokering. Developing the boundary infrastructure of a social learning system means paying attention to people who act as brokers. Are they falling through the cracks? Is the value they bring understood? Is there even a language to talk about it? Are there people who are potential brokers but who for some reason do not provide cross-boundary connections?

Boundary Objects

Some objects find their value, not just as artifacts of one practice, but mostly to the extent that they support connections between different practices. Such boundary objects can take multiple forms.

- *Artifacts,* such as tools, documents, or models. For instance, medical records and architectural blueprints play a crucial role in connecting multiple practices (doctors/nurses/insurers, architects/contractors/city planners).
- *Discourses.* A critical boundary object is the existence of a common language that allows people to communicate and negotiate meanings across boundaries. This was an important thrust behind the quality movement, and it was typified by the six sigma discourse at Motorola.
- *Processes.* Shared processes, including explicit routines and procedures, allow people to coordinate their actions across boundaries. Business processes, for

instance, are not just fixed prescriptive definitions. At their best, they act as boundary objects that allow multiple practices to coordinate their contributions.

Boundary objects do not necessarily bridge across boundaries because they may be misinterpreted or interpreted blindly. Rethinking artifacts and designs in terms of their function as boundary objects often illuminates how they contribute to or hinder the functioning of learning systems. An organizational structure, for instance, is often considered as an overarching umbrella that incorporates multiple parts by specifying their relationships. But, in fact, it is more usefully designed as a boundary object intended to enable multiple practices to negotiate their relationships and connect their perspectives.

Boundary Interactions

- *Boundary encounters.* These encounters – visits, discussions, sabbaticals – provide direct exposure to a practice. They can take different forms for different purposes. When one person visits, as in a sabbatical, it is easier to get fully immersed in the practice, but more difficult to bring the implications home because the very immersion into a 'foreign' practice tends to isolate you from your peers. GM, for instance, has had difficulty learning from people sent on sabbatical at its more experimental units such as NUMMI and Saturn because their transformed perspectives could not find a place back home. When a delegation of two or more people visit, as in a benchmarking expedition, they may not get as fully immersed, but they can negotiate among themselves the meaning of the boundary interaction for their own practice, and therefore find it easier to bring their learning back home.
- *Boundary practices.* In some cases, a boundary requires so much sustained work that it becomes the topic of a practice of its own. At Xerox, as in many companies, some people are charged with the task of maintaining connections between the R&D lab and the rest of the corporation. They are developing a practice of crossing these boundaries effectively. Of course, the risk of these boundary practices is that they create their own boundaries, which can prevent them from functioning as brokers. It is necessary, therefore, to keep asking how the elements of the boundary practice – its enterprise, its relationships, its repertoire – contribute to creating a bridge and how the community deals with its own boundaries. And, sometimes, a new practice in its own right does develop at these boundaries, which is worth paying attention to in its own terms.
- *Peripheries.* Communities often have to take steps to manage their boundaries to serve people who need some service, are curious, or intend to become members. Many communities have found it useful to create some facilities by which outsiders can connect with their practice in peripheral ways. Examples of such facilities include lists of 'frequently asked questions', visitors' rooms on websites, open houses and fairs. Some communities have even established 'help desks' to provide access to their expertise in a more efficient way. The idea behind many of

these facilities is to provide for some boundary activities without overwhelming the community itself with the task of accommodating outsiders' demands. For newcomers, some communities organize introductory events, mentoring relationships, or even formal apprenticeship systems.

Cross-Disciplinary Projects

In most organizations, members of communities of practice contribute their competence by participating in cross-functional projects and teams that combine the knowledge of multiple practices to get something done. Simultaneous participation in communities of practice and project teams creates learning loops that combine application with capability development. In these double-knit organizations, as Richard McDermott (1999) calls them, the learning and innovation that is inherent in projects is synthesized and disseminated through the home communities of practice of team members. The new knowledge can then be applied and expanded in new projects, and the cycle goes on.

Such a perspective brings up a different way of thinking about these projects. From the standpoint of the task to be accomplished, these projects are cross-disciplinary because they require the contribution of multiple disciplines. But, from the perspective of the development of practices, they are boundary projects. Indeed, participating in these kinds of projects exposes practitioners to others in the context of specific tasks that go beyond the purview of any practice. People confront problems that are outside the realm of their competence but that force them to negotiate their own competence with the competences of others. Such projects provide a great way to sustain a creative tension between experience and competence when our participation in a project leverages and nourishes our participation in a community of practice.

(Source: Wenger, 2000, pp. 232–238)

Extract 2 The Landscape of Practice

As communities of practice differentiate themselves and also interlock with each other, they constitute a complex social landscape of shared practices, boundaries, peripheries, overlaps, connections, and encounters. I want to [make] two points that are by now rather obvious but cannot be overstated. First, the texture of continuities and discontinuities of this landscape is defined by practice, not by institutional affiliation; second, the landscape so defined is a weaving of both boundaries and peripheries.

Practice as Boundary

Because communities of practice define themselves through engagement in practice, they are essentially informal. By 'informal' I do not mean that the practice is disorganized or that communities of practice never have any formal status. What I mean is that, since the life of a community of practice as it unfolds is, in essence, produced by its members through their mutual engagement, it evolves in organic ways that tend to escape formal descriptions and control. The landscape of practice is therefore not congruent with the reified structures of institutional affiliations, divisions, and boundaries. It is not independent of these institutional structures, but neither is it reducible to them.

- On the one hand, the boundaries of communities of practice do not necessarily follow institutional boundaries, because membership is not defined by institutional categories. Who belongs and who does not, how the boundaries are defined, and what kinds of periphery are open are all matters of engagement in practice over time, of the need to get things done, and of the formation of viable identities.
- On the other hand, an institutional boundary does not necessarily outline a community of practice. Careful scrutiny of its day-to-day existence may reveal that a work group, classroom, committee, or neighborhood does not actually constitute a community of practice. It may consist of multiple communities of practice, or it may not have developed enough of a practice of its own.

An institutional boundary may therefore correspond to one community of practice, to a number of them, or to none at all. In addition, communities of practice can also be found spread throughout organizations (e.g. a community of practice of specialists in one area of expertise who work in different units but manage to stay in close contact) or straddling the boundaries of organizations (e.g. communities of practice formed around an emerging technology by professionals from competing companies). Communities of practice that bridge institutional boundaries are often critical to getting things done in the context – and sometimes in spite of – bureaucratic rigidities.

Thus, even when communities of practice live and define themselves within an institutional context, their boundaries may or may not coincide with institutional boundaries. And even when communities of practice are formed more or less along institutional boundaries, they entertain all sorts of relations of peripherality that blur those boundaries. Institutional boundaries draw clear distinctions between inside and outside. By contrast, boundaries of practice are constantly renegotiated, defining much more fluid and textured forms of participation.

Boundaries and Peripheries

The terms *boundaries* and *peripheries* both refer to the 'edges' of communities of practice, to their points of contact with the rest of the world, but they emphasize different aspects. Boundaries – no matter how negotiable or unspoken – refer to discontinuities, to lines of distinction between inside and outside, membership and non-membership, inclusion and exclusion. Peripheries – no matter how narrow – refer to continuities, to areas of overlap and connections, to windows and meeting places, and to organized and casual possibilities for participation offered to outsiders or newcomers.

Boundaries and peripheries are woven together. I was allowed to enter the community of practice of claims processors with an openness that at times felt like full participation, but every so often elements of boundary would creep in to remind me that I was an outsider: an expression I could not understand, a mistrusting look from the supervisor, a reference to a past event, someone's panicking concern about production quotas (to which I was not subjected), or even a claims processor's sigh of relief at 5 o'clock when I knew that I still had to go to my office and type up my notes.

Peripherality is thus an ambiguous position. Practice can be guarded just as it can be made available; membership can seem a daunting prospect just as it can constitute a welcoming invitation; a community of practice can be a fortress just as it can be an open door. Peripherality can be a position where access to a practice is possible, but it can also be a position where outsiders are kept from moving further inward.

The access that claims processors have to medical professionals, medical records, and medical jargon as a matter of routine is a form of periphery that does affect their own doctor – patient relations. But their own experience of their peripheral access to medical practices reflects all the ambivalence of peripherality, as illustrated by the following dialogue.

ETIENNE: Does that make a difference for you now, when you go see a doctor? Do you feel different?

MAUREEN: No.

SHEILA: Well, you know more about what they are talking about. I think it's . . . when I went to the dentist yesterday, he told me that this joint and everything is kind of weak. And I knew exactly it was TMJ. I knew exactly. The way he was wording it.

MAUREEN: You're sort of, self-diagnosing yourself.

SHEILA: Yeah, exactly. I think I pay more attention going to the doctor. Look at all these people who get sick, you know, maybe I should go. Maybe, I don't know if . . . I haven't gone to the doctor in a long time, so.

MAUREEN: You read an operative report. 'Oh, I think I got this,' you know.

SHEILA: Or I think I get to be a hypochondriac. Oh, that sounds like me, better go to the doctor.

Claims processors do not become doctors. In fact, they usually keep a low profile about the knowledge they gain through their peripheral access to medical information. An old-timer, who was the mother of a young child, told me that knowing all the terms and having read many reports gave her critical insights into the work of the medical professionals she dealt with. Yet, with a tacit awareness of her need to cooperate in maintaining a traditional doctor-patient relation, she also confided that she usually tried not to show her own knowledge and not to ask too many technical questions. Along with the periphery, the boundary clearly remained. By weaving boundaries and peripheries, a landscape of practice forms a complex texture of distinction and association, possibilities and impossibilities, opening and closing, limits and latitude, gates and entries, participation and non-participation.

(Source: Wenger, 1998, pp. 118–121).

Extract 3 Identity in Practice

There is a profound connection between identity and practice. Developing a practice requires the formation of a community whose members can engage with one another and thus acknowledge each other as participants. As a consequence, practice entails the negotiation of ways of being a person in that context. This negotiation may be silent; participants may not necessarily talk directly about that issue. But whether or not they address the question directly, they deal with it through the way they engage in action with one another and relate to one another. Inevitably, our practices deal with the profound issue of how to be a human being. In this sense, the formation of a community of practice is also the negotiation of identities.

[There are many ways in which we define who we are in the context of practice:]

- Identity as *negotiated experience*. We define who we are by the ways we experience our selves through participation as well as by the ways we and others reify our selves.
- Identity as *community membership*. We define who we are by the familiar and the unfamiliar.
- Identity as *learning trajectory*. We define who we are by where we have been and where we are going.
- Identity as *nexus of multimembership*. We define who we are by the ways we reconcile our various forms of membership into one identity.
- Identity as *a relation between the local and the global*. We define who we are by negotiating local ways of belonging to broader constellations and of manifesting broader styles and discourses.

[Here I discuss just two of these ways: identity as a learning trajectory and as nexus of multimembership . . .]

Trajectories

I have argued that identity in practice arises out of an interplay of participation and reification. As such, it is not an object, but a constant becoming. The work of identity is always going on. Identity is not some primordial core of personality that already exists. Nor is it something we acquire at some point in the same way that, at a certain age, we grow a set of permanent teeth. Even though issues of identity as a focus of overt concern may become more salient at certain times than at others, our identity is something we constantly renegotiate during the course of our lives.

As we go through a succession of forms of participation, our identities form trajectories, both within and across communities of practice. In this section, I will use the concept of trajectory to argue that:

1. identity is fundamentally temporal
2. the work of identity is ongoing

3. because it is constructed in social contexts, the temporality of identity is more complex than a linear notion of time
4. identities are defined with respect to the interaction of multiple convergent and divergent trajectories.

In using the term 'trajectory' I do not want to imply a fixed course or a fixed destination. To me, the term trajectory suggests not a path that can be foreseen or charted but a continuous motion – one that has a momentum of its own in addition to a field of influences. It has a coherence through time that connects the past, the present, and the future.

In the context of communities of practice, there can be various types of trajectories:

- *Peripheral trajectories.* By choice or by necessity, some trajectories never lead to full participation. Yet they may well provide a kind of access to a community and its practice that becomes significant enough to contribute to one's identity.
- *Inbound trajectories.* Newcomers are joining the community with the prospect of becoming full participants in its practice. Their identities are invested in their future participation, even though their present participation may be peripheral.
- *Insider trajectories.* The formation of an identity does not end with full membership. The evolution of the practice continues – new events, new demands, new inventions, and new generations all create occasions for renegotiating one's identity.
- *Boundary trajectories.* Some trajectories find their value in spanning boundaries and linking communities of practice. Sustaining an identity across boundaries is one of the most delicate challenges of this kind of brokering work [...].
- *Outbound trajectories.* Some trajectories lead out of a community, as when children grow up. What matters then is how a form of participation enables what comes next. It seems perhaps more natural to think of identity formation in terms of all the learning involved in entering a community of practice. Yet being on the way out of such a community also involves developing new relationships, finding a different position with respect to a community, and seeing the world and oneself in new ways.

Learning as Identity

The temporal dimension of identity is critical. Not only do we keep negotiating our identities, but they place our engagement in practice in this temporal context. We are always simultaneously dealing with specific situations, participating in the histories of certain practices, and involved in becoming certain persons. As trajectories, our identities incorporate the past and the future in the very process of negotiating the present. They give significance to events in relation to time construed as an extension of the self. They provide a context in which to determine what, among all the things that are potentially significant, actually becomes significant learning. A sense of trajectory gives us ways of sorting out what matters and what does not, what contributes to our identity and what remains marginal.

For claims processors, being on a trajectory is an important aspect of their job. They know that improvement in their performance will mean advancement, and they value the fact that advancement is automatic because it gives them some degree of control over their trajectory. Moreover, their sense of trajectory extends beyond claims processing. Some of them view the job as their profession, hoping to move on to technical or managerial positions in due time; some are just paying their way through college and have no interest in a professional career in claims processing. These different trajectories give them very different perspectives on their participation and identities at work. So for them, processing a claim is not just a self-contained activity. Understanding something new is not just a local act of learning. Rather, each is an event on a trajectory through which they give meaning to their engagement in practice in terms of the identity they are developing.

Learning events and forms of participation are thus defined by the current engagement they afford, as well as by their location on a trajectory. A very peripheral form of participation, for instance, may turn out to be central to one's identity because it leads to something significant.

Paradigmatic Trajectories

The progression of a career offered by the company is not the only way claims processors define their identity as a trajectory, even within the confines of their job. Their community, its history, and its evolution shape the trajectories they construct. More experienced peers are not merely a source of information about processing claims; they also represent the history of the practice as a way of life. They are living testimonies to what is possible, expected, desirable.

More generally, any community of practice provides a set of models for negotiating trajectories. These 'paradigmatic' trajectories are not simply reified milestones, such as those provided by a career ladder or even by communal rituals. Rather, they embody the history of the community through the very participation and identities of practitioners. They include actual people as well as composite stories. Exposure to this field of paradigmatic trajectories is likely to be the most influential factor shaping the learning of newcomers. In the end, it is members – by their very participation – who create the set of possibilities to which newcomers are exposed as they negotiate their own trajectories. No matter what is said, taught, prescribed, recommended, or tested, newcomers are no fools: once they have actual access to the practice, they soon find out what counts.

From this perspective, a community of practice is a field of possible trajectories and thus the proposal of an identity. It is a history and the promise of that history. It is a field of possible pasts and of possible futures, which are all there for participants, not only to witness, hear about, and contemplate, but to engage with. They can interact with old-timers, who offer living examples of possible trajectories. A community of practice is a history collapsed into a present that invites engagement. Newcomers can engage with their own future, as embodied by old-timers. As a community of practice, these old-timers deliver the past and offer the future, in the form of narratives and participation both. Each has a story to tell. In addition, the practice itself gives life to these stories, and the possibility of mutual engagement offers a way to enter these stories through one's own experience.

Of course, new trajectories do not necessarily align themselves with paradigmatic ones. Newcomers must find their own unique identities. And the relation goes both ways; newcomers also provide new models for different ways of participating. Whether adopted, modified, or rejected in specific instances, paradigmatic trajectories provide live material for negotiating and renegotiating identities.

Generational Encounters

As a process of negotiating trajectories, the encounter between generations is much more complex than the mere transmission of a heritage. It is an interlocking of identities, with all the conflicts and mutual dependencies this entails; by this interlocking, individual trajectories incorporate in different ways the history of a practice. Different generations bring different perspectives to their encounter because their identities are invested in different moments of that history. With less past, there is less history to take into consideration. With less future, there is less urgency to reconsider history. Yet, the perspectives of old-timers and newcomers are not so simply delineated.

If learning in practice is negotiating an identity, and if that identity incorporates the past and the future, then it is in each other that old-timers and newcomers find their experience of history. Their perspectives on the generational encounter is not simply one of past versus future, of continuity versus discontinuity, or of old versus new.

- While newcomers are forging their own identities, they do not necessarily want to emphasize discontinuity more than continuity. They must find a place in relation to the past. In order to participate, they must gain some access – vicarious as it may be – to the history they want to contribute to; they must make it part of their own identities. As a result, newcomers are not necessarily more progressive than old-timers; they do not necessarily seek to change the practice more than established members do. They have an investment in continuity because it connects them to a history of which they are not a part. Their very fragility and their efforts to include some of that history in their own identity may push them toward seeking continuity.
- Conversely, old-timers have an investment in their practice, yet they do not necessarily seek continuity. Embroiled in the politics of their community and with the confidence derived from participation in a history they know too well, they may want to invest themselves in the future not so much to continue it as to give it new wings. They might thus welcome the new potentials afforded by new generations who are less hostage to the past.

Depending on how a community negotiates individuality, the generational encounter can have different effects – with different degrees of emphasis on continuity and discontinuity as old-timers and newcomers fashion their identities in their encounter. This encounter is always a complex meeting of the past and the future, one in which generations attempt to define their identities by investing them in different moments of the history of a practice. The new will both continue and displace the old. In each other, generations find the partiality as well as the connectedness of their personal trajectories, that is, new dimensions of finitude and extension of their identities.

The temporality of identity in practice is thus a subtle form of temporality. It is neither merely individual nor simply linear. The past, the present, and the future are not in a simple straight line, but embodied in interlocked trajectories. It is a social form of temporality, where the past and the future interact as the history of a community unfolds across generations.

In summary, the temporal notion of trajectory characterizes identity as:

1. a work in progress
2. shaped by efforts – both individual and collective – to create a coherence through time that threads together successive forms of participation in the definition of a person
3. incorporating the past and the future in the experience of the present
4. negotiated with respect to paradigmatic trajectories
5. invested in histories of practice and in generational politics.

Nexus of Multimembership

As I mentioned, we all belong to many communities of practice: some past, some current; some as full members, some in more peripheral ways. Some may be central to our identities while others are more incidental. Whatever their nature, all these various forms of participation contribute in some way to the production of our identities. As a consequence, the very notion of identity entails

1. an experience of multimembership
2. the work of reconciliation necessary to maintain one identity across boundaries.

Identity as Multimembership

Our membership in any community of practice is only a part of our identity. Claims processors do not form their identities entirely at work. They came to their jobs as adults or youths, having belonged to many communities of practice. Some have other jobs concurrently; some are students in community colleges; some are parents; some are church-goers; some are bar-goers; some have engrossing hobbies. In fact, for many of them, their work is a part of their identity that they tend to disparage.

Because our identities are not something we turn on and off, our various forms of participation are not merely sequences in time. Claims processors who are parents come to the office without their children, and they will return home at the end of the afternoon to be with them. Though there are sequential phases in their engagement in different locations, they certainly do not cease to be parents because they are at work. They talk about their kids; and, more generally, the tidbits of conversation they interweave with their exchanges of work-related information continually reflect their participation in other practices.

Our various forms of participation delineate pieces of a puzzle we put together rather than sharp boundaries between disconnected parts of ourselves. An identity is thus more than just a single trajectory; instead, it should be viewed as a nexus of multimembership. As such a nexus, identity is not a unity but neither is it simply fragmented.

- On the one hand, we engage in different practices in each of the communities of practice to which we belong. We often behave rather differently in each of them, construct different aspects of ourselves, and gain different perspectives.
- On the other hand, considering a person as having multiple identities would miss all the subtle ways in which our various forms of participation, no matter how distinct, can interact, influence each other, and require coordination.

This notion of nexus adds multiplicity to the notion of trajectory. A nexus does not merge the specific trajectories we form in our various communities of practice into one; but neither does it decompose our identity into distinct trajectories in each community. In a nexus, multiple trajectories become part of each other, whether they clash or reinforce each other. They are, at the same time, one and multiple.

Identity as Reconciliation

If a nexus of multimembership is more than just a fragmented identity, being one person requires some work to reconcile our different forms of membership. Different practices can make competing demands that are difficult to combine into an experience that corresponds to a single identity. In particular:

1. different ways of engaging in practice may reflect different forms of individuality
2. different forms of accountability may call for different responses to the same circumstances
3. elements of one repertoire may be quite inappropriate, incomprehensible, or even offensive in another community.

Reconciling these aspects of competence demands more than just learning the rules of what to do when. It requires the construction of an identity that can include these different meanings and forms of participation into one nexus. Understood as the negotiation of an identity, the process of reconciling different forms of membership is deeper than just discrete choices or beliefs. For a doctor working in a hospital, making decisions that do justice to both her professional standards and institutional bottom-line demands is not simply a matter of making discrete decisions; she must find an identity that can reconcile the demands of these forms of accountability into a way of being in the world.

The work of reconciliation may be the most significant challenge faced by learners who move from one community of practice to another. For instance, when a child moves from a family to a classroom, when an immigrant moves from one culture to another, or when an employee moves from the ranks to a management position, learning involves more than appropriating new pieces of information. Learners must often deal with conflicting forms of individuality and competence as defined in different communities.

The nexus resulting from reconciliation work is not necessarily harmonious, and the process is not done once and for all. Multimembership may involve ongoing tensions that are never resolved. But the very presence of tension implies that there is an effort at maintaining some kind of coexistence. By using the term 'reconciliation' to describe this process of identity formation, I want to suggest that proceeding with life – with actions and interactions – entails finding ways to make our various forms of membership coexist, whether the process of reconciliation leads to successful resolutions or is a constant struggle. In other words, by including processes of reconciliation in the very definition of identity, I am suggesting that the maintenance of an identity across boundaries requires work and, moreover, that the work of integrating our various forms of participation is not just a secondary process. This work is not simply an additional concern for an independently defined identity viewed as a unitary object; rather, it is at the core of what it means to be a person. Multimembership and the work of reconciliation are intrinsic to the very concept of identity.

Social Bridges and Private Selves

Multimembership is the living experience of boundaries. This creates a dual relation between identities and the landscape of practice: they reflect each other and they shape each other. In weaving multiple trajectories together, our experience of multimembership replays in our identities the texture of the landscape of practice. But this replay is not a passive reflection. On the contrary, as the boundaries of practice become part of our personal experience of identity, the work of reconciliation is an active, creative process. As we engage our whole person in practice, our identities dynamically encompass multiple perspectives in the negotiation of new meanings. In these new meanings we negotiate our own activities and identities, and at the same time the histories of relations among our communities of practice. The creative negotiation of an identity always has the potential to rearrange these relations. In this regard, multimembership is not just a matter of personal identity. The work of reconciliation is a profoundly social kind of work. Through the creation of the person, it is constantly creating bridges – or at least potential bridges – across the landscape of practice.

And yet, the work of reconciliation can easily remain invisible because it may not be perceived as part of the enterprise of any community of practice. Across boundaries, the parallelism between histories of practice and personal trajectories no longer holds. The experience of multimembership can require the reconciliation of a nexus that is unique and thus very personal. Indeed, this nexus may not, in its entirety, be relevant to any practice or even to any relationship we have with anyone. Even though each element of the nexus may belong to a community, the nexus itself may not. The careful weaving of this nexus of multimembership into an identity can therefore be a very private achievement. By incorporating into the definition of the person the diversity of the social world, the social notion of a nexus of multimembership thus introduces into the concept of identity a deeply personal dimension of individuality.

(Source: Wenger, 1998, pp. 149, 153–161)

Extract 4 Participation and Non-participation

I have argued that we know who we *are* by what is familiar and by what we can negotiate and make use of, and that we know who we are *not* by what is unfamiliar, unwieldy, and out of our purview. This is an important point. We not only produce our identities through the practices we engage in, but we also define ourselves through practices we do not engage in. Our identities are constituted not only by what we are but also by what we are not. To the extent that we can come in contact with other ways of being, what we are not can even become a large part of how we define ourselves. For instance, we define ourselves in a small but not insignificant way by our regular contacts with various professionals from whom we receive services. Though we remain mostly non-participants, our service encounters often let us know just enough about their practices to gain some sense of what it is we are not, what we wish we were, what we would not dream of being, or what we are glad not to be. In other words, non-participation is, in a reverse kind of fashion, as much a source of identity as participation.

Our relations to communities of practice thus involve both participation and non-participation, and our identities are shaped by combinations of the two. [Here] I will explore the notion of identity of non-participation by defining a range of interactions between participation and non-participation, and in particular distinguishing between peripherality and marginality [. . .].

Identities of Non-participation

Experiences of non-participation do not necessarily build up to an identity of non-participation. Because our own practices usually include elements from other practices, and because we inevitably come in contact with communities of practice to which we do not belong, non-participation is an inevitable part of living in a landscape of practices. In a world complexly structured by interlocked communities of practice, we are constantly passing boundaries – catching, as we peek into foreign chambers, glimpses of other realities and meanings; touching, as we pass by outlandish arrangements, objects of distant values; learning, as we coordinate our actions across boundaries, to live with decisions we have not made. Not all that we encounter becomes significant and not all that we meet carries our touch; yet these events can all contribute in their own ways to our experience of identity.

It would be absurd to think that we can or should identify with everyone and everything we meet. In a landscape defined by boundaries and peripheries, a coherent identity is of necessity a mixture of being in and being out. When participation and non-participation refer only to relations of insider and outsider, they simply reflect our membership in specific communities of practice and not in others. Realizing that you are not a claims processor may contribute in a small way to your sense of self but, unless you are trying to become one, that realization remains inconsequential. In such cases, participation and non-participation do not define each other and merely have distinct effects on our identities.

Experiences of non-participation are an inevitable part of life, but they take on a different kind of importance when participation and non-participation interact to define each other. For instance, for a novice not to understand a conversation between old-timers becomes significant because this experience of non-participation is aligned with a trajectory of participation. It is the interaction of participation and non-participation that renders the experience consequential.

More generally, it is useful to distinguish two cases of the interaction of participation and non-participation.

- In the case of *peripherality*, some degree of non-participation is necessary to enable a kind of participation that is less than full. Here, it is the participation aspect that dominates and defines non-participation as an enabling factor of participation.
- In the case of *marginality*, a form of non-participation prevents full participation. Here, it is the non-participation aspect that dominates and comes to define a restricted form of participation.

Peripherality and marginality both involve a mix of participation and non-participation, and the line between them can be subtle. Yet, they produce qualitatively different experiences and identities, so it would be wrong to associate them too closely [. . .].

The difference between peripherality and marginality must be understood in the context of trajectories that determine the significance of forms of participation.

- Newcomers, for instance, may be on an inbound trajectory that is construed by everyone to include full participation in its future. Non-participation is then an opportunity for learning. Even for people whose trajectory remains peripheral, non-participation is an enabling aspect of their participation because full participation is not a goal to start with.
- Conversely, long-standing members can be kept in a marginal position, and the very maintenance of that position may have become so integrated in the practice that it closes the future. We often find it hard to be grown-up participants within our own families of birth. Women who seek equal opportunity often find that the practices of certain communities never cease to push them back into identities of non-participation. In such cases, forms of non-participation may be so ingrained in the practice that it may seem impossible to conceive of a different trajectory within the same community.

Hence, whether non-participation becomes peripherality or marginality depends on relations of participation that render non-participation either enabling or problematic. Of course, there are degrees of each. From this discussion emerges the

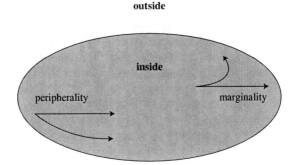

Fig. 8.1 Relations of participation and non-participation
(Source: Wenger, 1998, p. 167)

notion of a range of forms of participation with four main categories, as illustrated
in Fig. 8.1: full participation (insider); full non-participation (outsider); peripherality (participation enabled by non-participation, whether it leads to full participation
or remains on a peripheral trajectory); and marginality (participation restricted by
non-participation, whether it leads to non-membership or to a marginal position).
(Source: Wenger, 1998, pp. 164–167)

Extract 5 Participation in Social Learning Systems

The perspective of a social learning system applies to many of our social institutions:
our disciplines, our industries, our economic regions, and our organizations. This
view has implications at multiple levels.

- For individuals, this perspective highlights the importance of finding the dynamic
  set of communities they should belong to – centrally and peripherally – and to
  fashion a meaningful trajectory through these communities over time.
- For communities of practice, it requires a balance between core and boundary
  processes, so that the practice is both a strong node in the web of interconnections – an enabler of deep learning in a specific area – and, at the same time,
  highly linked with other parts of the system – a player in system-wide processes
  of knowledge production, exchange, and transformation.
- For organizations, this perspective implies a need to learn to foster and participate
  in social learning systems, both inside and outside organizational boundaries.
  Social learning systems are not defined by, congruent with, or cleanly encom-
  passed in organizations. Organizations can take part in them; they can foster
  them; they can leverage them; but they cannot fully own or control them [. . .]
  (Source: Wenger, 2000, p. 243).

References

McDermott, R. (1999) 'Learning across teams: how to build communities of practice in team-based organisations'. Knowledge Management Review 8(May/June):32–6.

Star, S.L. and Griesemer, J. (1989) 'Institutional ecology, "Translation," and boundary objects: amateurs and professionals in Berkeley's museum of vertebrate zoology, 1907–1939'. Social Studies of Science 19:387–420.

Wenger, E. (1998) Communities of practice: learning, meaning and identity. New York: Cambridge University Press, extracts reproduced with permission.

Wenger, E. (2000) 'Communities of practice and social learning systems', Sage Publications, 7(2):225–46. Extracts reproduced with permission.

Chapter 9
Learning Nursing in the Workplace Community: The Generation of Professional Capital

Mary Gobbi

Introduction

This chapter explores the connections between learning, working and professional communities in nursing. It draws on experiences and research in nursing practice and education, where not only do isolated professionals learn as a result of their actions for patients and others, but those professionals are part of a community whose associated networks enable learning to occur. Several characteristics of this professional community are shared with those found in Communities of Practice (CoPs) (Lave and Wenger, 1991; Wenger, 1998), but the balance and importance of many elements can differ. For instance, whilst Lave and Wenger (1991) describe many aspects of situated learning in CoPs that apply to nurses, their model is of little help in understanding the ways in which other professions as well as patients/clients and carers influence the development of nursing practice. Therefore, I shall argue that it is not just the Community of *Practice* that we need to consider.

At the heart of any discussion of communities and practice lie concepts associated with interpersonal relationships, the moral being and the purpose of community, the knowledge that is explicitly and implicitly communicated within a given community, and thorny discussions about what constitutes practice, theory and action. To attempt to address all of these components in a single chapter would be unrealistic, so I focus on the characteristics of communities of professionals, learning in professional workplaces, the professional capital that is generated, acquired and maintained as a result of that learning, and its relationship to CoPs.

Throughout the chapter I use vignettes from nursing practice and educational activities to illustrate the complexities of learning in workplace communities. The vignettes include examples drawn from fieldwork notes made as a participant observer on cardiothoracic and palliative care units whilst researching the learning and development of registered nurses,especially their use of intuition, reflection and

Source: Gobbi (2009)

C. Blackmore (ed.), *Social Learning Systems and Communities of Practice*,
DOI 10.1007/978-1-84996-133-2_9, © The Open University 2010.
Published in Association with Springer-Verlag London Limited.

thinking in practice. Other examples are from ongoing work with students learning in simulated hospital environments. The chapter commences with three vignettes from clinical practice that raise questions about the nature of CoPs, professional capital and the effects of linguistic and paralinguistic practices.

Vignette 1
The student [nurse) had a query as to whether a thoracic patient could be rolled onto their side or not. The registered nurse stopped, thought and then went to clarify for herself. She went to get the X-ray, looked at it and then checked with the houseman [intern]. They compared the X-ray with previous ones and discussed the situation; the registered nurse indicated that she wasn't happy to roll the patient. She verbally invited the ward sister's [head nurse] opinion, who agreed with her judgement. The sister then called to members of staff and students who were passing by to 'come and look at this' [meaning the X-ray]. This particular situation was not in the textbooks.

In Vignette 1, a student nurse seeks advice from her supervisor. This example indicates not only the particular nature of clinical decisions, but also the discursive manner through which decisions are made and, for others, the potential for learning occurs.

Does this typical example of A seeking a decision from B, who consults with others before a decision is reached, indicate that a CoP existed [...] in the way Wenger (1998) describes? Or rather, is this more an expression of individuals coming together in a team for a moment of decision making that, through leadership, opens the possibility of learning at work not only for those directly involved but also for others in the vicinity? The driver for learning and action is the need to make a decision about patients in their best interests. Is this a temporary CoP or pragmatic communal action where learning happens as a consequence? It is hard to say – just as it is in practice. Without the intervention of the ward sister, knowledge sharing with the local community would not have occurred. Indeed the cycle of learning and decision making arose from uncertainty about what action to take.

The decision required a 'judgement call'. Gadamer (1973, 1993) links the development of judgement with that of 'sensus communis' (the common sense). Judgement is described as a capacity to subsume 'a particular under a universal, recognising something as an example of a rule' (Gadamer, 1993, p. 31). However in Vignette 1, no one could offer the rule, although interpreting an X-ray in the context of the patient's diagnosis would have been guided by some rules. Gadamer (1993, p. 39) asserts that judgement cannot be learned theoretically 'because no demonstration from concepts is able to guide the application of rules'; rather judgement can only be 'practised from case to case'. The significance is that whilst judgement is about individual cases, albeit influenced by universals, judgement cannot be logically proven and its explanation may present the individual with discourse problems.

Professional judgements can be between or concerning isolated individuals or may be within groups of people. From Vignette 1, we can recognise the following features of learning and actions in groups:

- learning is provoked by a need to make a decision
- learning and decision making can involve discussion and consultation between members of a working community
- knowledge gleaned in practice can be shared through leadership
- situated learning takes place because the answer 'wasn't in a textbook'
- decision making can refer to the tacit presence of the 'other', namely the patient for whom the decision applies

Vignette 2

The SHO [junior doctor] attempted to put a line [intravenous line into a neck vein] in the neck, so I stayed by his [the patient's] head; I was now caught pragmatically in the middle by accident... By now I was literally trapped up beside the patient, next to the registrar [senior doctor] who was going to position the scope [fibre optic imaging device].... Around the patient [who was very sick], there were plenty of looks that were exchanged between me and the patient, between nurse L and me, and then between the doctors [whose preoccupation with what they were doing led them to be generally unable to converse with the patient]. Nurse S understood it; there was a lot of silent team work going on in the background... the unspoken acknowledgement that it was better for me to be with the patient.

(working with nurse V month 18)

Vignette 2 provides an illustration of how looks and gazes can be used in professional practice between different professionals and to and from the patient. Here I am working in a high-dependency unit with a patient who has begun to deteriorate seriously; the doctors are engaged in both diagnostic and treatment activities.

Vignette 2 reveals signs, signifiers and acknowledgement tokens exhibited through linguistic and paralinguistic devices that need to be learned and effectively employed in order to practice successfully. I found that the learning was embedded within experience, through observation, role modelling and perhaps the advice of others. We also see this in Vignette 3, where students are working in small groups to manage and respond to the stimuli presented by a computer mannequin 'SIMMAN' that provides numerous multi-sensory physical outputs, e.g. blood pressure, heart rate and voice/respiratory sounds.

> **Vignette 3**
> Observing the students around the bedside, one can see how some of them
> haven't yet learnt to manage and place their bodies. Their resting postures are
> ergonomically strained, their hands are awkward and they don't know where
> to put themselves in relation to the bed area. In contrast, others automatically
> move around the bed, control their hands, move equipment and furniture and
> position themselves to get the best view of the patient and each other. Some
> observe their mentor and emulate their movements; others seem oblivious to
> the mentor's actions.
>
>   (video observations, November 2006)

Each vignette offers us some clues about how professional practice incorporates
knowing, not knowing (what to do or why) and doing, as well as paralinguistic and
embodied skills that even include how to comport oneself. As such the vignettes also
offer clues as to the nature and content of professional capital for nursing, which we
will now explore.

Professional Capital

Professional capital can be described in two distinct ways, one economic and one
non-economic. From the economic perspective, professional capital is a dimension of human capital and refers to the skills and knowledge, including tacit and
embodied knowledge, necessary for the economic growth and development of the
profession. In this context, professional capital becomes, for example, associated
with longer periods of education or the requirement to maintain the professional
capital held by individual practitioners through mandatory updating or evidence of
demonstrable and current competence. Specialist knowledge (Leahey, 2006) and
knowledge from evidence-based practice (Goldenberg, 2005) develop professional
capital in this economic sense, ensuring that the skills and knowledge components
of professional capital are used effectively and efficiently.

Professions also contribute to the creation of economic capital through their role
in the production of new technology (Iyigun and Owen, 1999) and science. The
relationship between medicine and the pharmaceutical industry classically generates
this form of economic professional capital. Additionally, professional capital may
be exhibited through particular ways of looking, walking and using body language
(Exley, 2001). Such embodied knowledge can carry economic professional capital
since economic penalty may result if the wrong image is presented. Thus, the economic perspective of professional capital includes both professional knowing and
doing and the embodiment of professional practice.

The second approach, the non-economic one, has origins largely associated with
values and beliefs. I call this Personal Professional Capital. It is intrinsically associated with the self-concept of the individual professional and their relationship with
others and as McGregor (2004) proposes, it can be viewed as a dimension of a

person's philosophical well-being. Non-economic professional capital might include the connections, relationships of trust and mutual obligation and common language that are characteristic of a professional community, as suggested by Lesser and Storck (2001) who draw on the work of Nahapiet and Ghoshal (1998) to highlight this aspect of social capital among professions. Clearly, Personal Professional Capital may also be associated with economic benefit, so that, for example, the public recognition of 'good care' has the capacity to bestow not only personal value for the practitioner and kudos for the organisation but also monetary value by attracting clients to centres of good repute.

Communities of Professionals

As early as, Goode's (1957) sociological analysis of professions and their development described a profession as a contained community within a larger society. Although such professional communities may have no physical locus, he writes, many are associated with particular places or brand images with which they give themselves a recognisable way of being, whether liminal, virtual, real or imagined. This in turn enables the community to craft an identity that helps it to maintain a relationship with the wider society as well as provide structure to the community itself.

As a consequence members of a professional community, Goode suggests, are bound by their sense of identity, rarely leave, share common values, have acknowledged role definitions that are understood by members and non-members, share a common language only understood partially by non-members, have power exerted over them by the community itself, exist in a community expressed through social rather than physical or geographical limits and produce the next generation socially through their control over the selection of trainees and the form of their socialisation – a socialisation that might include periods of social isolation from the wider community. Here, it would seem, we already find the fundamental ingredients, as described by Lave and Wenger (1991), Brown and Duguid (1991), Wenger (1998) and Lesser and Storck (2001) of a CoP. In addition, one could argue that communities of professionals, by virtue of the way they learn together, develop a distinctive epistemology – their shared way of knowing about their world. As we shall see later (in Fig. 9.1), this epistemological dimension of a community of professionals is an important aspect of their professional capital. However, whilst agreeing that commonality is central to the community of professionals and CoPs, it is necessary to explore further the nature of this commonality within CoPs that comprise professionals like nurses.

Society, Communities Groups and Teams

Some time ago Macmurray (1961) argued that any human society is a unity of persons and that such unity is more than fact, it is a matter of intention. The society remains for as long as its members intend to maintain it. Furthermore he asserts, any human society is a moral entity whose basis is the 'universal and necessary intention to maintain the personal relations which make the human person and individual and his life a common life' (p. 128). He distinguishes between society and community according to the nature of the bonds between the persons who comprise the group. In society, the bonds of relationship between individuals are impersonal and arise from negative motivation, whereas a community is characterised by bonds based on positive personal motivation. Community members are therefore in communion with one another and are associated through fellowship, by practical transactions and by the way they act in relationship to one another.

In the more positive community-based personal relationships that Macmurray spoke of, there is trust. Individuals can think, feel and act together; people are comfortable being 'themselves', relationships can be more authentic and consequently people enjoy freedom as we have shown in the earlier vignettes. If conflict arises and is not completely resolved through the rebuilding of confidence and trust, the relationships may break down or they may be salvaged through the imposition of agreed, mutual restraint. This restraint, of course, diminishes the freedom to be authentic and caring, resulting in the creation of characteristics more akin to those of a society rather than those of a community.

Communities may then resemble the classical Greek concept of koinonia. Whilst koinonia nowadays has theological connotations of communion and fellowship, its root in community incorporates the concepts of sharing, fellowship, association, partnership and common interest. Typically, koinonia engages with beneficial activity that is optimally non-hierarchical and involves actions towards common altruistic goals. Perhaps those communities – such as communities of professionals with a strong sense of mission and vision arising from service or covenant roots – may share these features so that their learning will be orientated towards values and practices that uphold beneficent goals. A community of professionals is therefore a very different kind of entity from a society of professionals. This ontological dimension of a community of professionals – i.e. the essence of what it is to be that community – is another important component of professional capital, which like the epistemological dimension of the community discussed above, we will return to in Fig. 9.1.

In relation to the professional practice of nursing, clinical freedom comes with the authority and accountability that is held or accorded to the individual professional by the community of the profession. These professional authorities and accountabilities bring with them duties, responsibilities and obligations which may be recognised through discourse. Edwards and Potter (1992) demonstrate that although people who are discussing accountability can, at one level, assign broad responsibility for the events, at another level they are also concerned with the speaker's own accountability for their practice. The interaction between these two levels is shown to be managed according to the context within which it occurs. Vignette 4 provides an example of this.

> **Vignette 4**
>
> She [the relative] wanted me to sort of reassure HIM and I thought well
> next time, I'll probably say to the person: 'No, (.) I can't lie for you. I can't
> answer your query' [laughter]. It's not, not just how you actually deal with the
> patients; it's their relatives as well [ironic laughter].
>
> (with V month 5)

In this de-contextualised extract, several layers of accountability and belief are
perceived and implied through V's account. As speaker, V is stating that 'I can't lie
for you'; she indicates that she perceives or experiences contrasting accountabilities (responsibilities) between relatives, patients and herself. Learning in a community is often about appraising oneself against one's own and the community's, the
profession's and/or civic society's pre-existing values, beliefs and standards. The
emphasis is on the person as a moral, socially responsible and intelligible agent and
clearly articulates the community dimension of the Person, whose relation to the
Other engenders meaningful action (see Macmurray, 1961; Shotter, 1975). Within
the context of reflective practice, of course, the Other may be the referential self –
i.e. the inner voice that may arguably be speaking for the community.

As Kirkpatrick (1991) discusses, for Macmurray, community is for the sake of
friendship and the full expression of a relationship between people, whereas society
is for the sake of protection and presupposes fear being maintained by common
constraints, for example the law. It is evident therefore that professional communities have the capacity to oscillate between these two modes with implications
for the learning and development of their members, so practitioners need to learn
now to be a 'professional friend' as well as being an accredited, legitimate professional. Indeed, a legitimised professional community becomes 'professional'
society by definition because of its associated obligation to uphold the espoused
and formalised mores of the profession, as well as the laws of the state as they
relate to the profession. There is another way to see this: Sergiovanni (1998) cites
Sacks (1997) who argued that where a social *contract* is maintained by promises of
reward or threat, a social *covenant* is maintained by loyalty, fidelity, kinship, sense
of identity, obligation, duty, responsibility and reciprocity and that different types
of communities connect as either social contracts or social covenants. Indeed Bradshaw (1994) has analysed the covenant concept in the context of nursing practice.
This also suggests that, besides the epistemological and ontological dimensions of
community (discussed above), which is based more on covenant than on contract,
a community of professionals also entails an element of *society*, a formal structure
that the profession must espouse in order to be recognised as such. Again, as we
shall see later, the formal espoused aspect of a community of professionals is an
important aspect of their professional capital.[1]

---

[1] Some readers may see parallels between my usage here of the terms 'koinonia' and 'society', and
the widely used sociological concepts of *Gemeinschaft*, which roughly speaking refers to the bonds

The Latin roots of the word community denote 'sameness', 'common or shared by many', 'together' and 'performing services' (munis). These themes resonate with professional practitioners in person-based occupations who perform services with and for people, espouse common values and practice and frequently operate in co-located or virtual small groups, albeit now in more inter-professional and inter-disciplinary ways of working. In these communities, practitioners share together their professional woes, experiences, hopes, aspirations, achievements and joys in the context of their interactions with each other, their clients, related co-workers and the other persons who comprise the wider society. In order to achieve their espoused goal of professional recognition or status accorded by the relevant society, novices are required to enter, engage with and participate in these communities whilst achieving any personal goals associated with their intended aims. Furthermore, as Lave and Wenger (1991) noted, what distinguishes some professionals from others is the nature of their relationship with their clients. Analyse, for example, the differences and similarities between nurse and cancer patient, defence lawyer and the accused, engineer and industrial client. Vignette 5 demonstrates clearly how the motivational effect of caring for the person leads V to learn how to have the courage of one's convictions and to know how to go and 'get the doctor'.

> **Vignette 5a**
> You go through on your own, that's right. I was saying I would get her [senior nurse] to back me up before, whereas now I would go and bleep the doctor. I would go and get the doctor. That's the difference, I would go. It's having the courage of your convictions as well.
>
> (interview with V month 36)

This vignette echoes back to a prior developmental state where V sometimes had difficulty operating effectively within teams of professionals due to her clinical inexperience. But she was also unable to read and manage the signs of others and communicate in their professional discourse. In reflecting back to the same incident that occurred in month 4, V states as follows;

> **Vignette 5b**
> ...something in hindsight I'm aware of that was also stopping me then. Two things. Firstly knowing you can use the doctors to help you, actually getting access to them. And secondly, having the confidence to go ... I think the problem was I didn't know how to prepare my case properly.
>
> (V month 15)

---

of kinship and shared values and beliefs, and *Gesellschaft*, the bonds of social relationship that are necessary for social function but only in so far as they serve the individual interest. However, I have chosen to use koinonia and society in order to avoid the connotations of those terms that are unhelpful in the context of a community of professionals.

This vignette illustrated the learning that has to occur within different teams and communities of professionals, in this case the ability to present information in ways that others cannot ignore. V's Personal Professional Capital therefore not only includes a moral dimension, but is also dependent upon traits like courage, multilingual discourse practices and pragmatic knowledge. Experienced practitioners may be able to elicit information from others and thereby facilitate translation from one discipline to another. In addition, we see V's developmental progress acquired through analysing experiences, her own abilities arid the interactions occurring in teams both within and across communities of professionals.

Lesser and Storck (2001) discuss the often-confused distinctions between Communities of Practice and teams and refer to the characteristic differences highlighted by Storck and Hill outlined in the middle two columns of Table 9.1. When analysing these characteristics in the context of professional practice (column 4), it is evident that groups of individuals in practice can exhibit the characteristics of both team and CoP. This challenges us to consider what makes the difference – perhaps leadership (Vignette 1), personal commitment (Vignette 5) or individuals co-located in time who have the ability to share their embodied practice (Vignette 2).

Table 9.1 A comparison of teams, communities of practice and professional practice

Feature	Team (after Storck and Hill)	CoP (after Storck and Hill)	Professional practice
Relationships	Organisation assigns roles	Formed around practice	Formed around client and role
Authority	Organisationally determined	Emerge through interaction around expertise	Arises through client expectations as well as those of profession and organisation
Goals	Goals set by those not members of the team	Only responsible to their members	Responsible to clients, profession and team
Reporting processes	Determined by organisation	Develop their own	Develop their own in context

Linguistic Problems and Discourses of Professional Practice by Communities

We have seen that communities can generate their own sense of 'right and wrong' and thereby shape the individual's moral being. Malikail (2003) discusses how 'many aspects of moral life are a matter of imaginative vision and understanding one's own life by analogy to classic narratives' and, citing Aristotle, how the qualities of character are socio-teleological and relate to life in community. The generation, acquisition, transmission and communication of these common values and narratives can require sophisticated discursive practices. Goodwin (1994), for example, identifies the coding, highlighting, producing and articulating of material representations that enable the professional vision to be constructed. This professional vision is the socially organised ways of seeing and understanding events of the particular group: ways of seeing and understanding that need to be learned. Steier (1991:167) points out that patterns of tacit knowing 'may get unconcealed in conversations' and that attention to stories may reveal 'social ways of seeing and doing'. Analysis of the vignettes (including those that follow in this section) confirms this way of eliciting and learning the ways of 'seeing and doing' as represented through discourse and the analysis of experience as text.

Several of the vignettes have examples akin to Alice in Wonderland's account of *thinking in chorus*:

> Alice thought to herself 'then there's no use in speaking'. The voices didn't join in this time, as she hadn't spoken, but to her great surprise they all *thought* in chorus (I hope you understand what *thinking in chorus* means – for I must confess that *I* don't). (Lewis Carroll, *Alice in Wonderland*, p. 128).

This idea that one can 'think in chorus' indicates connections between silence, language, transmitted meaning and a socio-emotional way of being. As the vignettes demonstrated, occasionally practitioners (and their patients) may not actually verbalise something, but indicate that they shared the same thought as another person.

Ortega commented with respect to the concept of language that 'each language represents a different equation between manifestations and silences. Each person leaves some things unsaid *in order* to say others. Because *everything* would be unsayable. Hence, the immense difficulty of translation: translation is a matter of saying in a language precisely what that language tends to pass over in silence' (Becker, 1991, p. 226). Applying this to the discourses of practice and their translation implies that practitioners need to learn the purpose of what is said, what is unsaid and the meaning of silence in particular contexts of practice.

Discourses of practice may contain aspects of the 'sensus communis' (the common sense) in which 'feelings or intuition' have an established 'something' with common significance to the community (Shotter's analysis of Vico, 1993, p. 54). According to Shotter, Vico's 'common sense' arises from socially shared identities or feelings in which an experience/event/circumstance has generated a shared sense with a subsequent 'imaginative universal'. If we take this further, we can acknowledge that the sensus communis can also generate a variety of shared signs and significations that render visible the invisible – at least to a fellow practitioner. From a psychological perspective, a sense of community can be engendered or fostered through a shared emotional connection and is exemplified in the emotional outpourings witnessed at the death of Princess Diana in 1997. In the world of health care, nurses, other health care workers and patients can experience shared emotional connections that strengthen, or indeed challenge the bonds of community or fellowship. Community therefore can be developed through the emotional bonds and ties of practice.

Shared identity is a central element of the professional community; however, the experiences and knowledge of the professional are increasingly becoming available to, and influenced by, lay people. This exchange will shape professionals' knowing and competence and ultimately their professional capital, which in turn will influence the identity, discourses and meaning of being a particular kind of professional.

I have argued elsewhere (Gobbi, 2005) how, when learning to nurse, students and junior practitioners need to learn how to be bricoleurs, both metaphorically, literally, intellectually and technically. Learning how to convey, read and interpret the plurisensorial signs, signifiers and rules associated with what one practitioner described as the 'unsaid stuff of practice' occurs when the moral, relational, intersubjective and permissible or prohibited interactions of practice are exposed: in other words, the professional capital of nursing.

In some situations it seems inappropriate to verbalise the 'unsaid stuff' as this next example demonstrates (Vignette 6). I am accompanying T, a palliative care home nurse visiting a patient with cancer. T, the patient, his wife and I engage in silent acknowledgement tokens and the reading of movements and expressions. It is an incident that most practicing clinicians will identify with, even though, as I have argued above, it may not be possible to articulate verbally this 'feeling in chorus'.

Vignette 6
The patient began to talk about how his lower abdomen felt more 'full'. He rubbed his abdomen as he spoke, indicating and saying that he could 'feel things'. There seemed to be an acknowledgement by those present that there was deterioration [without a word being said].
(Field notes with T month 9)

This 'unsaid stuff' may include gazes that transmit messages like 'this patient is going to die,' 'come and help me'. They can involve the use of linguistic devices, one I call the 'it cannot be said device'. This device is used when messages need to be conveyed and for whatever reason, words either cannot be said or they cannot articulate a feeling, thought or sensation, e.g. expressing worry, 'there's something wrong with that man' where the purpose of the remark is to alert another practitioner to concerns that cannot be verbalised at the time. Furthermore, as Usher (1992) suggested, not all experiences can be communicated, particularly if one tries to read experience as if it were text. In Vignette 7, T reflected upon an occasion when we had worked together within a hospice setting. T outlines the complexity of experience and notes how it is not possible to 'write it all down' and 'learn it all from a book' reminding us of the inadequacy of the written word in the context of professional practice.

> **Vignette 7**
> I think that something like we experienced this morning, it's um- it can't be
> learnt from a book. You can't put all that goes on this morning, every dynamic
> of it – you can't put it down in a book and tell people what to do. . . . You are
> not going to be able to articulate it. . . . it's about getting to know individuals
> and getting to know PEOPLE as err en masse [almost whimsical voice]. If
> you know what I mean?
>
>   (Interview with T)

Foucault (1972, p. 27) advised attention to the 'silent murmuring, the inexhaustible speech that animates from within the voice that one hears, (to) re-establish
the tiny, invisible text that runs between and sometimes collides with them'. In the
collective and individual experiences of practitioners and their clients reside invisible texts, the 'unsaid stuff' that runs in and out of practice as exemplified by these
vignettes. The appropriate transmission and interpretation of these 'it cannot be said
devices' are essential to those present. Foucault claims that 'there is always a secret
origin, so secret and so fundamental that it cannot be grasped itself'. In the world
of practice and workplace learning, by applying Foucault's recognition that events
have 'movement, spontaneity, and internal dynamism' we can gain insights into
the learning and doing of practice by and between individuals as well as within
the community. It is also possible to analyse the 'continuities and possibilities'
present through the influence of others who may or may not be physically present.
These influences may be those of power, knowledge and hegemony or influences
of emotion and motivation as seen in the vignettes. Once again acknowledgement
of the tacit and personal knowing reminds us of their inarticulate and unspecifiable
elements and concepts like hope, commitment, obligation and responsibility that are
fundamental to community interactions (Polanyi, 1958, 1983).

The Community, Learning and Professional Capital

In summary, we have seen that communities have three significant dimensions. First
there is *personal membership* of the community by individuals, possibly working and learning (as in Vignette 1) in small teams, who are developing embodied practice. Second there is the nexus of internal community relationships, which
I earlier called *koinonia*, which provides the community with its distinctive but
intangible ontological and epistemological form. This is the dimension of the community that gives its individual members the cultural propensity to practise in
certain ways, whether alone or collectively, and to adopt communally approved
forms of both explicit and tacit knowledge.[2] Third there is the formal dimen-

---

[2] There is a parallel here with Bourdieu's concept of the *habitus*, which he first described in the
1970s, and which is the propensity for members of a culture to act in particular ways that they have
learned from each other over a lifetime (Bourdieu, 1990).

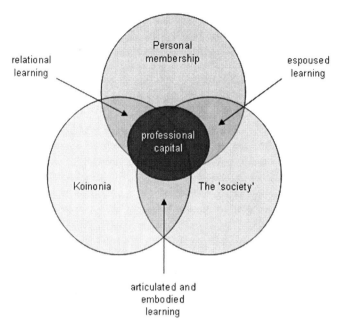

Fig. 9.1 The dimensions of community and learning as the basis for professional capital

sion of the community that conforms to the notion of *society*, as discussed above. Here we find the formal, contractual and regulatory dimension of the relationships between the individuals that may be the basis of a professional society and its espoused effect on the wider world. Figure 9.1 is an attempt to show how these three dimensions of a community of professionals integrate to generate professional capital.

This integration is achieved through the various types of learning that arise from the different dimensions of the community, which come together to create an active, emergent, and sometimes contested zone in which members generate and utilise their professional capital. More specifically, these types of learning include the following:

- *relational learning* between the individual members, generating and transmitting cultural, 'tribal', informal learning/knowledge and creating embodied action;
- *espoused learning*, which includes the formal and legitimised codes, ethics, practices, semantics and theories of the profession;
- *articulated/embodied learning*, which comprises the repository of collective formal and informal knowledge.

We have seen in the vignettes that the professional capital generated through learning is strongly influenced by professional (un)certainty and moral conviction, and that the learning of a range of linguistic and paralinguistic skills is also crucial. Foucault highlights this necessity 'because it means giving the key of a language that masters the visible' (Foucault, 1973, p. 114). Visible and invisible aspects of professional practice are exposed in the professional workplace as the medium not only through which learning, communication, action and reaction take place, but also through which professional capital is generated.

The Centrality of the Client in Generating Professional Capital

Learning is also inherently stimulated by the needs of clients, who play a key role in the accumulation of learning and professional practice and hence are vital to the creation of professional capital. Through their interaction and engagement with professionals, they play their part in each dimension of Fig. 9.1.

Personal membership of the profession allows each individual to have a personal portfolio of clients with whom they directly, indirectly or vicariously interact, learn about and learn from. This portfolio forms the basis of their professional and personal embodied practice and contributes to their Personal Professional Capital. Because personal membership inevitably results in involvement with the koinonia of specialist networks or communities (in Fig. 9.1, this is the intersection of 'personal membership' and 'koinonia'), they share a vicarious client group that gives them much more professional capital through their clients/or their representative user groups than they could ever achieve as individuals. Learning at this intersection is relational and allows the individual (student or qualified) access to the accumulated pool of knowledge from those clients. Depending upon the way the koinonia works, there may be a more or less accessible archive of client experience that is shared informally through such relational learning. Additional knowledge about (or from) clients may come from other professions/disciplines who relate directly to the community.

Moving round to the next dimension in Fig. 9.1, membership of the 'society' – the formal, regulatory aspect of the profession – is what gives the professionals direct access to their clients, since, for example, no nurse may treat a patient until s/he is formally licensed to do so. This formal access to clients is also regularised, constrained or augmented by the influence of a range of other stakeholders (for example, doctors, managers or politicians). Individual members of the community must formally engage in the community's espoused learning, mediated, for example, through curricula that delineate the theoretical strategies for interacting with clients. However, much of the formal learning overlaps with, and is mediated by, koinonia, and it is in this intersection that the professional is accorded access to the shared repository of client memories and archives. These may be acquired through many different media, such as individual client stories, the representations of user groups and, increasingly, information from digital repositories and interactive media. This gives the member a far wider repertoire of client experiences than would otherwise be possible.

So far, this chapter has explored aspects of learning and development in professional practice, using nursing as an exemplar. In so doing, it has proposed a view of professional capital that is integrally related to the client, for without the client there can be no meaningful professional capital for nurses. Professional capital may be both visible and invisible to its members and their associated clients or lay community, but it is learned, maintained and developed by professionals through the social practices of their communities.

The Relationship between Community, CoP and Professional Capital

Sergiovanni (1998) in the context of US schools has suggested that CoP could be cultivated as a way to generate professional capital as 'a fabric of reciprocal responsibilities and support' (Sergiovanni, 1998, p. 40) for both the members (i.e. the teachers and the students) and the community institution (school) concerned. Sergiovanni emphasises the importance of communities, the leadership of the communities and the learning that occurs within them. These elements are connected through learning in close proximity to others within a physical and social environment that allows people to focus on matters of importance.

This view is of course transferable to health care and more specifically to nursing where the professional capital associated with nursing is linked not only to the individuals directly involved in care – the nurse and the patient – but also to the impact that good (or poor) nursing care can have on the organisation in which care is provided. In transferring Sergiovanni's model to the health care context, one may see that CoPs could enable nurses to ask questions and learn together and also care together so that they are able to construct professional capital that helps them (and their organisation) navigate through the complex world of nursing. We saw this illustrated, for example, in Vignette 1. However, as we also saw in that vignette, and as I have argued above, one does not necessarily need to invoke the concept of a Community of *Practice* (except perhaps as a local subset of the community of professionals) in order to envisage how that team of nurses was able to generate the necessary professional capital.

Lesser and Storck (2001) describe how organisations benefit from CoPs, which have been shown to improve performance through the sharing of knowledge, through bypassing structural barriers by operating outside formal structures, and through their contribution to organisational memory. The communities/teams outlined in Vignettes 1, 2 and 5 show how organisational memory can be developed (1), exist (2) and be invisible to the neophyte (5). We saw how the nurses gained, or had the potential to gain, from using their community as a resource for learning and achievement, but it was also clear that this relied on all the facets of the wider community that I have been discussing.

Leadership of a community involves the mobilisation of the members to face problems, solve them and maintain the espoused standards of both the immediate CoP and the broader community of professionals. Sergiovanni uses the term 'head follower' to reflect the leader's role and obligation with respect to the professional community's ideals, purposes and commitments. It is in this sense that – whether or not it is a CoP – a community of like-minded people functions as a moral community drawing on similar values and ideas and generating professional capital.

The reciprocal influence shared by other influential communities may include mutually acknowledged obligations, but this does not always occur – as in Vignette 4, where those obligations were neither clear nor shared between the relatives and the nurse.

Professional Capital and Learning in the Workplace Community

In this chapter I have argued that learning among professionals operating in groups in the workplace needs to take account of the way they generate, disseminate and acquire professional capital within their community of professionals. Situated learning theory proposed by Lave and Wenger (1991) and Wenger (1998) has contributed significantly to the conceptualisation of learning outside formal educational institutions. Like Fox (2000), Lesser and Storck (2001) and Boud and Middleton (2003), I recognise the value of situated learning, but also that it is not a sufficient explanation of informal workplace and/or organisational learning. This is because situated learning theory focuses largely on cognition, meaning and concepts of identity and does not place sufficient weight on the effects of others, the developmental stage of the practitioner; the moral person and moral community. These factors also influence the decision-making processes, judgements, actions and discretionary practices. Furthermore as we have seen in complex workplaces, there are overlapping communities and the distinction between team, group, CoP and broader communities of professionals may be fluid in the context of the 'here and now' and the needs of clients.

Boud and Middleton (2003) remind us that learning at work comprises a major component of learning undertaken by adults. Theories of how adults are thought to learn and the conditions that foster learning in professional practice include work on learning in and from experience, developmental theories, the role of the organisation itself, socialisation and andragogy. Knowles et al. (2005) summarise the core principles of andragogy, namely the importance of a learner's need to know, their tendency for self-directed learning, the role of prior experiences, the person's readiness to learn, their orientation to learning and problem solving and finally their motivation to learn. They conclude however that 'learning is a complex phenomenon that defies description by any one model' (p. 202).

Boud et al.'s (1993) analysis of learning through experience outlines five propositions that underpin their work, namely that:

- experience is the foundation of and the stimulation for learning;
- learners actively construct their experience;
- learning is a holistic process;
- learning is socially and culturally constructed; and
- learning is influenced by the socio-emotional context in which it occurs.

Certainly, the vignettes in this chapter support these propositions, but also perhaps suggest that they underplay the importance of communication devices in workplace learning, along with the more widely perceived obligations of the profession and the associated drivers of personhood and moral conviction. Within professional communities, learning is intrinsically related to the nature of the professional's experience as well as the demands of professional competence and the influencing factors of others. Echoing Billett (2002, p. 4), the vignettes support the view that the 'structuring of experiences in workplaces is often inherently pedagogical (i.e. educational) as they are directed towards the continuity of the practice through participant learning'.

The vignettes suggest that leadership, role modelling, embodied practice/knowledge and professional vision may also be significant influences on both individual and community development and learning. Professional practice demands learning practices that are client focused, embodied, holistic, reflexive and can occur with or without cognition but always involve 'doing now' or envisioning the 'doing next time'. What is evident is that the analysis of professional capital allows us to understand better how that learning is stimulated, enabled, structured, archived, recognised and retrieved in communities of professional practice. Not only client needs but also the needs of the profession dictate that workplace learning for both neophyte and expert will develop and be reflected in nurses' emergent professional capital.

References

Becker, A. L. (1991) A short essay on languaging. In: *Research and Reflexivity* (ed. F. Steier). Sage, London.

Billett, S. (2002) Critiquing workplace learning discourses: participation and continuity at work. *Studies in the Education of Adults*, 34(1), 56–67.

Boud, D. and Middleton, H. (2003) Learning from others at work: communities of practice and informal learning. *Journal of Workplace Learning*, 15(5), 194–202.

Boud, D., Cohen, R. and Walker, D. (1993) *Using Experience for Learning*. SRHE and Open University Press, Buckingham.

Bourdieu, P. (1990) *The Logic of Practice*. Polity Press, London.

Bradshaw, A. (1994) *Lighting the Lamp: The Spiritual Dimension of Nursing Care*. Scutari, London.

Brown, J. S. and Duguid, P. (1991) Organizational learning and communities-of-practice: toward a unified view of working, learning and innovation. *Organization Science*, 2(1), 40–57.

Carroll, L. (1929) *Alice's Adventures in Wonderland. Through the Looking Glass and Other Works*. Marshall Cavendish Partworks Ltd [1987 Edition], London.

Edwards, D. and Potter, J. (1992) *Discursive Psychology*. Sage, London.

Exley, B. (2001) Teachers' professional knowledge: tensions within the accounts of off shore instruction. In: *Designing Educational Research: Theories, Methods and Practices* (eds. P. Singh and E. McWilliam). Post Pressed, Flaxton.

Foucault, M. (1972) *The Archaeology of Knowledge* [translated by A. M. Sheridan Smith]. Routledge, London.

Foucault, M. (1973) *The Birth of the Clinician – Archaeology of Medical Perception* [translated by A. M. Sheridan Smith]. Routledge, London.

Fox, S. (2000) Communities of practice, Foucault and actor-network theory. *Journal of Management Studies*, 37(6), 853–67.

Gadamer, H. G. (1973) Concerning empty and full-filled time. In: *Martin Heidegger in Europe and America* (eds. E. G. Ballard and C. E. Scott). Martinus Nijhoff, The Hague.

Gadamer, H. G. (1993) *Truth and Method* [translated by J. Weinsheimer and D. G. Marshall]. Second Revised Edition of the 1975 original. Sheed and Ward, London.

Gobbi, M. (2005) Nursing practice as bricoleur activity: a concept explored. *Nursing Inquiry*, 12(2), 117–25.

Gobbi, M. (2009) Learning nursing in the workplace community: the generation of professional capital. In *Communities of Practice in Health and Social Care* (ed. le May, A.). Blackwell Publishing, Oxford, pp. 66–82.

Goldenberg, M. J. (2005) Evidence-based ethics? On evidence-based practice and the 'empirical turn' from normative bioethics. *BMC Medical Ethics*, 6(11), 2621–32.

Goode, W. J. (1957) Community within a community: the professions. *American Sociological Review*, 22(2), 194–200.

Goodwin, C. (1994) Professional vision. *American Anthropologist*, 96(3), 606–33.

Iyigun, M. F. and Owen, A. L. (1999) Entrepreneurs, professionals and growth. *Journal of Economic Growth*, 4, 213–32.

Kirkpatrick, F. G. (1991) Introduction. In: *Persons in Relation*, Vol. 2 (ed. J. Macmurray) of The Form of the Personal. [Re-issue of the 1961 Edition with a new introduction by Frank G. Kirkpatrick, 1991]. Humanities Press International, Atlantic Highlands, NJ.

Knowles, M. S., Holton, E. E., III and Swanson, R. A. (2005) *The Adult Learner*, 6th edn. Elsevier Butterworth-Heinmann, London.

Lave, J. and Wenger, E. (1991) *Situated Learning: Legitimate Peripheral Participation*. Cambridge University Press, Cambridge and New York, NY.

Leahey, E. (2006) *Specialisation and Integration in Publication and Patenting Activity*. Paper presented at the NSF sponsored workshop using Human Resource data from SRS to Study the S & E Workforce, Arlington, VA.

Lesser, E. and Storck, J. (2001) *Communities of Practice and Organizational Performance. IBM Systems Journal*, 40(4), 831–41.

Macmurray, J. (1961) *Persons in Relation*, Vol. 2 of The Form of the Personal. [Re-issue of the 1961 edition with a new introduction by Frank. G. Kirkpatrick, 1991]. Humanities Press International, Atlantic Highlands, NJ.

Malikail, J. (2003) Moral character: hexis, habitus and 'habit'. *An Internet Journal of Philosophy*, 7, 1–22.

McGregor, S. (2004) *Philosophical Well-Being*. Working Paper. Available at: http://www.kon.org/hswp/archive/philosophical.pdf (accessed 5 December 2007).

Nahapiet, J. and Ghoshal, S. (1998) Social capital, intellectual capital, and the organizational advantage. *The Academy of Management Review*, 23(2), 242–66.

Polanyi, M. (1958) *Personal Knowledge*. Routledge and Kegan Paul, London.

Polanyi, M. (1983) *The Tacit Dimension*. Peter Smith, Gloucester, MA.

Sergiovanni, T. J. (1998) Leadership as pedagogy, capital development and school effectiveness. *International Journal of Leadership in Education*, 1(1), 37–46.

Shotter, J. (1975) *Images of Man in Psychological Research*. Methuen and Co. Ltd, London.

Shotter, J. (1993) *Conversational Realities: Constructing Life through Language*. Sage, London.

Steier, R (1991) *Research and Reflexivity*. Sage, London.

Usher, R. (1992) Experience in adult education: a post-modern critique. *Journal of Philosophy of Education*, 1(2), 201–14.

Wenger, E. (1998) *Communities of Practice: Learning, Meaning and Identity*. New York: Cambridge University Press, reproduced with permission.

Chapter 10
Graduate Professional Education from a Community of Practice Perspective: The Role of Social and Technical Networking

Linda G. Polin

[...]

Introduction

This chapter describes academic life at the intersection of three related topics: community of practice (CoP), a pedagogical model; digital culture, as embodied in the current and future student population; and post-secondary education, in particular graduate professional education. The aim is to illustrate ways in which social computing applications enable the use of a CoP model in graduate professional education. The illustrations are drawn from two hybrid, or blended, degree programs (a mix of face-to-face and online interactions) at the graduate school of education and psychology at Pepperdine University. These fully accredited programs have each been in operation for more than a decade. One is the MA degree in educational technology, begun in 1998; the other is the EdD degree in educational technology leadership, begun in 1995.

The Changing Face of Graduate Professional Education

The most recent study of graduate education in the United States, conducted by the National Center of Educational Statistics (NCES), is now nearly a decade old. Trends first seen in those data are now part of the reality of graduate professional education (NCES, 1996). Ten years ago, it was clear that students in master's and doctoral programs in professions other than law and medicine are increasingly older, working adults, in midcareer. These are students with professional identities anchored in their local practice. In the field of education, these include teachers, principals, curriculum supervisors, librarians, technology coordinators, special education instructors, counsellors, museum staff, and corporate trainers. They come to graduate education seeking professional development beyond what is available to them on their own at their local work-place.

Source: Polin (2008).

C. Blackmore (ed.), *Social Learning Systems and Communities of Practice*,
DOI 10.1007/978-1-84996-133-2_10, © The Open University 2010.
Published in Association with Springer-Verlag London Limited.

Ironically, in the field of education site-based isolation is keenly felt. Most practicing teachers, administrators, or managers are not involved in vital, active, engaged, professional communities. They do not attend conferences outside their locale. They do not subscribe to and read professional journals in their field. For many, even access to colleagues at the workplace can be quite limited by incompatible schedules that allow rare, brief opportunities to engage on matters of substance. Yet historically, these same full-time workers will not find any greater opportunity to connect to the professional practice when they come to the university as part-time students or commuter students. These students will not be working on campus with faculty as part of an externally funded project. They will not be available to engage with peers and near-peers in the campus coffee house, to occupy teaching assistant or research assistant positions, to accompany faculty to project meetings, to hear guest speakers and consultants on campus.

Like the students they teach or the colleagues they train, these educators arrive at the university classroom to acquire knowledge in one formal context in order to transfer it to another practical context at a later time. This traditional model of instruction in higher education has been, and largely remains, a model of learning as the acquisition of knowledge, transmitted from the faculty expert to the student novice, with the aid of text and, sometimes, audiovisual media.

New Ideas About Learning

Over the past 2 decades, learning theory itself has evolved as researchers have sought to understand the failure of cognitive transfer to deliver on its promise (Brown et al., 1989; Resnick, 1991). From studies of learning in informal settings (González et al., 2005) learning on-the-job (Hutchins and Klausen, 1998), in practitioner communities (Suchman and Trigg, 1996), and in everyday life (Lave et al., 1984), researchers from anthropology, sociology, sociolinguistics, psychology, and communication, have identified social engagement around shared work as a powerful mechanism for supporting learning. This research work has combined with Russian psychology to form a family of social learning theories (Cole and Engestrom, 1993; Lave and Wenger, 1991; Vygotsky, 1978). These are known variously as situated learning, cognitive apprenticeship, distributed cognition, activity theory, sociocultural historical theory, and communities of practice (CoPs). The first three focus on the scaffolding power of situativity, of experiencing learning in the context of its use. Available artifacts, peers and near-peers contribute to and shape the learning process (Lave et al., 1984). Activity theory, sociocultural historical theory, and the CoPs model move beyond the emphasis on context to consideration of social and historical influences as critical mediators of the learning process. For these social learning models, learning is viewed as a kind of enculturation of the individual into a system of practice. The additional benefit from these broader views of context is derived from the recognition that most impediments and challenges to learning tend to arise from the sociopolitical and cultural-historical roots of practice and practitioners. Though there are clear differences among variations of social learning theories, they share a powerful central premise: that learning is most readily accomplished through engagement with more knowledgeable other people and with objects in authentic practical settings.

One model in particular is appealing for its attention to both the individual learner and the larger context in which the learning takes place. That is, it offers an explanation of how the practice evolves, as well as how individuals develop and change within that practice. This CoP model describes learning as the transformation or development of the individual, as evident in his or her changing identity and practice. First proposed by Lave and Wenger (1991) as an analytic model for understanding how people learn in context, it has since become widely popular as a theory of learning. There are many interpretations and extensions of the original notion. These are extensively discussed elsewhere (Riel and Polin, 2004).

Two key notions are community and practice. In a CoP, the community can be defined as a group of people:

> whose identities are defined in large part by the roles they play and relationships they share in that group activity. The community derives its cohesion from the joint construction of a culture of daily life built upon behavioral norms, routines, and rules, and from a sense of shared purpose. Community activity also precipitates shared artifacts and ideas that support group activity and individual sense-making. A community can be multigenerational; that is, it can exist over time in the comings and goings of individuals. In short, a community differs from a mere collection of people by the strength and depth of the culture it is able to establish and which in turn supports group activity and cohesion (Riel and Polin, 2004, p. 18).

As used in the CoP model, practice refers, not to repetitive behaviours intended to increase memory, but to a body of practical knowledge used to accomplish work, that is, a domain or field of expertise.

Within a cultural framework, the CoP model describes ways in which the socio-cultural structures of a community mediate the development of the individual, from an initial novice state of limited participation to a fully developed identity of deeper participation. In addition to describing the development of the individual, the CoP model describes how practice communities also evolve or advance the practice itself, by continually accruing new members, tools, and experiences that inform and influence practice, and the body of knowledge upon which it relies.

Relocating Graduate Education in a Professional Practice Community

In this chapter, the central design application of the CoP model is in the re-conceptualisation or revitalisation of the practice of graduate programs in the field of education. The enterprise must recognise the larger profession of education as the central practice, to include research and development activities, as well as classroom teaching. In research universities, this is less of an issue, because these activities and identities are visible and available for full-time graduate students. For universities less centrally involved in research, with part-time students or commuting students, this requires a shift in practice. Graduate students must then be seen as coming to university to deepen their participation in the profession of education, not of schooling, and the design of their experience there must reflect that definition of the practice.

Historically, graduate students have come to the university as a continuation of their participation in the practice of schooling. They come as students. This is a practice though, at which they are already quite adept, as demonstrated by their participation at the highest level, that is, graduate school. They bring to campus a set of long-held notions of what it means to be a student, a set of expectations about what will happen in their classrooms, what their role will be, and what sort of participation structures will be there for them to engage. They behave as students, and traditionally, faculty members behave as teachers. This constrains graduate education within a practice of schooling.

If they were studying engineering, medicine or law, the discontinuity between their graduate school experience and their practical identity might be more evident, though in those professions, graduate education typically makes use of field experiences and real world cases as curricular material. However, since education students are educators in real life, the familiarity of roles, relationships and activities in traditional graduate education classrooms obscures the problem. Just as they find in their own settings, here at graduate school the practice relies upon an acquisition and transfer view of learning as the collection and storage of knowledge outside the context of its intended use.

The Special Problem of Education as a Practice

The practice of education is a varied one, ranging from the schooling of young children, to the professional development of working adults, to the science of research and theory development. Historically, though, this has not been a well-integrated community. There continues to be a perceived division of labour in which the university is the source of theory and basic knowledge, and the field is the location of practice and practitioners (Simon, 1992). With their own lived experience denied and marginalised in the face of formal theory, teachers, and other 'real world' educators who come to graduate classes are often faced with the choice of rejecting their own experiential knowledge or rejecting what they hear in class.

Ironically, this tension between worlds and identities represents the potential power of graduate education to be a transformative experience for the student. To do so, graduate professional education must open up its discourse to include the language of local, albeit limited, practice. Conversely, when welcomed in to the larger professional culture, students must be willing to problematise or question their own practical beliefs. When graduate education is reconceptualised as supporting engagement in a CoP, the discourse is recontextualised from a classroom transmission and transfer discourse to a discourse of collegial collaboration and negotiation around authentic work. Here, a social learning model can thrive as members of the same professional community, with differing expertise, engage in real world work.

Getting to Community of Practice

There are many cultural historical barriers that make it difficult to shift from a transmission conception of university learning to a socially constructed one. To begin with, students come to the university; the university does not come to them. The very locations in which groups meet to learn, structure particular participation opportunities and identities in the room. Rooms are designed to place the instructor at the front, behind a buffering piece of furniture. Learners sit in undifferentiated rows rarely in the same place twice. More critically, there is no enduring presence between class sessions; no place for shared or exchanged materials and artefacts to remain located in the room, and little opportunity for engagement outside the time parameters of the class.

University instructors' classroom activity is generally not representative of their expert practical activity; they do not talk in ways and about subjects they would with colleagues. They are behaving as teachers, working to convey a curriculum, talking about practice, not from within it. Education faculty members know their identity includes an active connection with professional organisations and with the peer reviewed journals and conferences those organisations sponsor. They know it means connecting with peers on projects and engaging in intellectual discussion of new and emerging ideas in the field. If instructors carried this identity into their classrooms, it would surely affect the nature of their engagement with the students they find there.

In our own graduate programs, we have reconceptualised our classroom teaching identities to more fully integrate with our professional identities in our field. That is, we take our role in the courses we teach as helping students experience, as much as possible in their novice condition, what it means to be, to know, in our field. Thus, the reason to study a particular curriculum is because in this domain, the professional community relies on this knowledge in this field, and to practice in the profession is to know and make use of these ideas. So too, we faculty members and our students must not only know about and talk about but know from use and talk from within real practice (Lave and Wenger, 1991).

Historically, this is more readily accomplished on campus with full-time graduate students. On campus, opportunities exist for graduate students to engage with faculty and outside experts through teaching and research assistantships, through attendance at guest lectures, and brown bag lunch discussions, and simply from hanging about in the hallways and coffee house frequented by faculty, postdocs, and fellows. In American graduate education, however, this tradition is at risk as an increasing proportion of graduate students are unable or unwilling to give up frill-time work to pursue their advanced degrees.

This trend is exacerbated, potentially, when graduate education moves online to accommodate students' need for flexibility. Such a move might seem to create an even broader divide between students and faculty, field and university. However, in online programs, few if any, preexisting traditional university structures exist. This grants us the freedom to construct structures that support different ways of participating and different roles to occupy (Polin, 2003). As will be seen later in this chapter, Web-based applications for supporting a CoP model of formal education are there for us to embrace. In some ways, it is easier to make this conversion through emergent networking technology than with traditional course tools in a traditional course setting on campus. The rest of this chapter will examine how the CoP model and new tools of the Web support a reconceptualisation and redesign of graduate education in our two hybrid programs that combine online and face-to-face formats.

Technology and Communities of Practice

If we look to the tools that are available to help us in this new role, we find the very same tool sets with which a growing digital culture is equipping our current and future students: tools that support networking, collaboration, co-construction, and community access. It is perhaps a wonderful coincidence that learning theory and Web technology have entered an era in which social engagement and community connections are leading concepts.

In 1992–1993, the Internet evolved the application we all now know the World Wide Web. In 2010–2011, children born with the Web will be heading to college. Already there is plenty of evidence to suggest that this generation experiences inter-action and handles information differently from prior generations (Gee, 2003; Ito et al., 2005; Prensky, 2001; Tapscott, 1998). While they are not yet in our graduate college classes, their influence is already being felt as they appropriate and repur-pose the Web to support their reliance on social networking. Although the Web was and is clearly about networking, connecting, linking, it has been primarily about doing so for information transfer and commerce. Since the rise of peer-to-peer appli-cations, most notably first for music file swapping, Web-based social networking applications have increased to the point where, in 2004, O'Reilly Media coined the phrase Web 2.0 to reference a new generation of Web functionality.

Applications that have emerged as Web 2.0 tools focus on collaboration and shar-ing, co-production and social networking. Among the most widely used applications are those listed here, but many more come into being every day. It is a difficult list to keep up to date. Indeed, we have a found a critical role in our own local community is that of the academic 'geek' the faculty member and his or her IT (information technology) support muse, both of whom thrive on exploration and experimentation on the cutting edge of peer-to-peer applications. As of this writing, the application functions listed here are employed in various ways in our programs:

- Wikis for collaborative, mediated, content production (writing and other repre-sentations) and organisation by a practice community
- Blogs and phone blogs for shared journaling, with commentary by readers
- Social bookmarking and tagging for storing and sharing collections of web sites, many include a reputation management feature that allows people to rate items in a thumbs up or thumbs down fashion
- Social networking sites for connecting peers with similar interests or needs

- Voice communication software for real-time small group voice interaction; often with the capability for file sharing on the fly
- Visualisation tools for graphic display of networks or concepts or both
- File sharing sites, often with reputation management features that allow users to upload, view, and rate homemade productions
- Virtual worlds for real-time, multiuser interactions in persistent yet modifiable settings that exist even after any particular user logs off

The affordances of ground-up social and technical networking tools support a shift in graduate education towards a CoP model. Moving to a hybrid of face-to-face and online learning, we can use these and other web-based community-oriented applications to support interaction and access to knowledge networks; and put peer-to-peer, or peer-to-near-peer, or novice-to-expert connections within reach. These tools also explicitly represent notions of continual modification of content through participation, a crucial counterpoint to typical student perceptions of university knowledge as static, dated, and isolated.

Convergence: Social Computing, Social Learning and Graduate Education

On the threshold of this socially and technically networking world, in 1995, we created a new doctoral program as a hybrid program combining face-to-face and online engagement. We understood and sought to employ a social learning model in the design, but had no idea how radically our teaching and our conceptions of course content would change as we immersed a formal learning program into a networked world.

With limited university resources, we looked to the growing pool of shareware and freeware tools. These applications are built by small groups or individuals, and donated or very modestly priced. They are notable in this context for two reasons. First, these are almost always need-driven developments, built from the users' point of view. Second, products that fill a strong need develop a community of programmer-users who continue to donate time and energy to maintain, debug, and extend the application. Almost all the compelling and successful Web 2.0 applications come from this heritage. These tools, widgets, and applets, are all about making it easier for people to interact, to communicate, to work together, to share material, to co-create.

It is no surprise that when we looked to the Web as a place for teaching and learning, we found ourselves choosing these applications over more traditionally oriented commercial products, such as course management systems (CMSs). CMS packages were designed to be sold to large schooling enterprises, and as such, they were built to reify the existing practices of schooling: lecturing, turning in papers, testing, and grading. These are the functions at which these packages excelled. We knew we wished to move in a new direction, not to simply port an existing program onto the Internet. We knew we hoped to create new participation structures for faculty and students. We knew that software packages that merely echoed traditional classroom practices were not going to work for us. Thus, we needed to turn to different technologies to accomplish the supporting structures of a CoP for our students.

A Closer Look at Virtual Worlds

Initially we were one of the few online programs that made any use, let alone extensive use, of virtual worlds as chat environments in our classes. For us, these places came the closest to providing the 'campus coffee house atmosphere' we desired for our students, that is, a casual, informal location for real-time conversation. Several applications offer voice over Internet (VoIP) chat or written text chat as part of their larger course management system. We have found these programs reify the existing power and authority structure of the university, giving control to the instructor who can 'pass the microphone' or otherwise call on students who 'raise their hand' or queue up in a line for a turn to speak. Instead we use a Web application called Tapped In®, a self-contained, browser-based, real-time, multiuser, virtual chat world designed and maintained by SRI (Schlager et al., 2002). Tapped In® was developed with the CoP model in mind, initially to support teacher engagement around science and mathematics education.

> As an online crossroads, Tapped In® has been quite successful in achieving its original goals of bringing together and forging new relationships among education practitioners, providers, and researchers from around the world on a daily basis. Thousands of different people log in each month to engage in activities that include course and workshop sessions, group meetings, and public discussion spanning a wide range of K-12 topics. (Schlager et al., 2002, p. 121).

As of this writing, we have also begun using a graphical version of a virtual world, Second Life. We have an island in this virtual world, which serves many functions: collaborative space for graphical project work, class meeting space, and even clubhouse for our student chapters of national organisations. This puts important professional links in tangible proximity. The ACM student clubhouse, the MA degree students' course projects and the doctoral program's classes occupy adjacent physical spaces, and hopefully, suggest adjacent conceptual spaces as well.

This virtual world chat environment differs from the traditional bricks and mortar classroom in other important and productive ways. First, of course, it does not contain the usual signs, tools, and symbols that structure power and authority. There is no 'front' to the room that is held by the instructor. Anyone can speak at any time, without raising his or her hand to seek permission. Furthermore, the nature of chat as a 'real-time' experience constrains the length of each person's written utterance to a sentence or two (for chat is truly written speech and not prose). This means it is difficult and clearly inappropriate for one person to take over the conversation with long displays of text. This confounds the tendency to rely upon lecture. Chat is best used for quick exchanges and emergent topics, some of which will be pulled into the foreground of discussion by participants as they take up the topics, whilst others will be pushed to the background. Any topic that arises can still be taken up should the instructor or student choose to carry it over into the asynchronous discussion area.

Our virtual world chat environments have been used to support guest speakers, and even guest classes. Guests are able to join us across time and space, at little cost. We have had faculty members from other universities visit, with and without their students, during our class time; we have engaged with authors and researchers about their work. Our guests do not come to lecture or make formal presentations to the class. They come to engage in dialogue. Typically, students will have had a research report or article to read before hand, and the conversation will unfold around that document. Perhaps because they have a live author/researcher to engage with, students tend to ask questions about the process rather than the content of what they have read. Why did the researcher make use of this instrument? Why do they think the study came out the way it did? These sorts of engagements are more powerful than typical guest speaker appearances because the constraints of the technology push the engagement into dialogue, and the visitors and students are talking from within an experience of the practice, not about it.

However, the very features that liberate the dialogue can also result in chaos. With a class of 20 students all talking at once, the result can be a mélange of topics, rapidly scrolling by in the text window. However, because we value these open expression of the chat environment, we have learned to manage the liabilities of the chat system. In our case, classes are partitioned into two sections, for purposes of the chat sessions. Each session is scheduled at a different time of day, depending on the time zone spread in the class.

Second, online chat classes tend to be very intense. Everyone is very focused. Talk in the chat room is, after all, written speech and is unconstrained by hand raising or passing the virtual microphone. Over the years of using chat environments with students in our master's and doctoral program, we have determined that the best duration for an online chat session is about an hour. At the end of an hour or so, students and their instructor are worn out. After an hour, the conversation tends to wander.

Third, we typically do not attempt to recreate the same class session in the morning and evening groups. We have found that it is much more useful to discuss related but separate topics, thus requiring students in one group to read the transcripts of the other.

The Expanding and Enduring Classroom

By moving instruction online, we are able to jettison many of the overt power structures and constraints of the university classroom, perhaps the most important of these is the time constraint of the course schedule. The lights never go off on the Internet. Students and instructors are never kicked out of the room to make way for the next class. In short, online class never ends, and like a normal collegial relationship, can extend in the wee hours of the night or the interstitial spaces in the workday. A powerful tool for supporting these extended relationships and engagements is the asynchronous, threaded discussion.

While chat is a wonderful tool for chat, the rapid fire and short bursts of 'talk' do not suit deeper discussion and thoughtful debate. For that, we rely upon asynchronous threaded discussions, also known as Web boards, forums, or group discussion spaces. Initially we employed an NNTP news server application of the sort that had historically been used on the Internet to support CoPs in such domains as wine tasting, feline diabetes, model train collection, home renovations, and skiing. When university concerns about security forced us into a commercial course management system, we balked at this instructor-centric reenactment of a knowledge transmission culture. However, we have found some ways bend the rules to suit our model. This includes, for instance, changing the status of all enrolled students in a class to 'teaching assistants,' thus giving them the power to modify content and menus, to initiate discussion forums and create group folders.

Threaded discussions do not in and of themselves transform didactic instruction into negotiated collaborations connecting practice experiences with expertise in theory. For that, we rely upon two pedagogical strategies. First, we make an explicit request for students to put words to their practical experiences and connect them with words from text and classroom conversation. Second, we do not ask students comprehension questions designed to see if they have done the readings. Instead, we ask them to co-construct and extend meaning.

A favourite instructional ploy requires students to select sections from course text, a quote that they like, resonate to, endorse or otherwise find compelling. They are asked to post that material, with page numbers, and then explain why they selected it. Likewise, they are asked to find a section of text they dislike, firmly disagree with, find confusing or otherwise irritating, and to post it, with page numbers, and an explanation. Students do this during the reading process, not after, to engage with the construction of meaning in the text, not just accept it on face value.

As they become adept at co-constructing meaning with peers, students are asked to anchor a selection of text with an example from the workplace, for an even more explicit effort to connect theory and practice. The example can raise questions when it does not conform to interpretations of the theory or models raised in the course, or it can serve as a case. Students are encouraged to use the formal language of theory to discuss their cases, thus also providing a space for trying out new language in a familiar context.

While our CMS does not include a reputation management system, which lets readers evaluate postings, we have borrowed and modified a clever strategy first heard from Dr. Sarah Haavind (personal communication, June 12, 2002). Periodically throughout their first semester, students are asked to find a posting made by a peer that helped them understand something or that otherwise moved the learning forward in the class. They must cite the selection and provide a justification for their choice. Then, they must find a posting they themselves have made, which they feel meets the same criteria. Again, they must cite and justify. This sort of activity directs students to see and to seek value in peer-to-peer conversation, as well as in text and teacher. It also opens up a discussion on what it means to engage in meaningful discussion on academic topics.

Access to Expertise and Generations

As the Web has evolved new technologies supporting community connections, we have embraced them. Most recently, podcasting has found its way into our online toolkit. Podcasting refers to the distribution of digital files in MP3 format, suitable for playback on an iPod or other MP3 player. The 'casting' part of podcasting refers to the distribution mechanism, a push technology called RSS 2. Listeners can subscribe to a podcast stream, which means new podcasts will be sent to them automatically.

Podcasting is not interactive. It is a broadcast medium, and when visual or written materials are also embedded, it makes a self-contained package of information, easily delivered and reviewed. Podcasting, when used to deliver lectures, does not offer any transformation of old style learning, of learning as transmission, a point lost on many faculty members. In a recent story in the *Los Angeles Times*, podcasting was severely criticised as the tool of student slackers (Silverstein, 2006). Professors found that podcasting lectures resulted in increased absenteeism in large lecture courses at universities. One instructor whose podcast lectures resulted in declining attendance responded by cutting back on her online offerings to force students to show up to get the material. At least one professor in the news article understood the absurdity and irony, and

> is working to enliven his lectures with material and interaction that students can't get on the audio or video 'coursecasts'; he wants to move to a Socratic teaching method and foster more discussion, while using technology to relay more of the basic information (p. 1).

The same story reports results of a UCLA survey of 142 schools taken in 2005, in which 43% of the respondents indicated that frequently they were bored and 58% had fallen asleep in class (Silverstein, 2006).

Web technologies such as podcasting and consumer appliances such as iPods are revealing the inherent weaknesses of old transmission style pedagogies. Why should a student show up in person just to listen to material that can be heard at a more convenient time and place? Frankly, why should the professor show up just to read her lecture? Does this mean there is no role for the podcast blast? No. It means the technology itself is not going to get you there.

My first homemade podcast was not to convey content, but to calm down a class of students that had worked itself up to near frenzy level about a large project coming due. I did not want to take up class time with one of those discussions in which students try to negotiate the assignment, but I did not want to let the innuendo and misconceptions slowly boil behind the scenes, between class sessions. Instead, I created a podcast offering a low-key, somewhat humorous explanation of project expectations. It did the job, and it did not take a lot of technical knowledge to accomplish.

My second podcast actually was focused on academics more than logistics: but not to convey a lecture. I wanted to offer students greater intellectual context for a very difficult text. Again, if I had taken class time, I would have felt compelled to limit my remarks due to time constraints. Via podcast, I was able to offer a bit of a history about the author, his academic lineage, his current work, and the role the book plays in a landscape of writing on the subject. I explained why I had selected the text and what my intentions were for them as readers. In this way I hoped to be able to not only help the students make meaning more easily, but also to connect them with a sense of the community of researchers pursuing this line of work. Later that semester we met with the author and one of his doctoral students through a video conference. They were both in England and my students were gathered for one of their occasional 5-day face-to-face sessions in Los Angeles. Interestingly, the most powerful part was the chance for the doctoral student to interact with another student nearing the completion of her dissertation process. She described her study, and thereby how she chose to use the theoretical model in a real world investigation.

The third podcast was not made by me. We require our students in both the master's and the doctoral program to attend a national conference as part of a course. The doctoral students were attending the American Educational Research Association meeting. I handed out six iPods, with microphone attachments, to student pairs, and asked them to interview speakers they heard and found interesting. They were responsible for determining their interview questions. Each night, they edited their podcast files and shared them through the RSS feed for the class. The MP3 file format of the audio recordings compresses the recording files and makes it fairly easy to distribute segments as long as 20 minutes.

The iPods in the third example functioned merely as a tool that enabled the students to negotiate access to researchers and other presenters at a national conference on education. The need to edit down the recordings required students to make choices about what was valuable to hear and what could be cut. The opportunity to share podcasts meant that everyone received more connection to the community as a group than they could have accomplished alone. The ability to archive these for future students meant that this participatory network would live and grow.

Reification and Participation: Blogs, Wikis, and LISTSERVS

A healthy CoP is a dynamic group. Even as expert practitioners ply their profession, the community and its practice are open to newcomers and journeymen, and to the new ideas and tools they bring in to the community by virtue of their co-membership in other communities. For instance, I am the mother of a 12 year old, as well as being a researcher interested in digital culture. From my 12 year old, I learn a lot about handheld gaming and game devices. That knowledge is with me when I am being the researcher, and I am likely to introduce it into the practice community. Because my 12 year old is a girl, I also bring an awareness of gender issues in technology to my work.

In a healthy community, the practice, the knowledge base and the tool sets are all open to influence and change from the co-memberships or concurrent identities that members bring to the community through new ideas, tools and artefacts. In this way, the practice can continue to evolve and not become brittle and cultish. However, where there is expertise and change, that change may be perceived as challenge. As community members participate and introduce changes into the practice, they are essentially challenging the acknowledged expertise. Lave and Wenger (1991) described this as a tension between reification (i.e., the freezing of knowledge in a concrete artefact) and participation (i.e., the variation of knowledge that arises in practice from the participation of diverse people). This tension can be a vitalising mechanism for communities. After all, there must be some solid core of domain knowledge that is captured and stable enough to be shared, but there must also be a dynamism that allows that knowledge base to continue to update, develop, and innovate.

Students of all ages tend to find school a place of frozen knowledge manifested in a predetermined curriculum of competence. Educational practitioners in schools experience the stress of new ideas that challenge their role and core knowledge, their very practice. They are not comfortable with the notion of an evolving practice, and yet, that is exactly what the practice is in the research arm of the community, to continue to evolve the practice through developing knowledge. For university faculty members, expertise is not static. New knowledge is constantly produced in the field, as evident in the never-ending parade of research grants and peer-reviewed publication. Clearly the fields in which university faculty claim expertise are continually evolving.

It would be very powerful for novice graduate students to have access to that tension, to see the mechanism of knowledge emergence, to hear the controversy and contention, to understand this tension as healthy and productive, and to learn to participate in it. Faculty see this in their professional lives; some suffer through it personally, for example, trying to publish qualitative work in peer-reviewed journals when ethnography was still an oddity. How can graduate students gain access to these experiences?

Many communities within the broad landscape of education run LISTSERVS, that is, subscription e-mail. Much like the threaded discussion LISTSERVS allow people to post and comment on postings via e-mail membership group. For instance, I am a member of LISTSERVS on information technology (ITforum), on communities of practice (com-prac) action research (PARnet) and a few others. In one of my courses, I require my doctoral students to join and lurk on the XMCA LISTSERV, which created in support of the *Mind, Culture and Activity* journal. The core group on this LISTSERV is comprised of experts and near-experts in activity theory, and yet a lot of the discussion that passes through that list focuses on disagreements, refinements, new ideas or extensions of theory, research paradigms, tools, and settings for theory in practice. There been semesters in which the postings in XMCA have served as a text for my course.

Often a LISTSERV community will decide to discuss a member's paper, or will select a paper from the current issue of a journal to discuss. Members will post questions and share resources. Sometimes discussion reveals the larger sociopolitical context of the topic from the point of view of the various countries in which members reside. They also announce postdoctoral openings, upcoming conferences, and related content from fields of inquiry in which they are also members. In short, this is a rich and vibrant nexus of practitioners and it is very accessible to students through their mere participation in the LISTSERV group.

LISTSERVS are not the only venue where students can participate peripherally in the dance of participation/reification. The venerable institution of peer-reviewed publication is becoming a more open process thanks in large part to the lure of online community publication and dialogue through reputation management applications. In a recent *Wired* article, Rogers (2006) describes a growing phenomenon altering the traditional process of peer review of academic publication. After describing the process, the time frame, and the errors in the current system, he describes several rigorous, peer-review processes in the scientific community that happen to be mediated on the Web by virtue of Web 2.0 applications such as Wikis, which allow commentary on posted articles. He concludes:

> An up-and-coming researcher can get more attention from the right experts by publishing something earthshaking on arXiv than by pushing it through the usual channels. Crazy ideas will get batted around in moderated forums, which is pretty much what the Internet is for. Eventually, printed journal articles will be quaint artifacts. Scientific papers will be living documents with data published on Web pages – commented on, linked to, and mirrored by labs doing the same work 6,000 miles away. Every research effort will have thousands of reviewers working in real time. Today's undergrads have never thought about the world any differently – they've never functioned without IM and Wikipedia and arXiv, and they're going to demand different kinds of review for different kinds of papers (pp. 30–32).

While his enthusiasm might be forgiven for being a bit excessive, he does make the point that new technologies are challenging the practices of venerable old communities in academe. Most importantly, they are opening up access to the community of practice in ways from which our novice graduate students can greatly benefit.

Future Trends

Current graduate students are not the group most au fait with Web 2.0. Often they are not particularly fluent with the Web at all. Recent data from the Pew Foundation's continuing study of the Internet and American life makes it clear that as of 2006 the actively peer-to-peer digital group is the 18–26 years olds (Lenhart et al., 2005). However, it also indicates that the Web-born, the preteens, those heading to college in 2010–2011, may well be the tipping point. These groups bring a sentiment, a culture, of production, and coproduction, of networking and collaboration. As faculty rethink programs and their own roles in those programs as brokers to a broader practice community, the upcoming students will be there to take advantage of the opportunities, ready with peer-review sensibilities from reputation management experiences; ready with publication and commentary as community norms; ready with the understanding of social capital through networking. It should be a very exciting time for us all and we must be ready to engage with them in these ways, or lose them to alternative educational enterprises that do understand learning as a social, situated, heterogeneous, collaborative, cultural experience, such as corporate universities and for-profit, private, start-up institutions (Meister, 1988; Schank, 2005).

Summary

This chapter has offered a perspective on graduate professional education as an activity arising in a community of professional practice. It has suggested the role of technical networks and tools in supporting social networks, and anchored those ideas with illustrations from current practices in two graduate programs offered as hybrids of online and face-to-face settings. However, these practices and the tools that support them will continue to evolve. The CoP model as a design touchstone helps us make reasoned choices that can be both strategic and innovative.

References

Brown, J. S., Collins, A., and Duguid, P. (1989). 'Situated cognition and the culture of learning.' *Educational Researcher*, 18(1), 32–42.

Cole, M. and Engestrom, Y. (1993). 'A cultural-historical approach to distributed cognition.' In G. Salomon (Ed.), *Distributed cognitions: Psychological and educational considerations* (pp. 1–46). London: Cambridge University Press.

Gee, J. (2003). *What video games have to teach us about learning and literacy*. New York, NY: Palgrave MacMillan.

González, N., Moll, L. C., Tenery, M., Rivera, A., Rendon, P., Gonzales, R., et al. (2005). 'Funds of knowledge for teaching in Latino households.' In N. Gonzales, L. C. Moll, and C. Amanti (Eds.), *Funds of knowledge: Theorizing practices in households, communities, and classrooms* (pp. 89–111). Mahwah, NJ: LEA.

Hutchins, E. and Klausen, T (1998). 'Distributed cognition in an airline cockpit.' In Y. Engestrom and D. Middleton (Eds.), *Cognition and communication at work* (pp. 15–34). London: Cambridge University Press.

Ito, M., Okabe, D., and Matsuda, M. (2005). *Personal, portable, pedestrian: Mobile phones in Japanese life*. Cambridge, MA: MIT Press.

Lave, J. and Wenger, E. (1991). *Situated learning: Legitimate peripheral participation*. New York, NY: Cambridge University Press.

Lave, J., Murtaugh, M., and de la Rocha, O. (1984). 'The dialectic of arithmetic in grocery shopping.' In B. Rogoff and J. Lave (Eds.), *Everyday cognition: Its development in social context* (pp. 67–94). Cambridge, MA: Harvard University Press.

Lenhart, A., Madden, M., and Hitlin, P. (2005). *Teens and technology: Youth are leading the transition to a fully wired and mobile nation*. Washington, DC: Pew Foundation, Internet and American Life.

Meister, J. (1988). *Corporate universities: Lessons in building a world-class work force*. New York, NY: McGraw Hill.

National Center of Educational Statistics. (1996). *Graduate and first-professional students. National postsecondary student aid study*. Washington, DC: U.S. Department of Education, Office of Educational Research and Improvement.

Polin, L. (2003). 'Learning in dialogue with a practicing community.' In T. Dully and J. Kirkley (Eds.), *Learner centered theory and practice in distance education* (p. 18). Mahwah, NJ: LEA.

Polin, L. (2008). 'Graduate professional education from a community of practice perspective: The role of social and technical networking.' In C. Kimble, P. Hildreth, and I. Bourdon (Eds.), *Creating learning environments for educators* (Vol. 2, pp. 267–285) Charlotte, NC: Information Age Publishing, Inc.

Prensky, M. (2001). *Digital game-based learning*. New York, NY: McGraw-Hill.

Resnick, L. (1991). 'Shared cognition: Thinking as social practice.' In L. Resnick, J. Levine, and S. Teasley (Eds.), *Perspectives on socially shared cognition* (pp. 1–22). Washington, DC: American Psychological Association.

Riel, M. and Polin, L. (2004). 'Online learning communities: Common ground and critical differences in designing technical environments.' In S. Barab, R. Kling, and J. H. Gray (Eds.), *Designing for virtual communities in the service of learning*. London: Cambridge University Press.

Rogers, A. (2006). 'Get Wiki with it: Peer review – the unsung hero and convenient villain of science gets a makeover.' *Wired*, 14(9), 30, 32.

Schank, R. (2005). *Lessons in learning, e-learning, and training*. Alexandria, VA: Pfeiffer.

Schlager, M., Fusco, J., and Schank, P. (2002). 'Evolution of an online community of education professions.' In K. A. Renninger and W. Shumar (Eds.), *Building virtual communities: Learning and change in cyberspace* (pp. 129–158). London: Cambridge University Press.

Silverstein, S. (2006, January 17). 'The iPod took my seat.' *Los Angeles Times*, (p. 1).

Simon, R. (1992). *Teaching against the grain*. Westport, CN: Bergin & Garvey.

Suchman, L. and Trigg, R. (1996). 'Artificial intelligence as craftwork.' In S. Chaiklin and J. Lave (Eds.), *Understanding practice: Perspectives on activity and context* (pp. 144–178). New York, NY: Cambridge University Press.

Tapscott, D. (1998). *Growing up digital: The rise of the net generation*. San Francisco, CA: McGraw-Hill.

Vygotsky, L. S. (1978). *Mind in society: The development of higher psychological processes*. Cambridge, MA: Harvard University Press.

Chapter 11
Communities of Practice and Social Learning Systems: the Career of a Concept

Etienne Wenger

The concept of community of practice was not born in the systems theory tradition. It has its roots in attempts to develop accounts of the social nature of human learning inspired by anthropology and social theory (Lave, 1988; Bourdieu, 1977; Giddens, 1984; Foucault, 1980; Vygotsky, 1978). But the concept of community of practice is well aligned with the perspective of systems traditions. A community of practice itself can be viewed as a simple social system. And a complex social system can be viewed as constituted by interrelated communities of practice. In this essay I first explore the systemic nature of the concept at these two levels. Then I use this foundation to look at the applications of the concept, some of its main critiques, and its potential for developing a social discipline of learning.

The concept of community of practice does not exist by itself. It is part of a broader conceptual framework for thinking about learning in its social dimensions.[1] It is a perspective that locates learning, not in the head or outside it, but in the relationship between the person and the world, which for human beings is a social person in a social world. In this relation of participation, the social and the individual constitute each other. When I refer to 'the theory' in what follows, I refer to this version of social learning theory.

A Social Systems View on Learning: Communities of Practice *as* Social Learning Systems

A community of practice can be viewed as a social learning system. Arising out of learning, it exhibits many characteristics of systems more generally: emergent structure, complex relationships, self-organisation, dynamic boundaries, ongoing

---

[1] Note that there are other dimensions of learning – biological, psychological, cognitive, as well as historical and political in the broad societal sense. The theory does not explicitly address these aspects, though it is, I hope, compatible with theories that do. It needs to be combined in a plug-and play fashion with theories that address these other dimensions to explain specific situations where they are salient.

C. Blackmore (ed.), *Social Learning Systems and Communities of Practice*, 179
DOI 10.1007/978-1-84996-133-2_11, © The Open University 2010.
Published in Association with Springer-Verlag London Limited.

negotiation of identity and cultural meaning, to mention a few. In a sense it is the simplest social unit that has the characteristics of a social learning system.

It is useful to start by looking at the assumptions about learning in communities of practice that give the concept such a 'systems flavour.'

Learning as the Production of Social Structure

Engagement in social contexts involves a dual process of meaning making.[2] On the one hand, we engage directly in activities, conversations, reflections, and other forms of personal *participation* in social life. On the other hand, we produce physical and conceptual artefacts – words, tools, concepts, methods, stories, documents, links to resources, and other forms of *reification* – that reflect our shared experience and around which we organise our participation. (Literally, reification means 'making into an object.'). Meaningful learning in social contexts requires both participation and reification to be in interplay. Artefacts without participation do not carry their own meaning; and participation without artefacts is fleeting, unanchored, and uncoordinated. But participation and reification are not locked into each other. At each moment of engagement in the world, we bring them together anew to negotiate and renegotiate the meaning of our experience. The process is dynamic and active. It is alive.

Participation and reification represent two intertwined but distinct lines of memory. Over time, their interplay creates a social history of learning, which combines individual and collective aspects. This history gives rise to a community as participants define a 'regime of competence,' a set of criteria and expectations by which they recognise membership. This competence includes

- Understanding what matters, what the enterprise of the community is, and how it gives rise to a perspective on the world
- Being able (and allowed) to engage productively with others in the community
- Using appropriately the repertoire of resources that the community has accumulated through its history of learning.

Over time, a history of learning becomes an informal and dynamic social structure among the participants, and this is what a community of practice is.

Through active and dynamic negotiation of meaning, practice is something that is produced over time by those who engage in it. In an inalienable sense, it is their production. Assuming that practice is an active production is not romanticising it. It is not to deny, for instance, that there are all sorts of constraints, impositions, and demands on the production of practice – external factors over which participants have little control. Nor is it to assume that the production of practice is always a positive process. Practitioners can be deluded or myopic. Subconscious forces can undermine the best intentions. A community of practice can be dysfunctional,

---

[2] For more in-depth discussion of this polarity, see Chapter 1 in Wenger (1998).

counterproductive, even harmful. Still there is a local logic to practice, an improvisational logic that reflects engagement and sense-making in action. Even if a practitioner follows a procedure, it is not the procedure that does the following. No matter how much external effort is made to shape, dictate, or mandate practice, in the end it reflects the meanings arrived at by those engaged in it. Even when they comply with external mandates, they produce a practice that reflects their own engagement with their situation. A practice has a life of its own. It cannot be subsumed by a design, an institution, or another practice such as management or research. When these structuring elements are present, practice is never simply their output or implementation: it is a response to them – based on active negotiation of meaning. It is in this sense that learning produces a social system and that a practice can be said to be the property of a community.

Learning as the Production of Identity

The focus on the social aspect of learning is not a displacement of the person. On the contrary, it is an emphasis on the person as a social participant, as a meaning-making entity for whom the social world is a resource for constituting an identity. This meaning-making person is not just a cognitive entity. It is a whole person, with a body, a heart, a brain, relationships, aspirations, all the aspects of human experience, all involved in the negotiation of meaning. The experience of the person in all these aspects is actively constituted, shaped, and interpreted through learning. Learning is not just acquiring skills and information; it is becoming a certain person – a knower in a context where what it means to know is negotiated with respect to the regime of competence of a community.

Participants have their own experience of practice. It may or may not reflect the regime of competence. Learning entails realignment. When a newcomer is entering a community, it is mostly the competence that is pulling the experience along, until the learner's experience reflects the competence of the community. Conversely, however, a new experience can also pull a community's competence along as when a member brings in some new element into the practice and has to negotiate whether the community will embrace this contribution as a new element of competence – or reject it. Have you ever come back from a conference with a great new insight or perspective? It can take quite a bit of work to convince your community to adopt it. Learning can be viewed as a process of realignment between socially defined competence and personal experience – whichever is leading the other. In both cases, each moment of learning is a *claim to competence*, which may or may not be embraced by the community.

This process can cause identification as well as dis-identification with the community. In this sense, identification involves modulation: one can identify more or less with a community, the need to belong to it, and therefore the need to be accountable to its regime of competence. Creating an experience of knowledgeability (or lack of knowledgeability) involves a lot of identity work. Through this process of identification and the modulation of it, the practice, the community, and one's relationship with it become part of one's identity. Thus identity reflects a complex relationship between the social and the personal. Learning is a social becoming.

The concept of identity is a central element of the theory, just as fundamental and essential as community of practice. It acts as a counterpart to the concept of community of practice. Without a central place for the concept of identity, the community would become 'overdeterminant' of what learning is possible or what learning takes place. The focus on identity creates a tension between competence and experience. It adds a dimension of dynamism and unpredictability to the production of practice as each member struggles to find a place in the community.

The focus on identity also adds a human dimension to the notion of practice. It is not just about techniques. When learning is becoming, when knowledge and knower are not separated, then the practice is also about enabling such becoming. Being able to interact with your manager is as much part of your practice as technical know-how. Gaining a competence entails becoming someone for whom the competence is a meaningful way of living in the world. It all happens together. The history of practice, the significance of what drives the community, the relationships that shape it, and the identities of members all provide resources for learning – for newcomers and oldtimers alike.

Of course, by the same token, these resources can become obstacles to learning. Learning, once successful, is prone to turning into its own enemy. The long beak that made a species successful can be its downfall if circumstances change. Communities of practice are not immune to such paradoxes. Remaining on a learning edge takes a delicate balancing act between honouring the history of the practice and shaking free from it. This is often only possible when communities interact with and explore other perspectives beyond their boundaries.

A Learning View on Social Systems: Communities of Practice *in* Social Learning Systems

Communities of practice are of course not isolated; they are part of broader social systems that involve other communities (as well as other structures such as projects, institutions, movements, or associations). So the social world includes myriad practices; and we live and learn across a multiplicity of practices.

It is useful to briefly review the conceptual tools that the theory offers to talk about learning as constituting both the emergence of such a system and the personal experience of it.

Learning as the Structuring of Systems: Landscapes of Practice

Learning as the production of practice creates boundaries, not because participants are trying to exclude others (though this can be the case) but because sharing a history of learning ends up distinguishing those who were involved from those who were not. They share an enterprise, an understanding of what matters, relationships, as well as the resources that their history has produced. Boundaries of practice are not geographical; and they are not necessarily visible or explicit. But if you have ever sat at lunch with a group of specialists engrossed in shoptalk, you know that a boundary of practice can be a very real experience. Because of the unavoidability of boundaries, there is an inherent locality to engagement and to practice.

As learning gives rise to a multiplicity of interrelated practices, it shapes the human world as a complex landscape of practices. Each community is engaged in the production of its own practice – in relation to the whole system, of course, but also through its own local negotiation of meaning. This process is therefore inherently diverse. The bounded character of the production of practice makes social systems dynamic and unpredictable. Such a perspective leads to a suspicion of uniformity in social systems. If a uniform pattern is observed across the landscape, the production of this uniformity needs to be understood in terms of local production and boundary interactions.

Our ability to know is shaped in such landscapes of practice. For instance, the body of knowledge of a profession is not merely a curriculum. It is a whole landscape of practices – involved not only in practicing the profession, but also in research, teaching, management, regulation, professional associations, and many other contexts, including contexts in which the clients of the practice develop their own views (e.g., patients' communities in medicine). The composition of such a landscape is dynamic as communities emerge, merge, split, compete, complement each other, and disappear. And the boundaries between the practices involved are not necessarily peaceful or collaborative. What researchers find, what regulators dictate, what management mandates, what clients expect, and what practitioners end up deciding, all these attempts to colonise moments of practice can be in conflict.

In such social systems, boundaries are interesting places. First they are an unavoidable outcome of any depth of knowledge requiring a shared history of learning. Without a shared history of learning, boundaries are places of potential misunderstanding arising from different enterprises, commitments, values, repertoires, and perspectives. In this sense, practices are like mini-cultures, and even common words and objects are not guaranteed to have continuity of meaning across a boundary. At the same time, boundaries can be as much a source of learning as the core of a practice. The meetings of perspectives can be rich in new insights and radical innovations. Still such new insights are not guaranteed, and the likelihood of irrelevance makes engagement at the boundaries a potential waste of time and effort. Indeed, competence in not well defined at boundaries. This means that the innovation potential is greater, but so is the risk of wasting time or getting lost.

In every practice, boundary processes require careful management of time and attention. Depth in any practice demands commitment, and time at the boundary can be seen as taking away from core engagement. Moreover, the very value of boundary processes depends on the depth of commitment to the practices involved. Local depth increases both the tension and the likelihood of interesting insights at boundaries. The qualities of practices and their boundaries are complementary aspects of learning. There is therefore a profound paradox as the heart of learning in a system of practices: the learning and innovative potential of the whole system lies in the coexistence of depth within practices and active boundaries across practices.

Modes of Identification

As we (and by extension our communities) negotiate our participation in broader systems, we need to make sense of both the system and our position in it. Doing so creates relationships of identification that can potentially extend across the whole system. It is useful to distinguish between different modes of identification[3] that position learning in the landscape:

- *Engagement*: This is the most immediate relation to a practice – engaging in activities, doing things, working alone or together, talking, using and producing artefacts. Engagement gives us direct experience of regimes of competence, whether this experience is one of competence or incompetence and whether we develop an identity of participation or non-participation.
- *Imagination*: As we engage with the world we are also constructing an image of the world that helps us understand how we belong or not. If you work as a social worker in a given city, you know that there are countless other social workers in other contexts and can use your imagination to create a picture of all these social workers and see yourself as one of them. We use such images of the world to locate and orient ourselves, to see ourselves from a different perspective, to reflect on our situation, and to explore new possibilities. The world provides us with many tools of imagination (e.g., language, stories, maps, visits, pictures, TV shows, role models, etc.). These images are essential to our interpretation of our participation in the social world. Imagination can create relations of identification that are as significant as those derived from engagement.[4]
- *Alignment*: Our engagement in practice is rarely effective without some degree of alignment with the context – making sure that activities are coordinated, that laws are followed, or that intentions are communicated. Note that the notion of alignment here is not merely compliance or passive acquiescence; it is not a one-way process of submitting to external authority or following a prescription. Rather it

---

[3] These modes were called 'modes of belonging' in Wenger (1998), but I now think that the term 'mode of identification' is more accurate.

[4] I use imagination here in the sense proposed by Benedict Anderson (1983) to describe nations as communities: it does not connote fantasy as opposed to factuality. Knowing that the earth is round and in orbit around the sun, for instance, is not a fantasy. Yet it does require a serious act of imagination. It requires constructing an image of the universe in which it makes sense to think of our standing on the ground as being these little stick figures on a ball flying through the skies. This is not necessarily an image that is easy to derive from just engaging in activity on the earth. Similarly, thinking of ourselves as member of a community such as a nation requires an act of imagination because we cannot engage with all our fellow citizens. But it is not less 'real' for involving an act of imagination. Benedict Anderson notes that people are ready to kill and die for their 'imagined' nations.

is a two-way process of coordinating perspectives, interpretations, actions, and contexts so that action has the effects we expect. Following directions or nego-tiating a plan are forms of alignment as are enlisting a colleague's collaboration or convincing a manager to change a policy. Whichever way they go, these pro-cesses of alignment give rise to relations of identification: applying the scientific method, abiding by a moral code, joining a strike, or recycling can all become very deep aspects of our identities.

All three modes function both inside practices and across boundaries. Engage-ment is typical of participation in the communities we belong to, but it can also be a way to explore a boundary if we can have enough access to the practice. Imagination functions inside a community as members make assumptions about each other and talk about their future, but it can also travel without limits and is a way to experi-ence identification way beyond our engagement. And a community's local regime of competence entails alignment, as do broader systems, such as setting the goal of an organisation or the laws of a country.

Identity in a Landscape of Practices

Learning can be viewed as a journey through landscapes of practices. Through engagement, but also imagination and alignment, our identities come to reflect the landscape in which we live and our experience of it. Identity itself becomes a system, as it were. From this perspective, identity includes the following characteristics:

- *Identity is a trajectory.* Over time, it reflects our journeying within some com-munities as well as transitions across communities. It incorporates the past and the future into the experience of the present. Over time it accumulates memo-ries, competencies, key formative events, stories, and relationships to people and places. It also provides directions, aspirations, and projected images of oneself that guide the shaping of the trajectory going forward.
- *Identity is a nexus of multimembership.* Identity also comes to reflect the mul-tiplicity of locations of identification that constitute it. Multimembership is sequential as we travel through the landscape and carry our identity across con-texts. It is also simultaneous as we belong to multiple communities at any given time. The experience of multimembership is thus inherent in the very notion of identity in a landscape. And so is the work of experiencing all these forms of identification at once and in one body – whether they merely coexist or whether they complement, enhance, or conflict with each other.
- *Identity is multi-scale.* Our identities are constituted at multiple levels of scale all at once. For instance, teachers can identify (or dis-identify) with the teachers in their school, district, region, discipline, country, and even with all teachers in the world. Identification is in some sense a scale-free process through which identity embraces multiple levels of scale. Resonance may be stronger at some levels than others; with some levels we may actively dis-identify. Nevertheless, through the

combination of engagement, imagination, and alignment many levels of scale do enter into the constitution of identity.

Through learning, the landscape shapes our experience of ourselves: practices, people, places, regimes of competence, communities, and boundaries become part of who we are. Identities become personalised reflections of the landscape of practices. Participation in social systems is not a context or an abstraction, but the constitutive texture of an experience of the self.

Knowledgeability as the Modulation of Accountability

The metaphor of a journey through a landscape suggests a variety of relationships to practices. Some we enter and some we leave behind. Some we only visit, merely catch a glimpse of, or ignore altogether. With some we identify strongly, with others lightly, and with many not at all.

The danger of the metaphor might be to suggest that these relationships are merely individual decisions. Some communities may welcome us, but others may reject us. In the course of our lives, we enter in contact with countless practices we have no competence in, and never will by choice or necessity. As characterised so far, identity is both collective and individual. It is shaped both inside-out and outside-in. Identification is both something we are actively engaged in negotiating and something others do to us. Sometimes the result is an experience of participation; sometimes of non-participation. Both types of experience shape our identities. We are constituted by what we are as well as by what we are not.

How we experience non-participation depends very much on our degree of identification with a practice. If you don't understand what your neurosurgeon friends are talking about, you don't go through an identity crisis. You may not even feel marginalised. You can just listen out of curiosity or daydream for a bit. You are not a neurosurgeon. You just know that a bit better now you have seen them in action. But you don't identify with that practice. Since your identity is not invested in it, you don't consider yourself accountable to its regime of competence.

The regime of competence of a community of practice translates into a regime of accountability – accountability to what the community is about, to its open issues and challenges, to the quality of relationships in the community, to the accumulated products of its history. When an academic community expects a doctoral student to contribute something new through a dissertation, it first expects that student to do a literature review. This is a way to honour the history of learning of that community. Becoming accountable to history also enables the student to discover the learning edge of the practice, the places where a contribution makes sense and is possible. It is this double accountability to the past and the future of the practice that equips the student to contribute to its evolution as a full participant.

This kind of in-depth accountability is hard work (not just for graduate students but for any practitioner, new or old). The willingness to do it depends on the degree of identification with the community and its enterprise. When one considers a whole landscape, the situation gets more complicated. Should a nurse be accountable to research, to management, to a curriculum, to regulation? To all of them? What about close colleagues? What about personal experience? This often depends on the situation. Does the regulation apply to this specific case? There is a sense in which a professional serving a client represents the whole landscape of practice for that person. In each moment of professional service, he or she has to resolve the question of where to be accountable. This is quite a dance of the self, especially where there are conflicts at boundaries in the landscape.

More generally, one way to conceptualise knowledgeability in landscapes of practice is to think of knowing as the modulation of identification among multiple sources of accountability.

As the world becomes more complex, there are an increasing number of locations in the landscape to which we may potentially need to become accountable. Should I follow that blog, read that scientific journal, follow that twitter stream, subscribe to that website, go to that conference, or join that community? Negotiating an identity of knowledgeability is becoming more complex.

The processes and the challenges of learning in a complexifying world become clearer if we conceptualise knowledgeability as a process of modulating identification across multiple locations of accountability. This involves a constant interplay between practices and identities. In a complex landscape, trajectories of practice and identity do not evolve in parallel. The two act as distinct but interdependent carriers of knowledgeability across time. Learning takes place when they dance.

Applications and Critiques

When my colleague Jean Lave and I coined the term 'community of practice' in the late 1980s, we could not have predicted the career the concept would have (Lave and Wenger, 1991). It has influenced theory and practice in a wide variety of fields in academe, business, government, education, health, and the civil sector. It is by now impossible to list all the applications of the concept, but it is useful to mention a few examples:

- In organisations in the private and public sectors, communities of practice have provided a vehicle for peer-to-peer learning among practitioners. It enables them to develop the portfolio of capabilities necessary for the organisation to achieve its mission. Communities of practice have always been there, of course. But having the concept makes the process discussable and then potentially more intentional.
- In education, communities of practice are increasingly used for professional development, but they also offer a fresh perspective on learning and education more generally. This is starting to influence new thinking about the role of educational institutions and the design of learning opportunities.
- In international development, cultivating horizontal communities of practice among local practitioners presents an attractive alternative to the traditional view of the vertical transmission of knowledge from north to south.

- In healthcare, communities of practice offer the potential of new learning partnerships that are not hostage to professional silos. The potential even extends to patients who are increasingly forming their own communities.
- New technologies, in particular the rise of social media, have triggered much interest in communities of practice. Indeed, these technologies are well aligned with the peer-to-peer learning processes typical of communities of practice.

Not everyone is happy with these developments. There have also been serious critiques of the concept, both from a theoretical standpoint in academic circles and among practitioners. These critiques are diverse, subtle, and complex. A just review and response would require a whole book. But at the risk of oversimplifying, it is useful to mention some of them here. And at the risk of sounding flippant, it is useful to sketch out my take on them. This is not to dismiss them, but on the contrary to acknowledge their validity and appreciate how their challenge can help sharpen the perspective.

A Powerless Concept: What about Power?

A common line of critique is that the concept of communities of practice, especially in its later formulations in my own work, does not place enough emphasis on issues of power. The term community here risks connoting harmony and homogeneity rather than disagreement and conflict, even though it is not the intention. The self-generating character attributed to communities of practice may seem to obscure the degree to which they are influenced and shaped by their context, be it institutional, political, or cultural. The formation of identity in practice may seem to make slight of broader discourses of identity, such as class, gender, and race. Versions of this critique have focused on institutional settings in capitalist modes of production (Contu and Willmott, 2003), use of language as a tool of power (Barton and Tusting, 2005), and propagation of influence in networks through which action is possible (Fox, 2000; Jewson, 2007).

It is true that the theory takes learning as its foundation and its focus, not power. It is a learning theory, not a political theory. Issues of power are part of that, however: they are inherent in a social perspective on learning. It is useful to review some of the concepts from the perspective of how they incorporate issues of power.

Economies of Meaning

When learning takes place in social systems such as communities of practice, issues of power are at the core of the perspective. The definition of the regime of accountability and of who gets to qualify as competent are questions of power. Every learning move is a claim to competence, which may or may not function – i.e. be considered legitimate by the community or change the criteria for competence that the community has developed. From this perspective, a community of practice can be viewed as an unstable equilibrium among a set of experiences, each with a more or less effective claim to the competence that defines the community. Learning and power imply each other.

The accountability and identification that form the basis for power in communities is horizontal, mutual, negotiated, often tacit and informal. But this does not mean that it is less effective than more visible form of power, such as vertical hierarchies. In particular there is nothing that says that communities of practice are egalitarian, at least not in any simple way, or harmonious. Conflict can be a central part of the practice. The very existence of a community means that there is a competence for learners to lay claim to, something common to struggle over, meanings to define and thus appropriate. In the language of the theory, a community of practice creates an *economy of meaning*.

Economies of meaning do not operate inside communities of practice only. The power dynamics of learning and community also takes place in a landscape of practices. Beyond a given community, successful claims to competence inherit the position of the community in the economy of meaning in which its practice exists as a claim to knowledge – again a claim that may or may not be accepted. Belonging to a community of engineers confers you the right to design bridges because your practice has a history of doing so (mostly) successfully. Great success among your fellow gang members, however, may not confer much legitimacy to your perspective in other contexts. And in fact, it may be counter-productive or even disempowering in other contexts. In other words, there is no guarantee that a successful claim to competence inside a community will translate into a claim to 'knowledge' beyond the community's boundaries.

Reification is a process by which power can be projected across the landscape. Institutions, laws, and designs are examples of such projection of power through reification. But institutions as reifications do not carry their own meaning. The theory would expect that they require participation. They are a design that acts as a boundary object among the multitude of practices that in some way contribute to sustain the institution. Power needs to run through the formation of communities and the production of practice.

In a landscape, all practices are practices. Management and research are as much practices as technical communities. All practices are local and no practice can subsume another because they are all produced by practitioners. But what they produce has different value in the 'market' of knowledge, where for historical reasons, some practices have developed a greater ability to influence the landscape (e.g., management, government), to colonise an area of the landscape (e.g., engineers having a history of building bridges that don't collapse), or to make people accountable to their competence (e.g., math as a core subject for all kids). In this historical sense, the concept of community of practice is not relativist. But it is political.

Power and Identity

The pairing of identity and community is an important component of the effectiveness of power. Identification with a community makes one accountable to its regime of competence and thus vulnerable to its power plays. In academic circles you can make people feel very defensive by asking them what they think of this or that esoteric theory or author. But this works only if there is identification. Short of the threat of violence, the efficacy of power depends on your degree of identification with communities and their practice. Without a notion of identification, it is very difficult to theorise power and its exercise. Even the threat of violence depends to some extent on identification. For instance, once identification with the fear of death is removed, exercise of power through violence becomes very problematic. This is one reason why groups that have overcome the fear of death, such as early Christians or some terrorists today, are such a puzzle for state powers.

Because identification is a source of nourishment for the self, modulating it can be difficult and painful. It can also be caught in conflicting demands that make it counterproductive. For instance, the anthropologist Gillian Evans (2006) has observed some kids dis-identifying with school-based accountability because of their accountability to other communities they belong to on the street. Their street life, family life, and school life create a need to modulate their identification across contexts – a complex equation of identity, which they can only solve by 'misbehaving' in school. But whether empowering or not, the modulation of identity is an aspect of power. It is the personal counterpart of a regime of competence. It is what makes such a regime effective or irrelevant as a source of accountability.

Power in Learning Theory

The concept of community of practice yields an inherently 'political' view of learning, where power and learning are always intertwined and indeed inseparable. The only glimmer of optimism that the theory affords in regard to power is that practice, even under circumstances of utter control and mandates, is the production of a community through participation. This local production implies a notion of agency in the negotiation of meaning, which even the most effective power cannot fully subsume. It is a small opening, a crack that represents a limitation to the application of power: the creation of a practice takes place in response to power, not as an outcome of it. Similarly the concept of modulation of identification locates relations of power in the active production of identity. Again it is a kind of theoretical crack in the concrete through which the negotiation of meaning allows for an experience of agency in learning.

Perhaps it is this insistence on learning as the negotiation of meaning, as a crack of agency in the concrete of social structure, that critics find overoptimistic. But this insistence is not incompatible with theories (and related data) that consider the reproduction of power structures writ large. All that is required for these theories to become consistent with communities of practice is that they run their claims through the lived experience of participation in practice. If class, gender, race, institutional roles, government systems and other axes of power become part of our identities, they do so through learning as the production of practice, identity and meaning. This places the reproduction of institutional structure in specific contexts of practice, as advocated by Paul Willis (1977) in his detailed ethnographic study of why working class boys get working class jobs. The reproduction of class is a lived story of learning and identity that is more complex than simply the reproduction of class. Or perhaps it is the story of the reproduction of class, viewed as learning. When theories run through each other in such a plug-and-play fashion, they can each contribute what they do best to the telling of the story.

An Anachronistic Concept: Is it History?

Another line of critique is that the concept is anachronistic. For some, this critique is theoretical: communities of practice are introduced in an ahistorical fashion, but in fact represent a learning process associated with craft production and cannot play a prominent role in learning in a different era. In particular, the fluid nature of modern work calls for more dynamic structures (Engestrom, 2007). It is true that the concept reflects an attempt to capture something fundamental about human learning, which should not merely be the reflection of specific moments in the organisation of work. On the contrary, the concept is meant to provide a learning foundation for anchoring history in social practice. At the same time, it is also true that what is fundamental about the notion of a community of practice will manifest differently as societal contexts evolve. Along these lines other critics are concerned that there is too much emphasis on community for an adequate account of learning in a web-enabled glob-alising world. They prefer to think in terms of networks (Brown and Duguid, 2000; Jewson, 2007). Networks seems more adapted to a world where learning needs and connections are becoming increasingly fluid; when the internet sends its tentacles across the globe, the notion of community seems almost quaint.

Again there is an important insight to this critique. Some of us have probably overemphasised community in our attempt to account for the directionality of learn-ing. But it is a mistake, I believe, to think of communities and networks as distinct structures. I am often asked what the difference is between a community and a network. Rather than contrasting a community here and a network there, I think it is more useful to think of community and network as two types of structuring processes. Community emphasises identity and network emphasises connectivity. The two usually coexist. Certainly communities of practice are networks in the sense that they involve connections among members; but there is also identification with a domain and commitment to a learning partnership, which are not necessarily present in a network.

More generally, I find it more productive to think of community and network as combined in the same social structures – but with more or less salience. So the question is not whether a given group is a network or a community, but how the two aspects coexist as structuring processes. This is not only a richer way to think about social structures, it also has useful practical implications. Network and community processes have complementary strengths and weaknesses; they are two avenues for enhancing the learning capability of a group. If a community becomes too much of a community, too strongly identified with itself, prone to groupthink, closed, or inbred, then fostering connectivity to generate some networking energy is a good way to shake it up and open its boundaries. There is something random and unpredictable about the dynamics of networking processes, which is a good counterpart to community. A twitter message sends a question into the connectivity of a network and it boomerangs back with a totally unexpected response, and a brand new person to follow. This is the magic of network. Conversely, if a network remains too fragmented, undefined, and individualised, then developing its identity as a community is a good way to give it shape – to endow it with an ability to project a collective intention and commit to a learning partnership. It is inspiring to discover others who share a concern and to let this joint caring become a bond of identity. This is the power of community.

A Co-opted Concept: On the Instrumental Slippery Slope?

Indicating as I just did that the perspective has practical implications leads to another line of critique, which has to do with the shift from an analytical concept to an instrumental one. Indeed, the concept of community of practice started out as an analytical concept, giving a name to a phenomenon that already existed. Now it is often used with an intention to create, cultivate, or capitalise on the process – almost as a technique. Some critics deplore the potential loss of analytical sharpness in this transition. The concept in its original formulation was used to distinguish practice from prescription (in particular educational, institutional, or managerial prescriptions), and to view learning as inherent in practice rather than reified in an educational setting. If it becomes a 'design intention' or a 'prescribed process' then it loses the very insights that made it useful (Vann and Bowker, 2001). Furthermore, instead of becoming sharper and more coherent over time the concept is becoming diluted and heterogeneous as various disconnected groups use it to suit their needs (Hughes, 2007).

I am quite sensitive to this line of critique, both because the critics assume that I had a key role in the transition and because I live in both worlds in my own work (Wenger et al., 2002). The dangers these critics warn against are real enough. The concept has been adopted and used in ways that are not always consistent with its origins and the diversity of adoption means that the concept is in some sense 'out of control.' It is true that many people are using the concept without much care for the broader framework or underlying principles. And admittedly, most organisations are interested in communities of practice to be more effective at what they already do, not for a more profound transformation. Nevertheless I find that the discourse about communities of practice is having an effect even if it is still at odds with the ways organisations function. Self-governance, voluntary participation, personal meaning, identity, boundary crossing, peer-to-peer connections, all these concepts are slowly reshaping the discourse on knowledge and learning. To see so many traditionally hierarchical organisations in so many contexts show genuine interest in fostering horizontal communities and networks may not be a revolution, but it does have a transformative potential for the future of learning.

Note that practitioners also have their own critique from the other side. They find the concept good in theory, but difficult to apply in practice. Communities of practice still do not fit very easily within traditional hierarchical organisation. Culti-vating communities of practice and creating an organisational context in which they can flourish is difficult within these organisations. Many 'designed' communities of practice fail or die early. The concern is that their informality and the difficulty to measure their value lets them fall through the cracks and lose priority. The word 'community' itself sometimes arouses suspicion of clubs or unfocused groups. A manager declared that a series of self-organised groups sounded too much like chaos. And it is indeed difficult to find the right balance between enough formality to give them legitimacy in the organisation and enough informality to let them be peer-oriented, self-governed learning partnerships.

I do not know whether the growing popularity of the concept will lead to its demise. Perhaps uninformed applications will generate too many failures, causing disappointment with the whole idea in practical settings. Maybe the fragmented adoption and redefinition of the concept will discourage academics from using it. The process has probably gone too far for people like me to have much effect. But for myself, I find the combination of analytical and instrumental perspectives par-ticularly productive. It is a tension, no doubt, but one that pushes both perspectives. Emerging from this tension, I see the beginning of a new discipline focused on the learning capability of social systems.

Towards a Social Discipline of Learning

Learning capability may be one of the most important characteristics to cultivate in social systems. But it is still an elusive aspiration. We need a social discipline of learning. Such a discipline builds what we have learned from the theoretical and practical work on communities of practice. It also incorporates perspectives such as the systems one outlined in this essay and it takes seriously critiques like the ones I have addressed. It derives its rigor from combining more systematically analytical and instrumental perspectives. It focuses on network as well as community pro-cesses. And it provides conceptual tools to address issues of power more directly. But it does all this from a social learning perspective, that is, with a primary focus on understanding and enhancing learning capability in social systems.[5]

Practice: Learning Partnerships

The concept of community of practice is a good place to start exploring a social dis-cipline of learning. From an analytical perspective, it is the simplest social learning system. From an instrumental perspective, a community of practice can be viewed as a learning partnership. Its learning capability is anchored in a mutual recognition as

---

[5] The following contains extracts from an essay I wrote on learning capability in social systems (Wenger, 2009).

potential learning partners. The discipline of such a partnership deepens and builds on this mutual engagement:

- *The discipline of domain*: What is our partnership about? Why should we care? Are we likely to be useful to each other? What is our learning agenda? What specific set of issues does it entail?
- *The discipline of community*: Who should be at the table so the partnership can make progress? What effects will their participation have on the trust and dynamics of the group? How do we manage the boundaries of the community?
- *The discipline of practice*: How can the practice become the curriculum? How can it be made visible and inspectable? What should participants do together to learn and benefit from the partnership?
- *The discipline of convening*: Who will take leadership in holding a social learning space for this partnership? How can we make sure that the partnership sustains a productive inquiry? Who are the external stakeholders and what are their roles? What resources are available to support the process?

Such a partnership may be collaborative and harmonious, or it may be tempestuous and full of conflicts. A learning partner is not someone who agrees with you or who even shares your background necessarily. It is someone with whom focusing on practice together creates high learning potential: 'I can see the practitioner in you from the concerns you express, from the way you behave, and from the stories you tell.' There is a kind of trust that arises out of this mutual recognition. It is not necessarily a personal kind of trust – that you would trust the other with your bank account – but it is a significant trust that participants will come from a place of experience and therefore make contributions that are very likely to be relevant to practice. It is trust in the learning capability of a partnership.

Learning Governance: Stewardship and Emergence

Cultivating learning capability gives rise to issues of governance. Learning in social systems requires decisions about what matters, about what counts as learning, about direction and priorities. To the extent that learning suggests doing something better, the definition of 'better' is a contestable terrain. Governance here refers to the process by which a social system becomes a learning system: it is learning that drives governance, not the other way round.

Governance oriented to social learning capability must reflect the complementary character of network and community structuring. On the one hand, our imagination gives us the ability to project what we care about, individually and collectively, into the future and across social spaces. On the other hand, our knowledge and our visions are limited. Each of us is just one node in a network. We need to respond to and embrace the unexpected as part of our learning. This suggests two types of governance processes that contribute to social learning capability:

- *Stewarding governance*. This type of governance derives from a concerted effort to move a social system in a given direction. Championing a cause or pushing an issue is a typical example. Stewarding governance is a process of seeking agreement and alignment across a social system in order to focus on definite concerns.
- *Emergent governance*. This type of governance bubbles up from a distributed system of interactions involving local decisions. Market mechanisms are the quintessential example of emergent governance in that they produce decisions like prices of goods that emerge out of many transactions. Similarly, aspects of learning capability emerge as the cumulative effect of local decisions negotiated and spread by participants.

Like network and community, emergent and stewarding forms of governance have complementary strengths and weaknesses in their effects on learning. It is the combination of the two that can maximise the learning capability of social systems.

Power: Vertical and Horizontal Accountability

Governance inevitably conjures up issues of power. It is useful to distinguish two forms of power, especially when one considers institutional contexts. Institutional structures tend to be based on what can be called *vertical* accountability through hierarchies. By contrast, the regime of accountability of a community of practice could be defined as *horizontal* in that it exists in mutual relationships among participants. Power works along these two axes of accountability:

- *Vertical accountability*, associated with traditional hierarchies, decisional authority, the management of resources, bureaucracies, policies and regulations, accounting, prescriptions, and audit inspections
- *Horizontal accountability*, associated with engagement in joint activities, negotiation of mutual relevance, standards of practice, peer recognition, identity and reputation, and commitment to collective learning

A common mistake in organisations is to assume that horizontal relationships lack accountability – and therefore that the only way to create accountability is to overlay vertical structures. Participation in a community of practice can give rise to very strong horizontal accountability among members through a mutual commitment to a learning partnership. Even a good conversation creates accountability, albeit of a temporal and tacit nature. Participants are held to an expectation of mutual relevance: they can't just go off into irrelevant topics or statements without violating such expectation. In its own ways, horizontal accountability is no less binding and operative than formal vertical accountability.

Another common mistake is to demonise vertical accountability and romanticise local engagement in practice. A self-governed community of practice is not heaven. It can reproduce all sorts of undesirable things, such as racism or corruption. It can be a place of collective mediocrity or contribute to systemically counterproductive patterns. When a system becomes too complex for negotiating governance issues directly, horizontal accountability is not always the best means of fostering systemic learning capability. It is useful to have certain things that are non-negotiable across a social system to limit the effects of local dysfunctions and myopia. Vertical accountability can help structure and simplify local engagement. We don't need to each decide at every moment on which side of the road to drive or whether it is a good idea to grab someone's wallet. Not everything has to be negotiable and decided anew every time. There is more productive use of our learning capability.

Vertical and horizontal accountability structures are very different in nature. Vertical accountability works across levels of scale. It tends to favour tools that travel easily across a landscape of practice. Numbers are a good example. Horizontal accountability tends to favour processes that focus on substance in the context of mutual negotiation. Conversations are a good example. In many organisations, vertical and horizontal accountability function almost completely separately. To foster learning capability at a system level, they need to be brought in interplay, even though they unavoidably remain in tension.

One of the difficult issues is that the two forms of accountability are not easily visible to each other. Imagine a vertical and a horizontal plane: the intersection between them is just a thin line. In one organisation, the person cultivating communities of practice had developed the practice of making the horizontal plane more visible in the vertical structure. From time to time, when someone was recognised as a valued contributor to a community, she would just send a letter to the manager of that person to let the manager know about what the subordinate had done, which the manager may not be aware of because it is not part of the job description. A letter like this is typical of what I call *transversality*: the ability to increase the visibility and integration between vertical and horizontal structures. One of the challenges of a social discipline of learning is to understand and develop *transversal* processes and roles.

Identity: Learning Citizenship

The final chapter of a social discipline of learning has to be about the person. If learning capability is a desirable characteristic of social systems, then attempting to contribute to this capability as much as we can is a personal responsibility that comes with social participation. Given our limited resources of time, attention, and memory, we have to make decisions about how we participate in landscapes of practice. This is going to affect learning capability – ours and that of the social systems in which we participate. The concept of *learning citizenship* refers to the ethics of how we invest our identities as we travel through the landscape. Examples of acts of learning citizenship include:

- Managing one's membership in existing communities: how do I contribute to communities I belong to or could belong to?

- Seeing a boundary to be bridged and becoming brokers using multimembership as a bridge across practices
- Being in a unique position to see the need for a community with the legitimacy to call it into being and becoming conveners
- Connecting someone, like a patient or a student, to a community that will enhance their learning capability
- Providing transversal connections in a context where vertical and horizontal accountability structures are disjointed

Learning citizenship is the personal side of a social discipline of learning. Its ethical dimension arises out of a recognition that each of us has a unique trajectory through the landscape of practices. This trajectory has created a unique point of view, a location with specific possibilities for enhancing the learning capability of our sphere of participation. From this perspective, our identity, and the unique perspective it carries, is our gift to the world.

The question of how we act as learning citizens is an appropriate way to end this review of the concept of community of practice from a systems perspective. What a career for a simple, intuitive concept with a systems flavour – to end up challenging us to see ourselves as the learning contribution we have to offer.

References

Anderson, B. (1983) *Imagined Communities*. London: Verso.

Barton, D. and Tusting, K. (2005) *Beyond Communities of Practice: Language, Power, and Social Context*. Cambridge: Cambridge University Press.

Brown, J.S. and Duguid, P. (2000) *The Social Life of Information*. Boston, MA: Harvard Business School Press.

Bourdieu, P. (1977) *Outline of a Theory of Practice*. Cambridge: Cambridge University Press.

Contu, A. and Willmott, H. (2003) Re-embedding situatedness: the importance of power relations in learning theory. *Organization Science*, 14(3), 283–297.

Engestrom, Y. (2007) From communities of practice to mycorrhizae. In Hughes, J., Jewson, N., and Unwin, L. (eds.), *Communities of Practice: Critical Perspectives*. London: Routledge.

Evans, G. (2006) *Educational Failure and Working Class White Children in Britain*. New York, NY; London: Macmillan Palgrave.

Foucault, M. (1980) *Power/Knowledge: Selected Interviews and Writings*. Gordon, C. (eds.). New York, NY: Pantheon.

Fox, S. (2000) Communities of practice, Foucault and actor network theory. *Journal of Management Studies*, 37(6), 853–867.

Giddens, A. (1984) *The Constitution of Society: Outline of the Theory of Structuration*. Berkeley, CA: University of California Press.

Hughes, J. (2007) Lost in translation: the journey from academic model to practitioner tool. In Hughes, J., Jewson, N., and Unwin, L. (eds.), *Communities of Practice: Critical Perspectives*. London: Routledge.

Jewson, N. (2007) Cultivating network analysis: rethinking the concept of "community" within communities of practice. In Hughes, J., Jewson, N., and Unwin, L. (eds.), *Communities of Practice: Critical Perspectives*. London: Routledge.

Lave, J. (1988) *Cognition in Practice: Mind, Mathematics, and Culture in Everyday Life*. Cambridge: Cambridge University Press.

Lave, J. and Wenger, E. (1991) *Situated Learning: Legitimate Peripheral Participation*. Cambridge: Cambridge University Press.

Vann, K. and Bowker, G. (2001) Instrumentalizing the truth of practice. *Social Epistemology*, 15(3), 247–262.

Vygotsky, L. (1978) *Mind in Society: Development of Higher Psychological Processes*. Cambridge MA: Harvard University Press.

Wenger, E. (1998) *Communities of Practice: Learning, Meaning, and Identity*. New York: Cambridge: University Press.

Wenger, E., McDermott, R., and Snyder, W. (2002) *Cultivating Communities of Practice: A Guide to Managing Knowledge*. Cambridge, MA: Harvard Business School Press.

Wenger, E. (2009) *Social learning capability: four essays on innovation and learning in social systems*. Social Innovation, Sociedade e Trabalho booklets, 12-separate supplement, MTSS/GEP & EQUAL. Portugal, Lisbon.

Willis, P. (1977) *Learning to Labour: How Working Class Kids Get Working-Class Jobs*. New York, NY: Columbia University Press.

Part IV
Synthesis

This final part of the book comprises just one chapter, written by Chris Blackmore, the editor of this book. This chapter is a synthesis of the main points made in all the chapters of the book by all the authors. First the context of 'managing systemic change' and the relevance of social learning systems and communities of practice for that purpose are considered. This is partly because this book is intended to contribute to an Open University course with that focus. A range of distinctions made by authors concerning social learning and social learning systems is next discussed. Fourteen common themes are identified across the book as a whole. These themes are elaborated in a process of mapping *a landscape of social learning systems praxis*, drawing on Etienne Wenger's metaphor of a landscape of practice, (which is explained in Chapters 8 and 11). The chapter ends with a brief reflection on potential roles for social learning systems and communities of practice in addressing future challenges.

Chapter 12
Managing Systemic Change: Future Roles for Social Learning Systems and Communities of Practice?

Chris Blackmore

Managing Systemic Change

The Open University course that prompted this book, and for which it is part of the required reading, focuses on *managing systemic change*. The course is designed for people who want to develop their skills and understanding in systems thinking and practice, to be used in a range of different domains. Most of the examples in the course come from work-based settings. The idea of managing in this context is mainly about appreciating situations with others, recognising what actions are desirable and feasible and for whom, and getting organised, in order to affect or respond to change in a positive way. It has little to do with control. As Vickers (1978, p. 81) said 'I do not think it too much to hope that an understanding of systemic relations may bring us a better understanding of our limitations and even our possibilities.'

When I began my career, around the same time that Vickers expressed this hope, my experience of the word *systemic*, in popular usage, was more often associated with illness or weedkiller than with institutions or relations or with ways of thinking and acting. It was a term not used widely in the educational and development contexts in which I worked at that tme. I was first formally introduced to systems theories through my study of ecosystems though it was several years later before I began to recognise a much wider range of systems theories and approaches. However, again from my perspective, terms such as systemic change and systemic failure now appear to be in regular use, for instance, in the contexts of governance, economy, climate change, sustainable development, public services and policy.

Systemic change usually applies to change of a perceived system, or sub-system, as a whole rather than to its constituent parts. Making improvements to health and social care services, for example, might not be possible just through dedicated professionals doing their own jobs better. Individual cases of apparent neglect with unintended consequences can still arise where there are failings at another level of a system, for instance regarding overall communications or management, where interconnections or 'knock-on effects' are not understood or not kept in mind. An elderly patient receiving care and treatment for illness at home and in more than one hospital, for instance, relies on good communication and co-ordination among many different practitioners. The overall quality of a patient's experience does not

C. Blackmore (ed.), *Social Learning Systems and Communities of Practice*,
DOI 10.1007/978-1-84996-133-2_12, © The Open University 2010.
Published in Association with Springer-Verlag London Limited.

rest just with the individuals they see but on how well that patient's health care system functions as a whole, from his or her perspective.

Ackoff's (1995) observation that 'it is better to do the right thing wrong than to do the wrong thing right' captures the idea of systemic change in that however much attention is paid to doing something better at one level it might make little difference in systemic terms. Investment in equipment and technicians to monitor air or water quality to a high degree of accuracy might be an example of doing the wrong thing right if the investment makes little difference over the longer term to addressing any issues of air or water pollution that are identified. This example is over-simplified, if taking the language used in many professional discourses today as evidence that there is now widespread recognition of the need to appreciate interconnections, systemic relations and the possibility of unintended consequences of our actions. But when and even whether this recognition leads to action is another matter. Systemic change does not just happen all around us in a detached way, but we are often a part of it. This might mean that we are sometimes slow to recognise it yet as individuals and groups we often have the ability to affect as well as be affected by systemic change.

In this book, the chapter authors all indicate that we have a lot more to understand about our interconnected world, the ways we live and work in it and how we might make changes in order to meet the many challenges we face as individuals, groups and societies. These challenges range from how we organise or regulate ourselves to work more effectively and ethically, to how we improve our communications and negotiations with each other. They also range from how we – individually and collectively – respond to, for example, issues of climate change, threats of terrorism or financial breakdown and how we might mitigate more negative effects, to how we can design more robust and appropriate institutions for our current times.

In their different ways the authors each offer insights into how we can develop necessary understanding and what we could or should do, using the concepts of social learning systems and communities of practice (CoPs). These concepts appear to have much to offer. The work of Vickers and Schön illuminates processes of interaction and transformation. The Hawkesbury group's focus on areas such as ethics and epistemology offers insights into our different traditions of understanding. Their work raises questions about what *should* be done, the role of epistemic learning in bringing together our different kinds of knowledge and ways of knowing and how social learning might help us engage with institutional dilemmas concerning the unsustainability of modern societies. The CoPs perspectives offered by Wenger, Snyder, Gobbi and Polin highlight the importance of engagement and participation at a local level, to gain access to larger scale learning systems. Insights into the importance of boundary interactions, discourses associated with practice, and multi-membership of CoPs are offered. They focus on identity and interpersonal relationships and highlight a range of conceptual and practical tools for social learning.

Perhaps of greatest import, a need to learn how to learn our way together to bring about improvements in various situations and practices is identified by many of the authors. Underlying this and other needs recognised by authors, and the recommendations they make, is a range of perspectives on social learning and social learning systems which are next summarised and discussed.

Distinctions Concerning Social Learning and Social Learning Systems

Donald Schön's view of social learning, as expressed in Chapter 1 (Schön, 2010), focuses on public learning, which appears to be akin to *societal* learning. Linear 'knowledge transfer' and didactic 'instructivism' were the underlying traditions of the prevailing view of learning at the time of Schön's writing. However he draws on cybernetics and non-linear dynamics in his arguments, suggesting a constructivist view of learning where knowledge is developed rather than transferred. He recommends a fundamental conceptual shift from central government as a trainer of society, in a linear manner, to central government as facilitator of society's learning. He also argues against the separation of the formation and implementation of policy. In calling for us to develop learning systems and systems capable of their own continuing transformation for the benefit of individuals and society at large, Schön seems to be concerned here mainly with social learning as societal learning, though in his later work he went on to consider the learning of organisations.

Geoffrey Vickers approach to social learning also is constructivist and highly dynamic (Vickers, 2010). He too was clearly much influenced by cybernetics. Vickers' appreciative systems approach focuses both on group process and on individuals in their social contexts. He recognises both social and individual experience as contributing to social learning. Vickers' work is notable not just because of the distinctions he has made – between for instance facts and values, appreciation and action, events and ideas – but because of the way he combines them with standards and 'settings'. In a sense he does not 'freeze' the process to analyse it, but instead captures the dynamics of learning. I consider Vickers' model as a moving model rather than a static model which, to me, seems particularly appropriate to learning. Vickers appreciative systems model can be applied at the level of an individual or a group.

The characteristics of critical social learning systems distinguished by the Hawkesbury group are indicated in Richard Bawden's (2010b) Chapter 6 and at the end of his Chapter 3 (Bawden, 2010a) where he applies a generalised model to consider how an effective learning community might be distinguished. In an earlier chapter (Bawden, 1995) a learning system was proposed as:

- an organised and coherent group of people
- collaborating purposefully together to achieve high quality transformations and transactions
- with a deep appreciation of their own integrity
- a keen sense of emergence

- an acute consciousness of their shared processes, levels and states of learning
- as they design and create new and responsible futures together.

This concept has been expanded in Bawden and his colleagues' subsequent work, drawing on insights from further systemic praxis of the Hawkesbury group. For instance increased emphasis is placed on epistemological, ethical and emotional dimensions and, particularly in Bawden's Chapter 6, the significance of world-views and messy issues. Nonetheless, this 'summary version' provides an accessible overview. It is also useful here for the purpose of comparison both with the earlier traditions of Schön and Vickers and CoPs distinctions that were articulated by Wenger and his colleagues in parallel to this tradition. Vickers' distinctions relating to appreciative systems were among the many influences on the Hawkesbury tradition, as explained in Chapter 6, and the focus on transformations has some similarities with Schön's ideas. Several of the characteristics identified by the Hawkesbury group for a critical social learning system could also apply to CoPs.

Jim Woodhill (2010), in Chapter 4, recognises that while the concept of social learning is not new there is a need to articulate its meaning in more detail in the contexts of environment and development. He offers a definition of social learning that focuses on institutions and makes a sustainability dimension explicit: In Chapter 4 he indicates that he sees social learning as 'Processes by which society democratically adapts its core institutions to cope with social and ecological change in ways that will optimise the collective well-being of current and future generations.' He also offers clarifications of: what he means by the democratic and cognitive process of social learning; the sense in which he uses adaptation; his concern with institutions and his reasons for the purpose for social learning that he specifies in this definition.

Ray Ison's perspective on social learning also focuses to some extent on institutions and sustainability. His Chapter 5 (Ison, 2010) includes examples of social learning systems in practice. The SLIM water management project team that Ison refers to went on subsequently to develop the following shared understanding of social learning:

What is considered as social learning depends on what focus is taken; it can be on:

- The convergence of goals, criteria and knowledge leading to more accurate mutual expectations and the building of relational capital. If social learning is at work, then convergence and relational capital generate agreement on concerted action for integrated catchment management and the sustainable use of water. Social learning may thus result in sustainable resource use.
- The process of co-creation of knowledge, which provides insight into the causes of, and the means required to transform, a situation. Social learning is thus an integral part of the make-up of concerted action.
- The change of behaviours and actions resulting from understanding something through action ('knowing') and leading to concerted action. Social learning is thus an emergent property of the process to transform a situation.

SLIM (2004, p. 1)

Both Woodhill and Ison are concerned with collective learning and concerted multi-level action which they see as essential in their domains of practice, which include development, environmental decision making and natural resource management.

In contrast, Etienne Wenger's CoPs-based theory, discussed in Chapters 7, 8 and 11 (Snyder and Wenger, 2010; Wenger, 2010a, b), is as much concerned with individual as with collective learning and has been applied, in different ways, in a very wide range of domains. Wenger proposes a social theory of learning rather than a social learning theory. He distinguishes this theory by defining learning as a social and historical process (see his quote at the start of this book). In considering social learning systems his focus is specifically on CoPs, where effectiveness of these communities depends on the strengths of their structural elements of domain, community and practice. By distinguishing these elements rather than specifying particular domains or applications Wenger's theory has a generic quality. It has certainly resonated strongly with many practitioners around the world in many different domains. Wenger does not make a hard distinction between practice and learning, seeing learning as practice in the sense that he observes that individuals in work-based settings are more likely to talk about improving their practices rather than explicitly about their learning. Wenger's focus on learning at boundaries of CoPs is echoed elsewhere in this book, for instance in some of Schön's deliberations about the relationship between the centre and periphery of government. Wenger's distinctions between peripherality and marginality and identities of participation and non-participation help to identify where there might be opportunities and constraints regarding learning, when considering CoPs and social learning systems.

In several places in this book the terms 'social learning systems' and 'communities of practice' have either been separated or conflated. So it might be useful here to consider what distinctions concerning social learning *systems* do CoPs traditions make? In Chapter 11 Wenger observes that the CoP concept did not arise from a systems theoretical tradition though several of the disciplines in which it has its roots, such as anthropology and psychology, do include and value systemic understandings and these disciplines are among those that have informed systems theories. In Chapter 11 Wenger elaborates ways in which a community of practice (CoP) can be seen as a social learning system, identifying systems characteristics that a CoP exhibits. It can also be argued that a perceived social learning system can be seen as a CoP, where for instance the distinctions of community, practice and domain can be identified. But both a CoP and a social learning system can be framed in other ways so that they do not automatically map on to each other. For instance, a CoP might be perceived as a knowledge-based social structure, not explicitly as a system. A CoP might also have other purposes besides social learning so even when it is perceived as a system it might be seen as 'a system for improving practice' or 'a system to develop a professional community'. These various framings and purposes are of course not mutually exclusive and still imply learning, particularly when adopting Wenger's (Chapter 11) position of considering learning as the production of social structures or as the production of identity. But they suggest that while a CoP *can* be viewed as a social learning system this perspective is not automatic.

Snyder and Wenger (in Chapter 7) take the perspective of considering our world as a learning system and make three basic specifications of a world learning system which they describe as follows:

- *action-learning capacity* to address problems while continuously reflecting on what approaches are working and why – and then using these insights to guide future actions
- *cross-boundary representation* that includes participants from private, public, and nonprofit sectors and from a sufficient range of demographic constituencies and professional disciplines to match the complexity of factors and stakeholders driving the problem
- *cross-level linkages* that connect learning-system activities at local, national, and global levels.

They consider what a CoPs approach might mean in the context of a world learning system. Structural distinctions are again proposed, this time the idea of a fractal structure, and growing a community of communities, to increase the scale of a community-based learning system without losing core elements of its success.

Mary Gobbi's perspective on learning, working and professional communities focuses on professional capital, discourses of professional practice and interpersonal relationships (Gobbi, 2010). She does not use the explicit language of social learning or social learning systems though she does consider a range of distinctions concerning society, community groups and teams in relation to learning. She also relates her perspective to 'learning through experience' which has similarities with the experience focus in the work of the Hawkesbury group.

A social learning, CoPs-based, model is at the core of Linda Polin's work in design for graduate education (Polin, 2010). In her constructivist approach she reconceptualises graduate education as supporting engagement in a CoP, and in so doing, as she observes in Chapter 10, 'the discourse is re-contextualized from a classroom transmission and transfer discourse to a discourse of collegial collaboration and negotiation around authentic work.' There are some similarities here with Schön's efforts, in his case at the level of government, to reconceptualise public learning by moving away from a linear model of social learning to one that is more systemic.

In this section some of the distinctions made by authors concerning social learning and social learning systems have been noted, compared and contrasted. It is clear that all the concepts and theories discussed have been grounded in or emerged from practices of various kinds and they all build on other theories. The authors also identify a range of influences and in considering the book as a whole it can be seen which of these influences are shared or not shared with other authors. In the next section such commonalities and an emerging synthesis of ideas and practices are explored to map what I refer to as a *landscape of social learning systems praxis*. This term draws on Wenger's (Chapter 8) idea of a landscape of practice and his and several of the other authors' acknowledgement of the importance of praxis-based approaches with theories and practices informing each other. In common with Wenger's idea this landscape is not about institutional affiliation but about shared praxis. As with any landscape, the exact 'mix' of features varies from place to place, not all elements will be found in every part of the landscape and the 'view' of the landscape is often observer dependent.

Mapping a Landscape of Social Learning Systems Praxis

There are both commonalities and differences among the analyses, ideas, situations and practices described by the authors of the chapters in this book. Many recurring themes have emerged, viewed from different perspectives. Here I begin to map a landscape of praxis with reference to 14 of these themes. I discuss each in turn briefly, summarising and synthesising some of the main points made in the book. These themes are:

1. Institutions, organisations and institutionalising
2. Ethics, values and morality
3. Communication
4. Facilitation
5. Managing interpersonal relationships and building trust
6. Communities and networks
7. Levels and scale
8. Boundaries and barriers
9. Conceptual frameworks and tools
10. Knowledge and knowing
11. Transformations
12. Time lag and dynamics of praxis
13. Design for learning
14. Stability, sustainability and overall purpose.

1. Institutions, Organisations and Institutionalising

Most of the authors focused on institutions and organisations and needs for change as key aspects of their perceptions of social learning systems. The term 'institutions' is used in various ways, sometimes as synonymous with organisations and at other times to refer to a range of forms of enablement or constraint of social learning, such as legislation or rules or organisational culture, as discussed by Ison in Chapter 5. Vickers noted that our institutions, at international level, have become so interwoven that we may regard them as a system. With increasing globalisation this interweaving trend has continued though a contemporary institutional system will undoubtedly also differ from one perceived several decades ago.

The contexts of the authors' observations are significant in a variety of ways. For instance Vickers and Schön wrote at a time when institutions, and attitudes towards them, had emerged from the post-second world war era and responses to events in the mid-twentieth century. New institutions and changed attitudes have evolved since then, influenced by, for instance, increasing globalisation, increasing world population, environmental degradation and new information and communications technologies. We now have trans-national corporations that operate internationally, beyond the control of any one national government. Less hierarchical, participatory modes of governance have also arisen, with more direct engagement of non-governmental organisations and citizens with issues that they might previously have been left to governments or perhaps ignored altogether. I doubt that today there would be widespread agreement with Schön's idea of public learning as '. . . a special way of acquiring new capacity for behavior in which government learns for the society as a whole.' Contemporary governments are quick to point out that other stakeholders besides themselves need to learn, in order for societies as a whole to change.

Yet Schön's call for institutions that do not separate policy development and implementation is still echoed in many places today. The linear metaphor of 'rolling-out' policy, with its attendant imagery of 'squashing' all in its path, is still with us in contexts ranging from health to environmental management to information technology and beyond (as can be seen from an Internet search). In this book Bawden's identification of the need for institutional reform; Woodhill's analysis of the institutional causes of unsustainability in modern society and Ison's discussion of how understandings become institutionalised, all draw on earlier analyses and identify certain factors that appear not to have changed, in spite of previous insights. For instance, the needs these authors identify: for institutions to change their focus to take account of systemic factors; to engage with the causes of the ecological unsustainability of modern society, and for some individuals to relinquish their perceived power and control in the interests of social learning. In relation to calls for change in power structures, Wenger's suggestion that it is a common mistake to demonise the form of power he calls 'vertical accountability' associated with traditional hierarchies and romanticise local engagement in practice provides another perspective on what might need to change.

However, many of the examples detailed in this book also show how other institutional factors have changed over time to encourage learning. Snyder and Wenger's description of the way that many organisations have had to confront large-scale learning issues to compete in the knowledge economy is a case in point. They consider institutions as part of a proposed learning system. One of their focuses is at the civic level, where they note that a challenge for civic learning systems is that there may be no clearly defined institutional context or financing model for process support. They suggest mapping CoPs as a way of considering the bigger picture and their model of a re-imagined city as a learning system (the second diagram in Chapter 7) puts infrastructure (including institutional factors) at the model's centre.

2. Ethics, Values and Morality

Ethics, values and morality take on a range of different forms and emphases in ideas about social learning systems. All the chapter authors consider ethics either explicitly or implicitly but to varying degrees. Vickers both integrates into his ideas, and makes explicit, the ethical and values aspects of 'our appreciated world'. Bawden is concerned with moral judgements, with worldviews that make beliefs and values assumptions explicit and with the notion of being critical – which implies comparison of what occurs with what should occur. Gobbi refers to a process of 'appraising oneself against one's own and the community's, the profession's and/or civic society's pre-existing values, beliefs and standards' as a key part of learning in a community. This appraisal process has some parallels with processes that Vickers describes when using and developing standards of fact and value in appreciating a situation.

Some ethical aspects of social learning systems are inevitably connected with how responsibility is viewed, including where responsibility lies. Gobbi compares a professional community that is responsible to clients, a profession and a team, with a CoP that is only responsible to its members. This largely depends on the wider purpose of a group. Professional communities can work as CoPs, as Polin's chapter shows in relation to education. Members of a CoP are also likely to be responsible, at an individual level, to other individuals and groups.

From a philosophical perspective, ethics can focus on 'being good'; 'doing the right thing', what 'ought to be' and on how we 'should' live and treat others. But these focuses are not necessarily the main focuses of learning. For instance, it is possible to learn how to be bad and to do the wrong thing. It is important to recognise that a community that serves its members' interests does not automatically have to have an ethical brief. However, many practices do include an ethical dimension so working with others to improve those practices will involve engaging with ethics. Working as a CoP that functions as a social learning system in the way that Wenger and his colleagues envisage is also likely to include an ethical dimension, for instance in the processes of welcoming newcomers, valuing boundary interactions, exploring and establishing shared values and regularly re-evaluating the purposes of the CoP.

3. Communication

Communication emerges as another significant theme and as an important part of this landscape of social learning systems praxis. It is at the core of processes of interaction and essential to development of our knowledge and understanding. The discipline of cybernetics which has had a major influence on ideas about systems and about learning involves the study of communication and control in both living organisms and machines. Understanding how communication occurs among humans and how it does or does not lead to action is central to developing an understanding of social learning. For Vickers, what changes when we communicate with each other, and how, was a major focus in developing his concept of an appreciative system. He observed the way that human social and individual experience had been amplified by symbolic communication and the way that individuals' ability to represent their contexts formed a basis for communication. As he saw it, '. . . the appreciated world mediates our communication, as well as guides our actions' (Vickers, 1972).

Other authors in this book also focus on communication: for instance, Bawden (in Chapter 3) on sources of distortion of communication; Ison on languaging and dialogue and on providing a biological explanation of communication, with particular focus on communication that leads to action; Gobbi on verbal and non-verbal communication, on the inadequacy of the written word and on linguistic and paralingusitic devices; and Polin is concerned with the social and technical networking tools that can help communication and learning.

4. Facilitation

Arising partly out of the importance attached to communication, needs for facilitation of social learning are widely recognised by authors in this book, particularly in relation to the kinds of social learning that lead to collective and concerted action. Without facilitation, existing power dynamics and patterns of interaction can constrain or even prevent the multi-level interactive learning processes that such social learning requires. In complex and messy situations, such as management of scarce natural resources, stakeholders need to develop shared knowledge and understanding and harmonise their actions, drawing on their different ways of knowing. This kind of social learning requires interaction across rather than within levels of a hierarchy. This interaction tends not to just happen as a result of participation but needs active and purposeful facilitation. A case in point is how local-level participation in 'Landcare', discussed by Woodhill, did not lead to this approach becoming part of the mainstream. Hence Woodhill focuses on the design of systems to facilitate social learning.

Schön identifies a need for government to facilitate social learning and Bawden is concerned with the need to facilitate the transformation of communities to learning systems, with concurrent transformation of worldviews. The CoPs perspectives on social learning in this book also identify needs for facilitation of knowledge development and a range of CoPs processes that require both facilitators and co-ordinators. For instance, the process of brokering between communities, as discussed by Wenger, is a particular type of facilitation. Facilitators are usually people. But tools, such as web-based tools are also recognised both by Snyder and Wenger and Polin as having a role in facilitation, as are the boundary artifacts discussed by Wenger.

5. Managing Interpersonal Relationships and Building Trust

With significant emphasis on communication and facilitation, it is not surprising that managing interpersonal relationships and building trust is referred to by many of the authors, particularly in the contexts of CoPs perspectives. Snyder and Wenger observe that informal learning and personal relationships are hallmarks of CoPs. They argue that this kind of learning depends on developing collegial relationships with those you trust and who are willing to help when you ask. They give examples of workshops that enabled trust to be built through face-to-face interactions and teleconferences that have helped in building trust and reciprocity. The process of building trust plays an important part in their idea of a fractal community, where brokering of relationships between levels and communities works 'because trust relationships have a transitive character: I trust people trusted by those I trust' (see Chapter 7). Gobbi's focus on building trust in professional communities is around developing 'non-economic professional capital'. Trust also features strongly in positive community-based personal relationships. For Bawden, addressing issues of lack of trust that affect how development is approached and the need to build trust in order to improve this situation, is part of the justification for critical social learning systems. Other authors, including Polin and Ison discuss some of the challenges in changing actual and perceived power structures that can hinder social learning. Vickers identifies a social system as a pattern of relationships – internal and external with each of us a part of several subsystems. Schön suggested re-modelling governments with a view to facilitating different interactions and enabling different relationships to be built. The emphasis of many of the authors on relationships and interaction to build trust leads us on to the strong focus on communities and networks.

6. Communities and Networks

The body of work in this book relating to CoPs, professional communities and learning communities modelled on principles of critical social learning systems all offer perspectives on how social learning can be brought into effect. Community implies a grouping of people that identify themselves as having some sort of unity and the term community is usually seen in positive terms. To be 'community-minded' or to make a contribution to the community, whether at home or work, often implies an ethical dimension connected to being a responsible citizen (Reynolds et al., 2009). Gobbi also observes that there is an emotional connection of communities. Yet communities and their learning can serve many different purposes, besides those described in this book. Wenger, in general, adopts a broad but critical view of community. By taking this approach Shaw (2002) claims 'he is in no danger of romanticizing notions of community'.

Wenger (in Chapter 11) discusses how communities and networks co-exist, not as different structures but as different aspects of social structuring. Wenger's (Chapter 8) discussion of multi-membership of communities and Polin's analysis of social and technical networking draw out dimensions of community and networking processes that have particular relevance to a systemic view of social learning because both concern the interconnections within and between networks and communities. Wenger's observation that we define who we are by the way we reconcile our multimembership into one identity I find a useful reminder that theories of social learning systems can apply at the level of an individual as well a collective. This brings to the fore notions of networks and communities operating at different levels and scale.

7. Levels and Scale

The idea of levels is central to a systems view of the world and to ideas about learning and, thus, to social learning system praxis. Vickers' work on systems claims we distinguish systems as comprising a whole hierarchy of over-lapping sub-systems, each exemplifying a different kind of order (Vickers, 1970). In a constructivist tradition, system, sub-system and wider system are relative terms and the choice of level for observation and analysis always depends on an observer (Checkland, 1999, pp. A23–A24).

Building on Bateson's (1978) work on levels and orders of learning and Kitchener's (1983) focus on level 3 learning, Bawden uses the idea of level in relation to both systems and learning. He describes a systems hierarchy of three levels of *learning*: learning about the matter in hand, *meta learning* i.e. learning about the processes of learning and *epistemic learning* which applies to the beliefs and values that affect the other two levels. Hence, this tradition emphasises epistemic cognition and knowing about the nature of knowledge.

Snyder and Wenger and Woodhill link the ideas of level and scale in considering how local-level participation can affect and be affected by other levels so that, as Snyder and Wenger comment in Chapter 7, the 'scale [of . . .] learning systems can leverage their full potential and match the scale of the problems they address'. Local level participation is recognised by both as essential to learning. Snyder and Wenger suggest a fractal structure as a means of using community-based approaches across different levels and accessing larger scale learning systems. There are some similarities between this view and Woodhill's idea of 'local-global dialectics'. As noted earlier in this chapter, Snyder and Wenger see cross-level linkages that connect learning-system activities at local, national, and global levels as one of the three basic specifications of a world learning system.

8. Boundaries and Barriers

A range of different kinds of boundaries and boundary activities are considered by authors in this book. For instance, 'boundary judgments' as part of a critical learning systems approach as discussed by Bawden, and in the sense of recognising limitations and barriers as discussed by Polin, in relation to making conceptual shifts and when considering removal of constraints to learning. An example from Polin is the way that cultural-historical barriers make it difficult to shift from a transmission conception of university learning to a socially constructed one. Boundary is a recognised systems concept, when the term system is used in a technical sense. As such, what is perceived as within a system and outside it, in its environment, defines a system, Hence Wenger's deliberations concerning boundaries (Chapter 8) including brokering, boundary artefacts and boundary interactions, are particularly relevant to social learning systems. Re-negotiating boundaries of systems of interest is an important iterative process in social learning, usually indicative of the changing purposes of a system or sub-system or changes in stakeholders or responsibilities.

For instance, re-negotiation of roles and responsibilities might take place among health care or education practitioners. In this way, consideration of boundaries and barriers are key determinants in shaping extant praxis.

9. Conceptual Frameworks and Tools

Chapter authors have offered a wide range of conceptual frameworks and practical insights into social learning systems and CoPs. These insights primarily concern: the use of a systems orientation, the development and use of models of learning and of learning to learn, and the role of technical tools.

In relation to systems, Bawden identifies a checklist of systems characteristics that provide a framework for the sets of conversations and discourse which guide a community. He also draws out various assumptions concerning our ability to act systemically and specifies what we need to learn in terms of *critical* and *social* and *learning* and *systems*. Ison considers practices that arise from a systems perspective and distinguishes first and second order research approaches.

Consistent with Polin's observation that learning cannot be explored using just one model, a range of models of learning and of learning to learn are considered in this book. Polin herself considers a range of social learning theories and models including those (such as activity theory, sociocultural historical theory, and the CoPs model) where as she says 'learning is viewed as a kind of enculturation of the individual into a system of practice.' Other models of learning in this book include Vickers appreciative systems model and Schön's critiques of prevailing models of governments and public learning and suggestions of alternatives, mentioned earlier in this chapter. Bawden (Chapter 3) proposes a range of models of learning and suggests that meaning emerges as the result of 'interactions' between the process of *experiential learning* on the one hand, and *inspirational learning* on the other with these processes in turn involving the concrete world of experience. In his later Chapter 6 he refers to what he sees as the two vital conceptual models relating to learning and knowing – Kolb's experiential model and Kitchener's model of cognitive processes that led to the 'three levels of learning' framework already described in this chapter (in the section on levels and scale). He also details a set of five beliefs that came to be held collectively by the Hawkesbury group concerning learning. These beliefs are about the role of experience, how we make sense of the world around us, the limitations imposed by our worldviews that 'filter' our 'sense-making'; how worldview perspectives can develop and what affects our ability to act systemically in the world.

Wenger's social learning theory, which includes the CoPs concept, is the main conceptual framework considered in Part III of this book. However, as he discusses in Chapter 11, the CoPs concept, which was developed in the context of modelling learning in apprenticeship, has been used in many different ways and contexts. As part of his overall theory in Chapter 8 Wenger provides a range of conceptual tools associated with social learning systems and CoPs. This range includes various conceptualisations of practice and identity such as the concept of a trajectory as a continuous motion through time that connects the past, the present, and the future. Use of this 'temporal' conceptual tool can help in understanding individuals' identities in relation to a CoP and the behaviour of the group as a whole.

In Chapter 11 Wenger argues that we need a social discipline of learning that will take account of some of the perspectives on CoPs and social learning systems that he discusses. His primary focus is on understanding and enhancing learning capability in social systems. Wenger sees such a discipline as building on learning through experience with CoPs. He suggests one of this discipline's purposes would be to provide conceptual tools to address issues of power more directly. In addition to her conceptual use of the CoP model, Polin considers the role of technical tools in a practical sense. Her analysis of how applications that have emerged as Web 2.0 tools focus on collaboration and sharing, co-production and social networking includes both conceptual and practical aspects.

All in all the authors reveal, as an important part of the landscape, a diversity of conceptual and practical tools to assist us with the challenge of, in Bawden's words in Chapter 4, 'seeing the world differently'.

10. Knowledge and Knowing

An invitation to see the world differently is carried through in the traditions of both the Hawkesbury group and CoP perspectives which focus on knowledge and our ways of knowing. Epistemology, in particular our assumptions about the nature of knowledge and of knowing, has a major influence on our worldviews and in our abilities to learn how to learn, which Bawden sees as one of the main factors that constrains social learning. Ison considers how knowledge is developed in the context of traditions of understanding, through use of metaphors and through dialogue.

Different CoPs perspectives are concerned with developing, disseminating and stewarding different kinds of knowledge and many examples of how this is or could be done are included by Wenger, Snyder, Gobbi and Polin. Roles of knowledge in practice are identified, for instance the relationship between knowledge and managing strategic capabilities which according to Snyder and Wenger in Chapter 7 'entails supporting self-organizing groups of practitioners who have the required knowledge, use it, and need it.' They also observe that 'practitioners themselves are in the best place to steward knowledge in collaboration with stakeholders' and that 'developing and disseminating certain kinds of knowledge depends on informal learning much more than formal – on conversation, storytelling, mentorships, and lessons learned through experience'. In these ways, knowledge and knowing become key elements of a range of transformations, that are discussed next.

11. Transformations

The idea of transformation is central to Schön's view of a learning system. He recognised, in Chapter 1, that 'transformations of local systems influence one another and may be supported in doing so' and that 'the gradual transformation of the system as a whole influences the context in which each local system experiences its own transformations'. In describing how 'the broad process can 'go critical' as ideas underlying the family of transformations come into good currency and as the numbers of learners and extenders multiply' he argued that 'a system capable of behaving in this manner is a learning system'.

Many different kinds of transformation are discussed by the authors for instance transformations of: discourse, practices, systems for collaborative working, world-views, nature, traditional society, and roles.

Most of these transformations have at least been alluded to in the previous themes so here I will just discuss one, the transformation of roles. Snyder and Wenger comment on our dependence on expert practitioners to connect and collaborate on a global scale. Yet the roles of these experts have changed over recent years, not just because of the need to operate at a range of different levels but because of a more general transformation in the roles of 'experts' (whether teachers, nurses, scientists, organisational leaders or farmers). Perspectives of social learning systems, CoPs and networks and their underlying theories of knowledge and knowing, challenge traditional understandings of experts and expertise, proposing a less hierarchical structure. This challenge is evident for instance in Polin's approach to graduate education. Vickers also focused on transformation of roles, exploring the boundary between personal and institutional roles.

12. Time Lag and Dynamics of Praxis

Several authors identified issues concerning time lags between the emergence of ideas and related practices, captured for instance by Schön in discussion of 'ideas coming into good currency' and by Vickers in considering 'feed forward and feed-back' in appreciative systems. From the perspective of praxis where practices and theories inform each other, this kind of time lag could be seen as an essential part of the dynamics of praxis. Bawden's considers 'tensions of difference', for instance among different beliefs and worldviews, as important to interactive learning. Although not just time related, they could also be considered as part of these dynamics. As noted earlier in this chapter, Wenger's notion of trajectory helps to develop a connected sense of past, present and future and offers potential for insight into the relationship between time lags, praxis and assigned purpose at any given moment of time in the landscape. Issues concerning time lags and dynamics of praxis are among those that need to be taken into account in design for learning.

13. Design for Learning

Design for learning is a strong theme in the work of Wenger (1998), where he argued that learning, of itself, cannot be designed but is something that happens, whether designed or not. He focused instead on designing social infrastructure that fosters learning, claiming that there are few more urgent tasks. In his contributions in this book, particularly with Snyder in Chapter 7, responsibility of design and design requirements for a world learning system are explored. They even go as far as proposing a *discipline* of world design.

Members of the Hawkesbury group also explore what principles should underpin the design of systems to facilitate social learning. Several other authors make 'design for learning' considerations. Polin, for instance, considers factors in design of graduate education and student's learning experiences. Ison details two independent sets of design considerations for the design of learning systems and Woodhill considers institutional design. Most of these latter authors link facilitation and design which is also consistent with Wenger's position that learning cannot be controlled and designed, but it can be encouraged to emerge from a designed process.

14. Stability, Sustainability and Overall Purpose

Design considerations are entwined with notions of purpose. Schön and Vickers were both advocates of social learning systems (in their different forms) in the context of *stability* which reflected their post-war contexts. The Hawkesbury group's focus on sustainability has some similarities with the stability focus. Both viewpoints are highly dynamic and are specific about what needs to be stable or sustained. There is no suggestion that we can control rates of change, but it is possible to engage in purposeful design for learning that takes account of a range of dynamics in learning and in situations. In the CoPs tradition a similar concern with sustainability is expressed by Snyder and Wenger in making the case for our world as a learning system when proposing the idea of a fractal structure, and growing a community of communities, as a design principle to preserve a small-community feeling at a range of levels.

Snyder and Wenger's chapter also introduces the idea of '*strategic* social learning systems to steward civic practices at local, national, and global levels.' A link here could be made to some of the political and institutional aspects of other chapters, such as those of Woodhill and Ison and it raises an important distinction about the *purpose* of social learning systems.

Quite a range of purposes is presented by authors in this book. Yet from my perspective, all the authors seem concerned in their different ways not just with understanding current situations, but with making improvements to bring about a better world where we nurture, rather than undermine, the variously perceived systems on which we depend.

These 14 themes are not comprehensive, in terms of what could be distinguished as a landscape of social learning systems praxis. For instance, themes around 'meaning' 'governance' and 'power' could apply in their own right. But this mapping exercise represents a start on which to build. All of the themes identified present challenges for the future and imply potential roles for social learning systems and CoPs. In conclusion, I consider what roles these concepts might have in future.

What Future Roles for Social Learning Systems and Communities of Practice?

Social learning systems and CoPs are described variously in this book as perspectives, theories, praxis, traditions, approaches, constructs and as if they existed out there in the world. It is evident from the different authors' contributions, which detail how these ideas are being used in different domains today, that they mean different things to different people. The landscape of social learning systems praxis described here is also part of a larger landscape. A social learning system or CoP might also be recognised through theories and praxis of both social learning and systems other than those that appear in this book. For many practitioners, it is the diversity of ways in which social learning systems and CoPs can be thought about or used that accounts for part of their strength and increasing appeal.

I selected the chapters in this book because to me they all offered descriptions, analyses and examples with potential to be of use to current and future practitioners in making sense of, influencing and managing the kinds of systemic changes that rely on high quality and multi-level individual and interactive learning. Social learning systems and communities of practice seem to me to have much to commend them to those who want to interact with others in meaningful ways to bring about changes perceived as necessary at a range of different system levels. These changes might include improving a national health service, adapting to or mitigating the effects of global warming, approaching development more systemically, re-designing the social infrastructure of cities; increasing opportunities for students to realise their potential and extend the boundaries of their learning, or more generally, increasing opportunities for individuals wanting a different relationship with the world around them.

Any landscape can evoke very different responses in individuals, depending on, for instance, different experiences and worldviews. Individuals with different perspectives might also identify different features and processes as those that are changing or that need to change. In this book, the landscape mapped appears to have been viewed on both sunny and cloudy days. Among the perspectives articulated are: belief that social learning systems and community-based approaches can influence change in a positive way; determination to learn and influence change; and exasperation at what does not appear to be changing, in spite of what we appear to know. Social learning systems and communities of practice appear to have many future challenges to address – conceptual and practical, collaborative and individual, professional and personal. While these are demanding, in mapping a landscape of social learning systems praxis, this book offers insights into new ways of being and acting in the world in relation to each other which arise from both old and new understandings of communities, learning and systems. It is from these insights that the possibility of influencing and managing systemic change for a better world emerges.

References

Ackoff, R.L. (1995) 'Whole-ing' the parts and righting the wrongs', *Systems Research*, 12, 143–6.

Bateson, G. (1978) *Steps to an Ecology of Mind*. Paladine, London.

Bawden, R. (1995) *Systemic Development: A Learning Approach to Change*. Centre for Systemic Development, University of Western Sydney, Hawkesbury, Occasional Paper No. 1.

Bawden, R. (2010a) 'The community challenge: the learning response.' Chapter 3 in Blackmore, C. (ed.) *Social Learning Systems and Communities of Practice*. Springer, Dordrecht.

Bawden, R. (2010b) 'Messy issues, worldviews and systemic competencies.' Chapter 6 in Blackmore, C. (ed.) *Social Learning Systems and Communities of Practice*. Springer, Dordrecht.

Checkland, P. (1999) 'Soft systems methodology – a thirty year retrospective.' In Checkland, P. and Scholes, J. *Soft Systems Methodology in Action* (2nd edn.). John Wiley, Chichester (1st edn. 1990).

Gobbi, M. (2010) 'Learning nursing in the workplace community: the generation of professional capital.' Chapter 9 in Blackmore, C. (ed.) *Social Learning Systems and Communities of Practice*. Springer, Dordrecht.

Ison, R. (2010) 'Traditions of understanding: language, dialogue and experience.' Chapter 5 in Blackmore, C. (ed.) *Social Learning Systems and Communities of Practice*. Springer, Dordrecht.

Kitchener, K. (1983) 'Cognition, meta-cognition, and epistemic cognition: a three level model of cognitive processing.' *Human Development*, 26, 222–232.

Polin, L.G. (2010) 'Graduate professional education from a community of practice perspective: the role of social and technical networking.' Chapter 10 in Blackmore, C. (ed.) *Social Learning Systems and Communities of Practice*. Springer, Dordrecht.

Reynolds, M., Blackmore, C. and Smith, M.J. (2009) *The Environmental Responsibility Reader*. Zed Books, London.

Schön, D. (2010) 'Government as a learning system.' Chapter 1 in Blackmore, C. (ed.) *Social Learning Systems and Communities of Practice*. Springer, Dordrecht.

Shaw, P. (2002) *Changing Conversations in Organisations – A Complexity Approach to Change*. Routledge, London.

SLIM (2004) Introduction to SLIM Publications for Policy Makers and Practitioners. *SLIM Policy Briefing*. http://slim.open.ac.uk/objects/public/slimpbintrofinal.pdf

Snyder, W.M. and Wenger, E. (2010) 'Our world as a learning system: a communities of practice approach.' Chapter 7 in Blackmore, C. (ed.) *Social Learning Systems and Communities of Practice*. Springer, Dordrecht.

Vickers, G. (1970) *Value Systems and Social Process*. Penguin Books, London. [First published by Tavistock Publications, London in 1968].

Vickers, G. (1972) *Freedom in a Rocking Boat*. Penguin Books, London. [First published by Penguin: Harmondsworth in 1970]

Vickers, G. (1978) 'Some implications of systems thinking.' in Vickers, G. (ed.) *Responsibility – Its Sources and Limits*. Intersystems Publications, Salinas, CA.

Vickers, G. (2010) 'Insights into appreciation and learning systems.' Chapter 2 in Blackmore, C. (ed.) *Social Learning Systems and Communities of Practice*. Springer, Dordrecht.

Wenger, E. (1998) *Communities of Practice: Learning, Meaning and Identity*. New York: Cambridge University Press.

Wenger, E. (2010a) 'Conceptual tools for CoPs as social learning systems: boundaries, identity, trajectories and participation.' Chapter 8 in Blackmore, C. (ed.) *Social Learning Systems and Communities of Practice*. Springer, Dordrecht.

Wenger, E. (2010b) 'Communities of practice and social learning systems: the career of a concept.' Chapter 11 in Blackmore, C. (ed.) *Social Learning Systems and Communities of Practice*. Springer, Dordrecht.

Woodhill, J. (2010) 'Sustainability, social learning and the democratic imperative: lessons from the Australian Landcare movement.' Chapter 4 in Blackmore, C. (ed.) *Social Learning Systems and Communities of Practice*. Springer, Dordrecht.

Index

Lightning Source UK Ltd.
Milton Keynes UK
07 July 2010

156695UK00002B/2/P